Union

Union

A Democrat, a Republican, and a
Search for Common Ground

JORDAN BLASHEK &
CHRISTOPHER HAUGH

Little, Brown and Company

New York Boston London

Copyright © 2020 by Jordan Blashek and Christopher Haugh

Hachette Book Group supports the right to free expression and the value of copyright. The purpose of copyright is to encourage writers and artists to produce the creative works that enrich our culture.

The scanning, uploading, and distribution of this book without permission is a theft of the authors' intellectual property. If you would like permission to use material from the book (other than for review purposes), please contact permissions@hbgusa.com. Thank you for your support of the authors' rights.

Little, Brown and Company
Hachette Book Group
1290 Avenue of the Americas, New York, NY 10104
littlebrown.com

First Edition: May 2020

Little, Brown and Company is a division of Hachette Book Group, Inc. The Little, Brown name and logo are trademarks of Hachette Book Group, Inc.

The publisher is not responsible for websites (or their content) that are not owned by the publisher.

The Hachette Speakers Bureau provides a wide range of authors for speaking events. To find out more, go to hachettespeakersbureau.com or call (866) 376-6591.

ISBN 978-0-316-42379-3
LCCN 2020930306

10 9 8 7 6 5 4 3 2 1

LSC-C

Printed in the United States of America

To our mothers, Carolyn and Holly

CONTENTS

Contents

AUTHORS' NOTE

Earlier today, we submitted *Union* to our publisher, concluding more than three years of work. Tonight we will celebrate the Fourth of July at Chris's childhood home near Berkeley, California, with a smattering of family and friends. Sharing one another's lives like this has become the heart of our friendship. This book is a record of those rituals, and our way of sharing them.

Union is a story about the road. But these trips weren't always meant for a book. When we first set off for California from New York City in 2016, it was a lark. Neither of us imagined we would spend the next three years together writing about what was to come. As a result, this book is part memoir and another part reporting. By the midpoint of our drives, we were taking copious notes, snapping a number of photos, and recording as many interviews as we could. But *Union* will always be a fusion of both memory and reporting. It's about the experience of meeting people and listening to their stories. We didn't write an exhaustive account of who we met and where they came from. We wrote about our impressions of these encounters—how they made us feel, and what we discussed with each other afterward.

Over many thousands of miles, the fog of the highway inevitably sets in. *Union* is our good-faith effort to tell the story as it happened. Thankfully there are two of us, and we were rarely shy in correcting one another's memories. Everything in this book is the best attainable version of the truth, as one of Chris's mentors often puts it. Some quotes in the book are reconstructed from memory. Others are derived from transcripts. More yet are pulled from our daily notes. We don't distinguish among them for a very particular reason: we went back and checked our recollections with as many people as possible, then employed two fact-checkers to do the same.

We decided to write *Union* in the third person, like a novel, so readers could more readily understand our frames of mind and emotions in the moment. We considered writing it in the first-person singular, bouncing back and forth between our two voices, but ultimately decided to leave that to William Faulkner.

On our journeys, we chose places to travel for a variety of reasons: there was a story we wanted to report, an event we had to see, or simply a place we had always dreamed of visiting. Along the way, we met people by appointment and also by chance. Some of them we sought out because of mutual connections, or research on our part. None of them were chosen because they stood in for larger trends; they were just people. People who welcomed us into their homes, who shook our hands despite our differences, and who let us see them at their strongest moments and their most vulnerable.

We never paid anyone or promised anything, except an adherence to the truth.

But we did participate in the lives of the people we met. Jordan moved tackle and boxes for a lobsterman, Chris dialed a trucker's phone while he drove, and we both volunteered in a Tijuana free kitchen. Sometimes we went even further. Chris edited a speech. Jordan bought a handbag made by former inmates of a women's prison. Perhaps that compromised us as journalists, but this project was always meant to be participatory. We engaged, and that mattered to us.

Writing *Union* was the last leg of our journey. Until we wrote it, and reflected on what we saw and did, we couldn't fully process what we had experienced. For three years, this work mattered to us most, so we worked multiple jobs in order to stay on the road. We took conference calls for our day jobs from the car, then stayed up well past midnight at highway-side motels finishing work that should have been done earlier in the day. The road is a hard place. We recognize it might have been even harder if we weren't white and male. But it is also profound, beautiful, and instructive. There was nowhere we'd rather have been.

Somewhere along the way, we realized that these road trips had changed our friendship, and that our friendship had changed the way we both saw the country. There are still things about America on which we'll never agree, and we nearly parted ways over them. But unspoken values emerged in our actions and the voices of the people we met along the way. Out there, we also found there's more to America than gladiatorial politics. When we listened, we heard a nation being shaped by millions of voices, each with ideas and wisdom more complex than can be captured by the steady drumbeat of television segments, radio features, and social-media posts.

Time and again we witnessed expressions of faith in this country. At times these expressions were unique and at other times conflicting, but on the road something resembling reverence existed for a collection of higher ideals—ideals that might best be called America's civic religion. Beneath the words of our founding texts—and in the canon of American speeches and literature, the melodies and lyrics that make up our musical heritage, or even the ways we explain ourselves to one another—there is a deep well of feeling that brings us closer to a singular identity: that of American.

On our last road trip, a musician in New Orleans told us something beautiful: Music brings people together, he said, because you can come at it, interpret it, and appreciate it from infinite points of view. There is no "right way" to take in and fall for a tune. All that matters is that you do, and what you bring to it in turn. After all these years on the road, we have come to much the same view about this country. The story of who we are as Americans can be told in a multitude of different ways, each with its high and low notes. There is no right way to look at this country and its people, just as there is no "right way" to tell that story. This just happens to be ours.

Our hope is that *Union* will play some small part in an ongoing effort to bring Americans a little bit closer together. We wrote it, and reported it, and remembered it with that in mind.

Sincerely,

Christopher Haugh & Jordan Blashek

PART I

New Haven

Chris had a dream that he was flying and woke with a start at the absurdity of the idea. Jordan was at the wheel of the boxy, sea-blue sedan, and Chris was splayed out on the passenger seat. We passed into Pennsylvania along fast, narrow roads moments before midnight.

Chris shot a look over at Jordan, whose eyes were fixed on the slalom road ahead. It was empty except for us and the long-haul trucks on their way up and down another lonesome freeway.

Earlier that evening, we had meandered down the sidewalks of New York City toward Jordan's Volvo S60, which he had inherited from his aging grandfather.

"It's not much," Jordan said. "The steering grinds when you make a tight turn and it's missing a few parts, but it runs."

"Spacious," Chris said, opening the door.

"And she can't make a U-turn—feels like steering a boat."

Our plan for the week was to drive across the country from New York City to Berkeley, California, where Chris had grown up, a few hundred miles north of Jordan's family home in Los Angeles. As we shot down the avenues of the Upper East Side under orange streetlights, we threw around possible stops like Yellowstone, Glacier National Park, and parts of the Pacific Northwest.

"Let's get to Chicago by morning," Jordan had said as we merged onto Harlem River Drive, and Chris had laughed aloud. But there we were, pressing on toward the Midwest through the dark woods of the Poconos a few hours before dawn.

Chris had come to know over our brief eight-month friendship how Jordan operated according to his own mysterious logic. A bleary-eyed, unending drive seemed true to form. So Chris kept quiet as we drove into the gloom of morning. We had six more days on the road together, and there would be plenty to disagree about later on.

It had also occurred to Chris in those first hours just how little he knew about Jordan. The two of us had become close at law school, but school friends are often just acquaintances. And as Chris thought it over, he couldn't come up with Jordan's parents' names or even what kind of a driver Jordan was. Would this Marine make them drive all night, every night?

We slid down the grades of Pennsylvania hills, the tail lights of the trucks ahead making us squint through the windshield. Our own headlights illuminated white trees with feathery leaves on the shoulder. Purple mountains flanked the road. A moonless sky merged with forested ridgebacks decorated with eerie crosses lit from below by pale floodlights.

Jordan shifted his position in the driver's seat. Like Chris, he had his reservations. Had it been a mistake asking Chris to come along on this trip? Jordan had never driven cross-country before, and spending days on end in a close space with a law-school peer was unsettling. It didn't help that Chris had talked nervously for the first hour. Jordan had asked on a whim, and there we were, many miles down the way.

Distracted by his thoughts, Jordan let the car reach a pace that brought us close behind an 18-wheeler. The truck's brake lights flared;

Jordan rode his own, and we drifted back. As we did, a second truck flashed past the passenger window and Chris flinched. For a beat, our car was boxed in by two multiton machines just as the less-harried truck in our lane caught a slick in the road, sending its trailer fishtailing toward the cab of the one to its right.

Chris gripped the arm rest. Jordan pushed down even harder on the brakes. And in the sickening moment of inertia—when the door panel of the truck beside us nearly collided with the flank of the one ahead—we both screamed.

Then, as fast as it had lost control of its load, the truck in front righted its lashing fishtail and took off down the road, the slower of the two trundled on into the night, and the two of us swallowed what was left of our shrieks.

Two years earlier, under the very different circumstances of Yale Law School, Jordan looked down at his trembling right hand. *Why am I shaking?* he thought. Behind him on the walls of the classroom were oil portraits of judges in black robes and academics in tweed suits in front of mahogany desks. Eighty pairs of eyes settled on him, including those of a professor a few dozen feet away.

Jordan felt exposed, and Jordan, like any Marine, did not like to be exposed.

"Mr. Blashek," the professor bellowed. "Where are you?"

It was the first day of law school in the fall of 2014. And out of the 200 or so new students that year, the civil procedure professor had asked Jordan the first question—or cold call—of the year.

"Yes, here," Jordan said.

"Mr. Blashek, why are laws necessary in a free and open society?"

Jordan's mind raced.

"Wait," she continued. "Before you answer, I have something for you."

The professor walked across the room, up some stairs, and handed Jordan a garbage bag. Jordan reached into the bag and pulled out a toy rifle. He gripped its handle and wrapped his finger around the trigger housing. A rifle—a real one—had been his near-constant companion on deployment in Afghanistan just a year earlier.

"Well?" the professor said.

Jordan's mind went blank.

"We have laws," Jordan said haltingly, "so that we don't resort to violence."

"Mr. Blashek," the professor continued. "Do you know how to use one of those?"

"A toy gun?"

"No, a real one."

"Yes, I do."

The professor's brow furrowed.

As she moved on with the lecture, a wave of relief washed over Jordan. He sat there, hand still wrapped around the dimpled grip, as his classmates scribbled notes and nibbled on pens.

Holding the cheap plastic gun, Jordan felt torn between two worlds. In one he was a student again, raising his hand, puzzling over exams, and writing papers. In the other he was an infantry officer with two tours of duty overseas and friends for whom he would give his life—and they for him.

And some of them still needed him. For weeks, texts had flashed across Jordan's phone at odd times of the day and night.

"Sir I'll be in clear water FL after noon," one read in an Afghan's new English.

The texts were from his Afghan interpreters, who spoke of college, booking plane tickets across the globe, and settling into new lives thousands of miles from home. Some were hopeful. Others, though, were less sanguine.

"I need someone to show me how to get room," one wrote. Jordan could picture the young man, who spoke trembling English, in a strange city where he knew no one, unable to find a place to escape the autumn frosts.

In that world, the one Jordan descended back into with each text, he was *Sir* or *Captain Blashek*. But at law school he was simply *Jordan*.

Slowly he started waking up later and letting his stubble grow longer. That change in appearance did little, however, to ease his sense of loss. He missed his fellow Marines, and the mission the uniform had given him.

At the start of his second year, Jordan was with several classmates at a local bar with a back patio illuminated by a string of light bulbs. On Friday nights that patio became the center of the law school's social calendar, a place where students of all years would mingle under the open sky and drink discounted Miller Lite and Sierra Nevada. Law students would usually occupy a few plastic tables beside a brick wall, which muffled the music from a student cabaret and the African American Cultural Center just beyond its rampart.

That night Jordan was making the rounds when a friend of his approached with a stranger by his side.

"I want you to meet someone," the friend said. "His name is Chris."

"You're Jordan?" Chris, the stranger, said. "We're supposed to know one another."

"Oh, right," Jordan said. "Chris."

Lauren, Jordan's cousin who had worked for the government, had told Jordan about Chris in a brief email mentioning that a young colleague was matriculating.

Chris looked nothing like what Jordan had expected. He had tousled hair. Studs protruded from both earlobes. A big smile was broken by the faint hint of a scar on his upper lip. He looked like a person who didn't take himself too seriously.

"It's nice to meet you," Jordan said.

New Haven

A few hours earlier, Chris had gazed out on the New Haven Green from his studio in the Taft apartments. It was September, and the humidity of the summer had long ago subsided. At night Chris could throw open the windows and listen to the murmur wafting up from the streets below. The elms along College Street, once a brilliant green, had turned orange and red, and the streetlights, which always seemed to flicker, glowed through the thinning branches. Chris spent many nights looking out that window. That view was his sanctuary, and it helped soothe the fever of embarrassment raised by his first few days of class.

"Is there a *Chris* here?" a professor had said from her podium a day or two before.

Oh no, Chris thought from the back row.

"Chris?"

"Yes, he's—I'm here."

"Chris," the professor said, looking down at her notes. "Tell me, where does judicial review come from?"

It was a straightforward—some might say charitable—question. Chris had actually done all of his reading the night before, too. He had cracked an enormous red-bound tome on constitutional law and digested cases such as *Marbury v. Madison* and *McCulloch v. Maryland.* But as fast as Chris's brain raced, no answer emerged.

"The Supremacy Clause?" Chris offered.

The professor busied herself with her papers as Chris stewed over the answer he'd given, which was evidently incorrect.

"Well," the professor said at length. "Anyone else?"

That night, Chris puzzled over whether he was cut out for law school. For weeks he had pined for his former job at the State Department in Washington, D.C., where he had a purpose as a small part of a much larger machine. Each day he was engaged in a project to make things better for people around the world. Law school had not yet given him that same thrill, and Chris felt its absence like a hunger.

Away from this work, Chris gravitated toward writing. He read

Edward R. Murrow's *This Is London,* the journalist's wartime reporting from a city under siege, and Timothy Crouse's *Boys on the Bus,* about the reporters covering the 1972 presidential election. Chris came to believe that getting back to his own reporting might restore that sense of purpose. The only hurdle was the classes and exams he had voluntarily taken on all over again.

One month in and Chris felt far from what mattered.

And so, later that night, Chris made his way to that very same patio bar where even the most hard-charging law-school types eased somewhat, or never showed up at all.

"I want you to meet someone," his friend said, approaching a student with a crew cut and broad shoulders. "Chris, this is Jordan."

Jordan had a face dotted with freckles and a military-trained confidence similar to what Chris had come to recognize living on Capitol Hill, where Marines and soldiers sported telltale shaved scalps and taupe T-shirts. But Jordan also had a warmth about him that broke through the studied posture and Marine gait.

"It's a pleasure," Chris said.

Jordan stuck out his hand.

"When you get settled, let me buy you a drink," Jordan offered.

"It's a plan."

A few weeks later, Jordan arrived at an Irish pub and settled in at a wobbly table with a dewy surface. Chris found him there and took a seat.

The conversation sputtered to life while the bartender busied himself with the drinks.

"So how's it been for you?" Chris asked. "Law school and all."

"It's funny," Jordan replied. "If you had asked me that just a few months ago, I would've given you a very different answer. The first year was rough."

The bartender put two tumblers on the table.

"But second year has been much better," Jordan said. "I've made some great friends here, and found a few professors who are supportive of what I want to do."

"And what's that?"

"A lot of things," Jordan said with a smile.

Chris waited for an answer as Jordan took a sip of his drink.

"Have you heard of Jim Webb?" Jordan continued.

"The senator from Virginia?"

"Yeah, former. That's the life I want, or something close to it. He was a Marine, wrote half a dozen novels, went to law school, became a journalist, and was appointed Secretary of the Navy. He eventually ran for Senate to oppose the Iraq War."

The bartender clinked glasses behind us and the street beyond shed noise from the passersby—couples draped over one another, raucous crew boys in turtlenecks, and professor types with swollen briefcases.

"How about you?" Jordan said.

"Write," Chris said.

"Heck of a place to end up, then."

"Yeah, a bit of a left turn. When I dropped out of grad school—"

"Dropped out?"

"Yeah, I went straight to Oxford after graduating from college, because I wanted to be a war correspondent and haunt those London bars where war reporters like Dexter Filkins and Marie Colvin used to gather. But instead I was writing papers about Foucault, so I left."

"What happened to becoming a war reporter?" Jordan asked.

"I still want to," Chris said. "Maybe someday."

One drink turned into three, which was something of a surprise to the two of us, since all we knew ahead of time was that we didn't share politics. Chris was a Democrat, Jordan a Republican. Yet in that moment our partisan allegiances seemed less relevant. There was something else at work—Jordan was grappling with a recent heartbreak, and Chris was clawing his way out of something similar. Things we could no longer control had eroded our guards. So we discussed what was deeper and unvarnished. Things like our most cherished memories, the influence of our mothers, and whether law school was the right path. We talked about history and learned that we shared a passion for great novels and beautifully rendered reporting.

It was a unique moment—a fortunate one for forging new friendships.

"Jim Webb," Chris said later on. "You said he's your hero, right?"

"Yeah."

"Interesting."

"Why?"

"He's a Democrat."

———

After that first night, Jordan drew Chris into a larger circle of friends and classmates. One evening while the weather was still warm, he took Chris along to a curbside patio at the Owl Shop, a New Haven smoking establishment. Almost every Tuesday, Jordan and his friend Hilary met for a cigar, a glass of whisky, and a set by The Red Planet, a Grateful Dead cover band. There, she and Jordan would unwind together, which to them meant spirited debates over another kind of spirit. Chris tagged along more and more and, as he grew familiar with the back and forth, he even felt like he might belong.

On those nights Chris would often talk about the stories he wanted to write, and Jordan the companies he hoped to build.

Still, our political differences were there; as we sat at the Owl Shop's curbside patio, those views emerged into full view every once in a while.

"It really bothers me that Democrats frame every argument about climate change as if the opposition were either ignorant 'deniers' or corporate shills," Jordan said one warm fall night.

Jordan often argued with his more liberal classmates and had developed a measured tone for navigating delicate conversations.

"It belittles legitimate criticism," he continued.

"But what is that legitimate criticism?" Chris asked.

Chris was more hesitant to engage this way with Jordan and his classmates.

"All I'm saying," Jordan responded, "is it's okay to express humility about what we can know or predict about something as complex as the earth's climate over decades."

"But there's complete consensus among experts on this issue," Chris said. "How does one quibble with 97 percent of climate scientists?"

"That number is misleading. And not a single climate model has made an accurate prediction to date."

"The evidence is overwhelming that climate change is real and man-made."

"I'm not denying that humans have an impact on climate, maybe even a huge one, but that's not the issue. The issue is what to do about it. Dramatically slowing economic growth to prevent some unknown harm a century from now causes serious harm to people today, especially the most disadvantaged."

"But not doing anything would be catastrophic. Millions of people could die."

"How can you know that? We have decades to adjust, and you have no idea what technologies will be developed in the meantime."

"That's a hell of a risk to take. And nearly every climate scientist has said that we have a small window of time right now before the damage becomes irreparable."

Chris's face had turned crimson, while Jordan grew more combative.

"That sounds like scaremongering. If you had reasonable solutions, I'd be all for it. But nothing proposed by the Left would actually solve anything."

"What? There are dozens of policy options. How about a carbon tax...investment in more clean power...more global commitments to reduce emissions?"

"Most of those solutions affect low-income Americans by slowing growth. And none of them take into account the fact that countries like China and India can't afford to give up oil and coal when they have millions of people dying in poverty."

"Look, the U.S. has to lead by example if we want to make progress. We can't be the worst offender on carbon emissions. We can't set the tone like that."

"Leading doesn't mean we have to stifle domestic opposition," Jordan said. "We've made many bad decisions in the name of *U.S. leadership* because legitimate dissent was suppressed."

The argument trailed off from there. We never managed to settle our disputes at the Owl Shop. Disagreements lingered, and over the next few months they would only grow deeper and more painful.

By January 2016, the presidential election had consumed the law school. Hillary Clinton was marching toward the Democratic nomination, and scores of students took Metro-North into New York a few days a week to volunteer for her campaign. On the other side of things, the presumptive favorite for the Republican nomination, Jeb Bush, had stumbled and faded. His impressive arsenal of funders proved inadequate next to Donald J. Trump's bombast.

Conversations at our weekly cigar nights, which had grown in size, became more cutting. Odds were placed on Trump and then viciously debated. The tone grew less collegial and more pugilistic, much like the broadcasts that flickered from a television mounted on a wall behind whichever bar we were patronizing.

We often found relief from it all in the purple of night, when a quiet set in over New Haven. On some evenings, the two of us would lounge on kitty-corner couches in Jordan's apartment, down by the train tracks and overlooking a parking garage. It was far from the Owl Shop and even further from the law school.

"I've been thinking about something," Jordan said one night.

"Oh yeah?" Chris said.

Jordan's decision to go to law school never really made sense to his friends and family. It seemed like a detour, especially since he also planned to go to business school and spend his career building companies. But Jordan loved politics—especially weighty issues like war and peace—and the law seemed like a good place to wrestle with those things. Just one year earlier, while advising the Afghan National Army, Jordan had watched as the absence of the rule of law, among other problems, had led to endless civil war. It felt urgent to him to understand why.

"I really like the idea of the Constitution as a *covenant,* something that binds us together in a society of mutual trust and collective responsibility," Jordan said. "One of my professors describes it as 'an intergenerational project in which every American has a role in helping to achieve a more perfect union.' It's a beautiful concept—but how does it actually work?"

"I used to hear a similar refrain in Washington all the time," Chris said. "That 'America is a great experiment' and each generation has to renew it and give it new meaning."

"But what does that mean?" Jordan continued. "Around here we talk about legal theory, and balancing tests, and principles that most people don't know. What actually binds us together? I feel like there's almost a spiritual dimension to all of this."

Earlier that year, Jordan had started learning more about his Jewish faith. He would frequently quote his favorite rabbi, noting the parallels between the United States and the story of the Jewish people.

"I think it happens out there," Chris said. "It's people who move this country. Leaders and artists and thinkers and people—just people."

"Right," Jordan said. "We find meaning in things that matter to everyone. Things like religion and art and culture and work, and even politics. But right now, all we seem to focus on is our differences.

"With all the division in the country, I guess I wonder what's being lost."

Chris considered it. Since watching Barack Obama's first inaugural speech on a screen jerry-rigged across Sproul Plaza on the UC-Berkeley campus, Chris had believed in the president's rhetoric that we are ultimately all one people and, while imperfect, our country is engaged in a democratic project worth perfecting. That Americans can understand one another and, together, reinvent the ways in which we interact. But Chris had come to fear that this might no longer be the case. The evidence he saw around him did not add up to that worldview. Conversations were becoming less tolerant by the day. Division was undeniable, no matter one's faith in a greater democratic purpose.

"That's something I've thought a lot about too, given what's happening right now," Chris added. "My impulse is to go out and see things—to experience what's happening and draw a conclusion or two from that."

It was apparent to both of us that we were missing an essential piece of the larger story. Our fields of view were just too limited. Still, one thing was clear: something was amiss.

"To be honest, it's why I've gone so quiet at the Owl Shop," Chris continued. "Everyone seems to have an idea of what's going on out there, and I don't. I couldn't tell you what's going on in Iowa or Alabama or Oregon. All I know is what's happening here, and even that's complicated."

"Agreed."

"And that's dangerous," Chris said. "Because if you haven't seen it, then what can you really know about it?"

Jordan nodded and leaned back.

One night at the Owl Shop, a visitor with long hair and a black coat began to shout. One of our friends had brought him along that evening, and the two of them were debating the limits of free speech.

"Unbelievable," the visitor snorted, his hair falling in locks over his face as others jumped in. He sank back against the wicker of his chair.

"If you want to have a dialogue, then stop interrupting me," our classmate insisted.

"Don't police my affect," came the reply.

A few days earlier, Donald Trump had emerged as the favorite to win the Republican nomination. As he cruised toward the convention, Hillary Clinton was struggling to finish off Bernie Sanders.

All the same, the two of us had grown closer. Our career paths diverged and our politics rankled the other, but we often found ourselves sharing and listening. Jordan was on his way to a summer job in Los Angeles, then Stanford business school in the fall. Chris was taking his first steps back into the media with a summer position at *The Atlantic*, for which he was already blocking out stories with Post-it notes on the walls of his apartment. But we still felt drawn to one another, drawn to this unlikely friendship.

Yet New Haven was suffocating. Chris's silence in these debates had grown, and Jordan's frustrations with the progressives of the law school had deepened. Even Jordan's patience for the political duels he had once relished was slackening.

The yelling at our patio-side table that night reached a new pitch. While multiple classmates tried to intercede with the warring parties, Jordan looked over at Chris, who was gazing up the street.

"Hey," Jordan said, thwacking Chris across the chest. "Wanna go on a road trip? I have to be in Los Angeles in a week, and I was thinking of driving."

Chris pondered the question. His job in D.C. didn't start until

June—three weeks from now. Like Jordan, Chris was perched at the edge of the conversation. A friend to his left was trying to butt in with a point while another classmate repeated himself. The visitor with the long hair was morose and sneered from behind his drink. In a flood of clarity, Chris made a decision.

"When do we leave?" he said.

Idaho

The Volvo ran out of engine coolant on a flat stretch of South
Dakota highway in the gathering dark. We were tearing across
I-90 somewhere between Chamberlain and Murdo when a threat-
ening red light flashed on the dash. A highway exit appeared on the
right, but Jordan was moving too fast in the far left lane to make it
in time.

"Dammit," he breathed. There was no telling how long it would be
until the next one.

"Do you know what coolant does?" Jordan said, turning to Chris.

"Cools the engine, I assume."

Jordan glared.

"I don't know, man," Chris shrugged.

"What if I just go really slowly?" Jordan said and veered right, across
the white lines on the two-lane highway, and settled into the slow lane
at thirty-five miles an hour. The sky was already black. Lumbering
18-wheelers crashed by at twice our speed, and the car shuddered
violently with each pass.

"Jesus," Chris said. "We're going to die."

"How far until the next gas station?"

Chris thumbed his phone, but the map wouldn't load. There was no cell service in the vast open space on either side of the highway.

"There's got to be something within the next few miles, right?"

Chris didn't speak. He didn't know much about cars, but something was wrong, and there was a good chance it was due to the blistering speed his new friend kept. But no matter what put the two of us in this predicament, we were in it and Jordan had the most to lose.

That morning, Jordan's mother, Carolyn, had called.

"Jordan, you know Jenna's wedding is in five days."

"I know, Mom."

"And where are you?"

"We're just leaving Chicago."

"And you're going to get to Los Angeles by when?"

"The day before the rehearsal dinner, Mom. I'm not going to miss my own sister's wedding, don't worry."

"I'm worried."

"Don't worry, Carolyn," Chris said, piping up. "I'll get him there— I promise."

"I'm on speaker phone?"

"Yep."

"Well, Chris, it's nice to meet you. Jordan has told us so much."

"You, too, Carolyn."

"You promise you'll make it back?"

"I give you my word."

Carolyn still sounded skeptical.

"Five days, Jordan," she said and hung up.

"She only let me go on this trip because I told her you're a speechwriter," Jordan said.

"Not because I'd look after you?"

"Well, in a sense."

"How so?"

"I told her you'd help me write my wedding toast."

Hours seemed to pass as we crawled along the South Dakota

highway, the car's hazard lights blinking, before we saw a sign for Badlands National Park. Jordan steered the car off the highway and stopped at an intersection to search the map for a place to stay.

"Well, there's one motel about thirty minutes away," he said. "We'll have to drive through the park to get there."

"Hope they have a room," Chris said.

"With our luck today?" Jordan laughed.

As we entered the Badlands, Journey came on the radio—"Lovin', Touchin', Squeezin'"—and suddenly the mood shifted, as it often did when the end of a long day of travel approached.

We opened the windows and blasted the music as we snaked our way down into the bowels of the labyrinthine park. Towering sandy totems rose out of the night. At one point, we pulled over to touch one of the pillars. The sandstone crumbled like shortbread through our fingers.

"We should come back and see this at sunrise," Chris said, and we pledged to set our alarms so we could hit the trails in the dark.

Journey was still playing on the radio as we pulled into the parking lot of a two-story motel with a blinking VACANCY sign. The office was dark and the door locked. Jordan found a number on a sign and started dialing. Five minutes later a man in pajamas emerged from a nearby trailer, rubbing his eyes, and opened the office.

"This is an odd time for y'all to get in," he mumbled.

———————

The next morning before the sun came up, we stood shivering on a large rock outcropping somewhere on the edge of Badlands National Park. The desert air was brisk, and we jumped up and down to stay warm. One mile into our predawn hike, we found a vista that looked down upon the towers of clastic and across a flat desert leading away from the park. We hopped back and forth on the boulders and ledges until we found a perch to watch the sunrise.

"This time of day is really important in the infantry," Jordan said, breaking the still. "The moment just before light crests. In the old days it was the perfect time to attack an enemy—you could use the cover of darkness to get into position, and the first light to coordinate the assault. Commanders would have their entire unit wake up before dawn and 'stand-to' in defense against these possible surprise attacks. We used to do that in training all the time."

"But if the enemy soldiers were all at 'stand-to,' doesn't that make it a bad time to attack?"

"That's what makes combat so hard."

Jordan was at his most passionate when he had a chance to talk about the Marines, and Chris often marveled at what it must feel like to belong so wholeheartedly to something.

"I've spent a lot of time on bluffs like this," Chris said.

"For bird-watching?"

"Yeah, exactly," Chris said. "When I was eleven, my mom, she used to practically carry me out to the car and drive to Point Reyes so I could volunteer at an ornithology lab that banded birds to track their migrations."

Jordan listened.

"So we'd often find ourselves on some hillside somewhere, pulling birds out of this nearly invisible mesh—they call it mist netting—and putting them in little cloth bags to bring back to the lab to measure and weigh. The real scientists, they would stand there, warming their hands just like us, and listen."

A cacophony of bird sounds echoed up the ravine.

"And they'd call out species names as each piped up—robin, California towhee, wrentit."

"*Wrentit?*"

"Yeah—*wrentit.*"

We listened for a moment.

"I think I hear a wren," Chris said at length. "That scratchy, throaty one."

"I hear it."

"Its Latin name is *troglodytes*. The little guy never really comes out of the bushes it lives in. A troglodyte."

"What else is out there?"

Chris listened.

Peach-blue light filled the horizon. Our conversation trailed off in anticipation of daybreak. A few birds sang in the hollow below as wind whistled past the sandcastle towers of the Badlands. On that plateau at sunrise, a stillness held us both.

From the moment we entered the lower Dakota, painted wooden billboards for Wall Drug cropped up every mile or so. FREE ICE WATER, read one. ALL ROADS LEAD TO WALL DRUG, proclaimed another. After seeing our umpteenth sign, we decided a visit was mandatory.

We stopped for breakfast there, and it was filled with oil paintings of Western tableaux and colorful headdresses and decor. Older men and women in jeans and cowboy hats lounged at tables over steaming hot coffee.

We returned to the car with full stomachs and a jerrican of coolant.

"Where does it go?" Jordan said, jiggling the container of green-blue liquid.

"You're asking me?"

We poked around under the hood.

"Right there," Jordan said, pointing at a plastic cap.

Chris rolled up a newspaper like a funnel and looked at Jordan.

"Pour away."

Half of the saccharine-smelling liquid ended up in the radiator, the other half on Chris.

"Is this toxic?" Chris said in a slight panic. Both of us belly-laughed as Chris hopped around, smelling his arms and T-shirt.

Chris washed up in a truck-stop bathroom and soon we were back on I-90, headed for Black Hills National Forest and the giant stone faces of Mount Rushmore. A few months earlier Jordan had given Chris a copy of *American Places* by William Zinsser, one of Jordan's favorite books. Inspired by those who "hit the road, going in search of the founding ideals they felt the country had lost," Zinsser had made his own pilgrimage to 16 iconic American places, beginning with Mount Rushmore.

We pulled the car into a crowded parking lot and made our way to the park entrance. We zigzagged through the tourists, walking down a colonnade of flags that cracked in the wind and up slowly rising stairs until we were right under the visage of the fathers. We tried to look straight ahead or down so that our first sight of the facade would be up close. And then, together, we looked up.

"That's it?" Jordan said.

The place felt almost insignificant. Above a field of rock and scree dotted with evergreens were the lifeless, deeply grooved faces, distant and small. We attempted to admire them among the jostling crowd. These were totems of our democracy. Famous men who helped carve out what it means to be American.

"Well, not much to see, I guess," Chris said.

The whole visit lasted less than 20 minutes.

Back in the car, Jordan felt a twinge of guilt about having been so unmoved at an American "holy site." And that guilt came out in a particularly truculent way.

"I wouldn't be surprised if there were a movement in the near future to try to get Jefferson and Washington removed from Mount Rushmore," he said, as we pulled out of the parking lot and back onto the downward slope of the road.

"Why?" Chris asked.

"Because they owned slaves," Jordan said. "It's like Calhoun."

For most of the school year, students at Yale had waged a campaign to have Calhoun College renamed. John C. Calhoun—seventh vice president of the United States, secretary of war, secretary of state, and

both a congressman and a senator from South Carolina—was an una-
bashed defender of slavery in the antebellum South. It had become a
frequent topic of conversation among our friends, and the two of us
seemed to fall on opposing sides.

The debate over Calhoun had come up a month earlier when Peter
Salovey, the president of Yale, announced that Calhoun's name would
remain on the college.* He argued that students would be better
prepared for the challenges of the present and the future if they were
forced to reckon with the legacy of slavery, rather than erase it from
memory.

"Universities have to be places where tough conversations happen,"
Salovey told reporters. "I don't think that is advanced by hiding our
past."

At the same time, Salovey declared that the title of *Master* at the
residential colleges would be changed to *Head of the college* to avoid any
connection to the appellation for American slave owners. The hedge
left no one satisfied.

There in South Dakota, the old debate reignited.

"It's a half measure," Chris said of Salovey's decision.

"I agree—it's the easy way out."

"Sure is."

"But that doesn't justify breaking things or screaming at professors.
The students' actions are out of proportion to the issue. It makes them
seem too radical."

"I appreciate what they're up to even if I don't always agree with
their tactics," Chris said. "I think it's healthy to have loud, well-
organized activists keeping the pressure up."

"But there needs to be a limit," Jordan said. "Otherwise, activists
end up hurting the very communities they claim to represent."

"I mean, I don't disagree. At Berkeley, when students would protest

---

* On February 11, 2017, Yale renamed the college after pioneering computer
scientist Grace Murray Hopper.

rising fees and tuition, some people would pull fire alarms, break windows, and otherwise wreak havoc. That was counterproductive—they were just wounding the thing they loved."

"But that's why I think the tactics have to be in proportion to the issue at stake," Jordan said. "Some injustices are so big they're worth dying for—like ending Jim Crow. But others just aren't, and when the same rhetoric and tactics are used for both, they lose their effect."

"Right, it's a question of degree."

"Yeah, totally."

We paused.

"So we agree?"

"I guess we do."

Still, certain things were left unsaid. New friends have a way of inoculating each other against argument. We pulled our punches, modulating our arguments so the differences seemed less severe. We used our toes to muddy the lines that divided us, but the lines were still there.

As we emerged from the gulches of the Black Hills, Jordan unfurrowed his brow.

"Look, if Yale changes the name," he said, "it should happen through a deliberative process that takes into account the traditions and history of the school, the perspectives of the alumni, and the interests of the current students. And I hope it's done in a way that's about choosing to honor someone else, rather than tearing down the memory of Calhoun out of hatred."

"I agree," Chris replied. "On the process bit, at least."

"Process is the key," Jordan said. "Activists play a role in pushing society forward. But if they push for too much too fast, they risk provoking a backlash that can hurt people."

"I'm not an activist," Chris said. "But I was raised by one, and I believe in them. For a long time it troubled me that I didn't count myself among them; how could I think that way and not join in? But everyone has a role. It seems like activists are supposed to be loud and transgressive and take extreme, sometimes uncomfortably idealistic positions. And it's the job of a university administration to do what is best for the college. That's the thing—that's democracy: a big, loud, messy conversation with competing ideas."

"Look man, I want progress too," Jordan said. "I just want to do it right. I think there's a lot of good and a lot of wisdom in those who came before us and the institutions they set up. They got a lot wrong too, and we should change those things. But we shouldn't throw away all the good with the bad."

"I agree with you," Chris said. "Sometimes things need to go slowly. The name change requires wisdom and listening and compromise. I think a lot of people just want to be heard."

We kept gliding down long open roads framed by snowcapped mountains and protruding rocks, which the road hugged like a length of rope. Carved marble clouds passed over great expanses of sky in trailing thermal patterns.

A few days earlier, Trump had clinched the GOP nomination and surpassed Clinton in the polls for the first time. That week there would be skirmishes outside a Trump rally in San Diego, where supporters and detractors exchanged blows in the street. Thirty-five people were arrested. But in South Dakota, the two of us felt all of the 1,500 miles that lay between us and the politics of 2016.

"I don't think we're really that far apart," Chris said.

"Me neither."

The next few days were a blur of fields and mountain ranges. We spent time in Bozeman, Montana and explored Yellowstone National Park in a gentle rain. With Chris at the wheel, we passed into Idaho, where we swooped southwest across the pine ridges of the Sawtooths and the volcanic rocks of Craters of the Moon National Monument and Preserve.

In southern Idaho, we cruised along the long flat valleys—until a set of flashing blue and red lights filled the rearview mirror.

Chris spotted the state trooper's truck, its form blurred by the heat rising from the road, as it barreled up the black pavement a quarter-mile behind us. Chris looked down at the speedometer—95. His stomach turned. The speed limit was somewhere around 70.

"Shit," Jordan said, turning in his seat.

Chris pulled onto the shoulder, killed the engine, and leaned back, defeated.

"Don't worry, man," Jordan assured Chris, as we watched an officer in knee-high leather boots approach the car. "It was bound to happen at some point."

"Do you know how fast you were going?" the officer said after Chris rolled down the window.

"T-too fast," Chris stammered.

"License and registration."

Jordan rummaged through the glove compartment, muttering something, while the officer looked over Chris's license.

"You two been driving all night?"

"Nearly," Chris said.

"What brings you out here"—he glanced at the license—"Christopher?"

"We're driving across the country."

"Why?"

"Jordan here is going to be the maid of honor at his sister's wedding."

"Man of honor," Jordan corrected without looking up.

The officer stood mute.

"We are both at law school in Connecticut," Chris offered, trying to occupy the silence.

"Sir," Jordan interjected, his search frustrated, "I don't have my insurance card, but I can try to pull it up on my phone."

The officer frowned and said nothing.

"Yeah, it was my grandparents' car," Jordan continued. "They live in New York. I must have left it with them."

"Give me your license, too."

Jordan fished it out.

"Encino?" the officer said.

"I grew up there. Like the movie *Encino Man*?"

Jordan's quip fell flat.

"And you're from"—the officer looked down at Chris's license again—"Washington, D.C.?"

"Well, no, I'm from the San Francisco Bay Area," Chris said, "but I lived in D.C. for a few years after college."

"And now you're in Connecticut?"

"Yes, sir."

"But the car is registered in New York?"

"Yep," Jordan said, leaning down to smile at the officer through the window.

"Stay here."

We both watched as he turned and made for his truck, which sat at a skewed angle on the side of the road. The Volvo's engine clicked and popped loudly as it cooled in the spring heat. Chris watched intently through the rearview mirror. Jordan looked at him and laughed.

"Calm down, man, it's not a big deal."

"You never know," Chris responded, still eyeing the officer. As a teenager, Chris had been pulled over for running a stop sign in Berkeley. The policeman had made Chris and two friends sit on the curb as he turned his mother's burgundy sedan inside out. When the officer couldn't find anything, he had cursed and tossed Chris's wallet in disgust. "You got lucky," the man said, leaving the three of them on the sidewalk.

A moment later, the Idaho trooper returned.

"I'm going to have to ask you to get out of the car," the officer said.

Chris's eyes darted to catch Jordan's, which for the first time flashed with fear.

"Please step over there," the officer said.

Chris stepped out of the car. The officer gestured to the side of the road and walked a step or two behind Chris. One hand hovered over his holster.

Chris's eyes drifted off toward Idaho's chaparral plains. The two of us had passed through Wisconsin, which was wild and green. We had driven through statuesque rock formations emerging out of thick woodlands, and gorges filled with emerald water on their floors. In Montana, Chris had drifted off to sleep in the passenger seat as thunderstorms passed over green pastures and wheeled in the shadow of the mountain ranges that lined the road. Idaho was flat and stark. There on the side of the highway, Chris noticed the sand under his feet and how it gave way beneath him. It was rough, unlike the peat on the highway shoulder in Wyoming where Jordan had taken a photograph of an American flag jutting from a rock outcropping in the middle of a lake.

"Would you step into my car, please?"

The officer's command snapped Chris back to the present. He had dealt with police before but had never been invited into one of their cars. He tried the passenger door and found it unlocked. He stepped up and into the jumper seat. *Things could be worse,* he thought to himself. *He could have my hands cuffed and a palm on the back of my head.*

The cab was silent as the officer stepped around the truck to the driver's seat. He passed in front of our car, where Chris could see Jordan craning his neck to watch. Chris reached for the seat belt out of habit, then thought better of it. An array of weapons— shotguns and long rifles—stood upright between his shoulder and the driver's seat. Chris breathed deeply to steady his hands and calm his throbbing head.

"Kid," the officer said after settling into his own seat. The silence deepened as he made himself comfortable, his single word hanging in the stale air of the truck. He looked straight ahead.

"None of this makes any goddamn sense."

Sitting in the front seat of his truck, the officer explained his dilemma to Chris.

"You say you're from California, but you have a D.C. license. Jordan here is from Los Angeles with a California license, but his car is registered in New York—to a different name, no less. Not to mention you say you're both law students. But this guy Jordan is now starting business school, and you can't stop shaking."

He turned and peered at Chris over the shotguns. Chris suddenly wished he had cut his hair, or had at least changed his shirt, which displayed the phrase BERKELEY POLITICAL REVIEW across the chest.

Chris smiled weakly.

"It just doesn't add up, kid."

"I know it sounds crazy," Chris said. "Hearing it out loud, it sounds crazy to me, too. But it's the truth, sir. We're on a road trip. He is who he says he is, and so am I."

The officer had turned back around. Chris could see him eyeing the car, weighing our plea against the facts of the unusual situation.

"Besides," he continued, "why are your eyes so bloodshot?"

Again, he had caught Chris off guard. Perhaps his red eyes were due to our sleepless driving habits, or perhaps it was just a fishing expedition. Whatever the officer's intent, the stakes had just gone up.

"Sir, if you're implying that I'm high or something, I can assure you that I'm not," Chris said.

"I implied no such thing."

Chris slumped back. *Soon I'll be moved to the back seat, where the doors don't open from the inside,* he thought. *Why did I say that? Was that probable cause?*

Chris regretted his decision not to take criminal law the semester before.

"Stay here," the officer said and left the truck to approach Jordan. Chris watched from the passenger seat, relieved that the gruff man had left him alone, if only for a moment. Jordan got out of the car and faced the officer. Both of them had their hands on their hips. The man leaned in slightly while Jordan stood and faced him. The officer spoke, gesturing first at the car, then back at Chris, and finally to Jordan. Jordan responded with some hand-waving of his own. They both turned to look at Chris, and suddenly Jordan threw his head back and clapped his hands, a huge smile on his face.

"Damn it, Jordan," Chris said aloud.

But then the officer smiled, too. He beckoned for Chris to join them, and Chris leaped down from the truck.

"I'm letting you go," the officer said as Chris approached.

Chris was stunned. Jordan would later explain that the officer's suspicion dissipated after he learned that Jordan had been a Marine. He may not have understood us, but he respected Jordan's service, and Chris would reap the reward.

"A word to the wise, kid," the officer said, pumping Chris's hand. "Don't be so scared next time. You're a law student. You know what happens at a traffic stop. All that sweat and stammering made me suspicious."

"Of course, sir," Chris said, still shaken. "I guess it's just the badge, the uniform—it's intimidating."

"Good luck to you both."

We got back in the car as the officer pulled away with the grind of tires against gravel. His taillights soon disappeared around a rare curve in the otherwise empty highway.

Jordan looked at Chris with a triumphant smile.

"I knew we'd get out of it," he said.

"I'm done driving."

Chris tossed the keys to Jordan and made for the passenger side.

———

"I can't believe he just let us go," Chris said.

Twenty minutes after the encounter, he was still rattled. Jordan had brought the car back up to a terrific speed, tempered only slightly by the knowledge that these long, empty highways were, in fact, patrolled.

"And he was so—reasonable," Chris continued.

"Yeah, cops can be nice," Jordan laughed.

"I just haven't had a positive encounter like that in a while."

It was clear that the two of us had completely different understandings of law enforcement. For Jordan, the police were, in a sense, his people. The military and law-enforcement often share a deep respect born from their professions' similar perils. Though there were certainly bad apples here and there, Jordan believed that most police officers had good intentions and cared deeply about serving their communities. They deserved respect and gratitude for the dangers they faced.

Chris, though, had learned to be wary around cops. There had been an officer who handed out stickers and gave tours of his car to kids in Chris's neighborhood. But in high school, after his own run-ins, Chris had read all about the Oakland Police Department's checkered history and seen videos of police brutality online over and over again. Seared into his mind's eye was the image of Oscar Grant, a 22-year-old black man, lying handcuffed on the platform of the Fruitvale BART station just moments before Johannes Mehserle, a BART police officer, fired a bullet into his spine.

If Jordan's assumption was that law-enforcement officers were decent people trying to do a job in the most difficult circumstances, Chris's was that they could be dangerous—and, when they abused their power, deadly.

"Generally, if you're respectful to police when they pull you over, nothing happens," Jordan said. "If you call them *Sir* and act polite, they might even let you go."

"That's not true for everyone."

"What do you mean?"

"Well, it's one thing for you—or me—to say that. The situation might have turned out very differently if we were African American."

"Maybe the situation would have turned out differently if you weren't so nervous, or if I hadn't been a Marine. You're isolating one factor and making it all-important. My point is that if you're generally respectful and give police no reason to be suspicious, then the situation will nearly always turn out okay. Are there exceptions? Yes. And they are tragic, and horrible, and the cops who make mistakes should be thrown in jail. But they are the exception."

"I'm not sure we're talking about rare exceptions here," Chris said.

"My problem," Jordan continued, "is that exceptional cases end up dominating the conversation so that all police seem racist, or poorly trained, or whatever. It creates a vicious cycle where police feel like they are under public attack while certain communities feel distrustful and disproportionately targeted by law enforcement. And because both sides feel this way, it increases the chances that mistakes will happen."

"But they *are* disproportionately targeted by police," Chris said.

"Honestly, I don't know how to untangle the statistics," Jordan said. "Do you?"

"You don't even need to look at the statistics," Chris said. "Just look around. You can watch videos on YouTube of cops being overly aggressive, shooting when they aren't supposed to, firing tear gas into peaceful crowds. Or look at the long history of it or listen to the communities who deal with police on a daily basis."

"Those are exceptions. Horrible, tragic exceptions. And if there's malice involved, then that's evil, and those bad actors should be prosecuted to the full extent of the law. But that shouldn't mean we paint all cops as murderous or racist."

Things went on like this for an hour or so. Both of us dug in, frustrated that the other couldn't seem to accept points we felt were patently obvious.

By sunset, we passed Boise, ran out of steam, and stopped to find a bite to eat. The sun was hanging low in the sky as we parked at an Applebee's. We ordered teriyaki chicken to go, then looked for a place to watch the sunset. We found it in a spit of land just off the highway in the foothills of a long valley. Plastic takeout bags in hand, we scrambled up to the top of a bluff.

"Did you see that Lewis and Clark went through Idaho?" Chris asked.

"That would have been like 200 years ago."

Another moment of stillness. The battles of the day had subsided. Something about the golden view—the rustle of insects in the tall waving grasses, the muted sounds of the highway around the bend—washed away the worst of the day, even if a distance still existed between us.

How could we agree on so much, yet disagree on who an average police officer was? Or what racial violence looked like? How could we have felt the beguiling sensation of agreement in South Dakota, yet be so far apart come Idaho? Over the next few days, the two of us would keep revisiting the Idaho state trooper's exclamation: *None of this makes any goddamn sense.*

———————

We made our way out of the heat of the Oregon lowlands to Crater Lake, where ice and snow coated the high banks of the caldera's lip. Down below, a glassy purple surface mesmerized the two of us from our high vantage. Then it was back down into green forests that felt like the redwood groves of California, making Chris homesick for the first time.

"I think it's time," Jordan said, as we whizzed through the brown trunks and deep green leaves.

"For what?"

"For my speech."

Chris had thought of the wedding toast at various times throughout the trip, but the moment never seemed right. Only hours away from California, it finally did.

"Okay, then. Why not?"

Chris rifled through his bag and pulled out a notebook. He flipped through it, showing Jordan its empty pages and sporadic doodles.

"My notes from International Law."

"Seems about right."

"So what do you want to say?"

Jordan had imagined a joke or two—about apologizing for shedding some "manly maid-of-honor" tears, or about how his brother-in-law was now the family's favorite son because he played golf and was gainfully employed.

"That's good. That's good."

"But what do I say about Jenna?"

"Well, what does she mean to you?"

Jordan considered it.

"Jenna always protected me growing up," he said. "Which will surprise some people. She's warm and bubbly and was always caring for others—it's why she became a social worker. But she has a ferocious side, too. My favorite example was during *Bush v. Gore.* Jenna went to one of the most liberal high schools in the country, and there was a lot of Republican-bashing going on. At one point, she'd simply had enough. She got up during a school assembly and told 500 people, 'All of you need to stop it. My parents and my brother are Republicans, and they are still good people!' I'll never forget that."

Jordan smiled.

Chris held his breath. Jordan had an easy way about his stories of the service, but personal stories—the anecdotes of family and tender moments, and the possibility of once, just maybe, having not been a trained Marine—were fewer. Chris felt as if Jordan were ushering him in closer, which Chris welcomed.

As a child, Chris relied on friends much like family. His numerous "godmothers" would watch him when his mother got sick. Dan, his godfather, not only brought over pizza every Friday but taught Chris to shave, came to his soccer games, and slipped him cash for concerts in high school and college. His mother, a force in her own right, had folded these men and women into an extended family, and Chris had taken to doing the same as he aged into adulthood. Perhaps Jordan could become family, same as the kin Chris had come to know in Berkeley, Washington, and now, maybe, New Haven.

"When I was a freshman in high school," Jordan continued, "a senior bullied me. I was terrified to walk around school. I never said anything about it at home, but Jenna could tell that I was upset. We went to different high schools, but soon I had seven junior boys come up to me, all Jenna's friends, and tell me not to worry because they had my back. Two weeks later, Jenna berated the senior at a party. I have no idea what she said to him, but he never picked on me again."

"Well," Chris said, looking down at the jostled notes he had taken. "I think it's all there. You've got a nice dose of comedy up top. You've got a thoroughly touching anecdote, and a place to land. Bravo."

We fell silent again as we passed through old-growth forests and took a hook down a mountainside, crossing into California with a day to spare before the wedding. It was a satisfied quietude. There was no note of discomfort in the hum of the engine and the tinkle of the radio. With each passing mile, what started as an almost-friendship began to feel more like a brotherhood.

We both felt this outside Redding, among the tawny grass hills of California. We had seen much on the trip. We survived the car's swoon in South Dakota. We'd come to a skittering stop a few feet from a jumpy herd of sheep meandering across the highway, cajoled along by the teeth of a judicious pair of collies. We'd communed with a bull elk somewhere in the highlands of Yellowstone as its fur matted with the same mist that clung to our thin cotton layers. We'd exchanged looks with bronze-faced inmates in bright orange jumpsuits clearing underbrush as a wildfire burned oak trees and grass in the California foothills, sending ash curling up into the sky like fetid snow. And we had met both strange men and kind people—people who offered directions, meals, and beds for the night. We didn't know what to make of the trip quite yet. We knew there was something to the road—and the road taken in this way—but we couldn't put our fingers on it. We drove into Sonoma after all this, knowing our 3,000-mile journey was almost over.

"Let's do this again," Jordan said.

"I'd like that," Chris responded.

Phoenix

One year later—on August 22, 2017—the two of us were racing east in the Volvo down Highway 8. Jordan swerved off a frontage road and sent Chris sprawling against the window. He parked on a berm outside the Marine Corps Air Station in Yuma, Arizona, where we joined the agitated crowds that had formed along the fence line, and together we all watched Air Force One land and taxi.

A hushed silence had descended after the president's plane touched down. Then, after a short chorus of car horns and clapping, the brief moment of comity erupted into chaos.

"Trump just wants to protect our borders!" screamed a Navy nurse with flushed-red cheeks and a BUILD THE WALL sign. A group of protesters and supporters had knotted around her. "You can't have a country if you don't have borders. That's why we need the wall!"

"He's racist!" a young Hispanic man shouted back. The two of them approached each other. "Why doesn't he build a wall along Canada, huh? Because he hates Mexicans. He calls us rapists and murderers."

"Black Lives Matter is racist to me!" the nurse said, pointing at his shirt. "This isn't about race. This is about being red, white, and fucking blue." With each syllable, she pounded her chest with a fist.

An older woman with short white hair and a tie-dyed shirt waved a LOVE TRUMPS HATE sign around the nurse's ears. Cars honked their approval for indistinguishable placards, each blare eliciting halfhearted cheers from segments of the crowd.

This is what we had come to see: the ways in which Americans now conversed in a polarized world where triple-digit heat was no deterrent to speaking one's mind into someone else's face.

A few feet away from us, the nurse shook her head.

"I think we should be able to talk to each other. Can we not talk to each other?" she said. It was a change in tone, as if she had taken off a costume and revealed herself. "All I did was come over here to show that we can mix and not be violent. What does it say about our country that we can't have a conversation, that we can't talk?

"You have an opinion, and I have an opinion," she continued. "We're supposed to be able to sit here and have a discussion. The reason why America is dead is we can't sit here, and we can't talk together."

We wandered back to the car and waited for the air-conditioning to fight off the suffocating heat. Neither of us spoke right away—it was too hot to think—but our faces wore our concern with what we had just witnessed.

With a last glance at the writhing crowd, Jordan threw the Volvo in gear and gunned it down I-10 toward Phoenix, Arizona, where President Trump would hold a rally later that night.

––––––––––––

Earlier that day, we had awoken in a fifth-floor room at the Real de Rio Hotel in Tijuana, Mexico. Chris opened his eyes to find Jordan fully dressed and sitting upright on the edge of the other bed.

"What's going on?" Chris mumbled.

"Time to go," Jordan said.

We were on our second road trip, which had taken us from Northern California down through the Central Valley and out again to the coast. It was the first time we had seen each other in around eight months. Jordan was about to start his second year studying business at Stanford, and Chris had just flown to California after a summer of writing in D.C. We spent a few days in Los Angeles, where Chris introduced his girlfriend to Jordan's mother, and an afternoon at Camp Pendleton, Jordan's old base. A night of exploring in Tijuana followed.

Back on U.S. highways, we veered east along the border with Mexico. Highway 8 was austere. The road glided through mountain passes and desert valleys that stretched for miles. Hamlets no larger than a few city blocks, with names like Ocotillo and Coyote Wells, dotted its sparse exits. The rust-brown border wall wound like a copper vein through the primordial landscape.

We watched the border come and go and come again as we drove. Chris traced its span with his finger, smudging the window as he went. It looked like little more than a thin ribbon amid the mountains and sloping valleys. Jordan wondered aloud how something so small and arbitrary could become the focus of so much tension. This was an empty land, after all, with little to distinguish one side of the border from the other. Yet that line—drawn more than a century and a half earlier—had somehow become a main source of conflict in our politics.

It had been a little more than a year since that police officer pulled us over in Idaho, and we were back on the road. We started the trip with no agenda and no set stops, just a vague plan to swing through the Southwest. On the way to Tijuana, however, Chris had discovered that the president was going to hold a rally in Phoenix. Jordan was wary, but Chris was eager.

Both of us thought the rally might shed light on what was going on around the country. The 2016 presidential election had left little room for compromise. Neighbors who shared values and sometimes even meals were suddenly separated. Like that border wall in the Sonoran Desert, a dividing line cut sharply through society, making two out of one—even if some of us weren't sure why we were on one side or the other, or what the line represented in the first place.

So we drove east to Phoenix.

For months the two of us had fought about who was the bigger threat to democracy—Donald Trump or those who opposed him. Jordan argued that the constant hand-wringing over America's supposed authoritarian swing, or its upsurge in racism, was not just overblown but destructive. It was fueling an active resistance to a sitting president that was unprecedented in American history. Chris was less inclined to point the finger at those rallying in the streets. He heard dog whistles in Trump's language and policies, and recoiled from the offers Trump made to pay his supporters' legal bills if they "knocked the crap out of" protesters.

Even so, the two of us hoped we might find Americans still listening to one another in Phoenix.

———————

Chris spent much of the afternoon scrolling through Twitter, closely monitoring hashtags such as *#PhoenixRally* and *#Trump*. One local reporter claimed 50,000 protesters were expected. An article was circulating about an army of leather-clad motorcyclists—known as Bikers for Trump—descending on the city in full force. Chris came across a short video of the crowd already collecting downtown. The sound was too much for his phone's speakers, which scratched and squealed with the effort. He threw it down and watched the scrub fly by.

The timing of this rally was particularly controversial. A week before, a hundred or so young men from various white-supremacy groups had gathered on the University of Virginia's Nameless Field in Charlottesville, torches in hand, to protest the removal of a statue of Confederate general Robert E. Lee. They barked hateful slogans such as "Blood and soil" and "Jews will not replace us." Hundreds of counterprotesters mustered in opposition, and the convergence became a melee. Many feared the Phoenix rally would become the next battlefield.

Jordan was worried. For months he had tried to convince Chris that the country would return to normal. Trump would moderate his tone, he argued, and the #Resistance would lose steam. Things seemed to be going in the right direction after the president named John Kelly his new chief of staff in July. Kelly, a Marine Corps general, was known to Marines like Jordan as a competent manager and an even-tempered man. But Charlottesville shattered these hopes. Jordan had no doubt there would be violence where we were going. The only question was how much and against whom.

We took a taxi downtown to the convention center, where the rally was being held. Shouts and slogans ricocheted off the sand-colored walls of the buildings. Heavily armed police stood sentinel, and beige dump trucks lined the streets—a macabre reminder of the truck that had purposefully jumped a curb in Barcelona, Spain, only a week before, killing and injuring scores. The sidewalks were swollen with Trump supporters. Jordan felt tense in a way he hadn't since leaving Afghanistan. He knew from training and experience when a place is primed for violence, and Phoenix felt just so.

When traffic became too heavy, we exited into the choking heat. In line were groups of graying older men, parents with young children, and packs of teenagers. A number of them sported iconic red hats and gray T-shirts printed with mottoes such as CAN YOU HEAR US NOW?

We tried to find the end of the rally line, but it stretched for blocks and blocks. Chris looked at his phone—6:25 p.m. Trump was set to go on stage at seven.

"We're not getting in," he said, looking at Jordan.

Chris slumped down on a planter box and listened to the crowd.

Jordan turned toward the front, eyeing the entrance where throngs of people were shuffling through a narrow gate.

"What if we just go to the head of the line?" he said.

"Wait—" Chris started, but Jordan was off.

We picked our way through the crowd, stepping into the street and around barricades. We slipped past scores of people who lolled in the heat and watched us without a word. A haggard policeman met us at the front of the line; next to him stood a man in a white polo shirt, scanning tickets. Both of them were overwhelmed by the crush of people. "Go, go, go," the officer said, his earpiece abuzz, and we were ushered past the doorman.

We were getting in.

Beyond the checkpoint, the line snaked its way around the outside of the convention center through a series of roped-off pathways. We followed behind two men with shaved heads and dark sunglasses. The line rounded a corner, and then, in a burst of noise and energy, we found ourselves face-to-face with the rumored protesters. Across the heavily guarded street were thousands of people. They pressed up against the police barriers, at least six deep. A few hoisted colorful signs above their heads—NOT MY PRESIDENT; ONE DOES NOT SIMPLY PARDON RACISM; TRUMP COSTS AMERICANS MORE THAN MONEY; FUCK TRUMP—while someone howled calls and responses through a crackly bullhorn.

"Oh my God," Jordan shouted.

A call of *Shame* went up, and it became all we could hear.

What better way to express collective condemnation? Chris thought.

Chris had grown up among protests. On some weekend mornings, his mother would put him in a sweater and whisk him over to San Francisco to march down Market Street among thousands of like-minded people calling for an end to the Iraq War. On one occasion they made it all the way to the civic center, where they found a window perch high above the scene below. There, leaning out, Chris could see the cupola of City Hall rising above the broad square, where crowds of people mingled under knobby sycamore trees. The plaza was full of men, women, and children—singing, chanting, laughing. Chris remembered feeling the warm sensation of belonging. There were no battle lines in sight, no differences of opinions. On that morning, to a young boy, things seemed so simple, so straightforward.

Standing on the opposite side of the protest line in Phoenix, however, was more complicated. The barricades lining the street formed a barrier between him and those on the other side. They were screaming at him. Chris thought about jumping the police line and joining them.

We were both overwhelmed. But the two men with shaved heads ahead of us in line were more clearheaded. One of them unfurled an American flag and pushed out his chest. "Four more years," he bellowed back at the mass of protesters across the street, pumping the flag with a clenched fist. His friend joined him, and their display incited an equal reaction across the street, the crowd spasming with noise and raised fists.

"They hate us," Jordan said under the crowd's torrent. We slipped inside—and away from the chorus of sound.

"Our lives are too short to let our differences divide us."

The words echoed as we entered the convention hall.

"At the end of the day, our differences are nothing compared to our shared humanity and the values that unite us."

"That voice sounds familiar," Chris said.

"It's Ben Carson," Jordan said.

Carson stood at a narrow lectern flanked by dozens of people raising Trump signs, each illuminated by camera lights on the other side of the hall. A couple thousand people were corralled in the center by waist-high fences encircling the stage and the media pit. It felt like a boxing ring with two prizefighters on either side, the audience trapped in between.

Chris was surprised by the tenor of the speeches. From time to time, when he shut his eyes, he could imagine he was at an Obama rally. Words like *unity, love,* and *shared humanity* filled the auditorium. Some of the words may have been the same, but this crowd was mostly white, and it skewed older. Many sported short hair cuts, tattooed arms, and worn leather jackets. A few young couples looked on with arms around each other—notable exceptions in the middle-aged crowd.

As we acclimated, the sea of people came into focus. We saw individuals instead of a collective, and a few in particular caught our eyes. A handful of ominous characters prowled the margins with scowls on their faces. One with gnarled teeth and an oversize polo shirt walked in and out of the crowd, trying to get closer to the stage. On occasion he would unleash an outburst.

"Whoop them, Uncle Donald!" he squealed.

Though few in number, these men left us unsettled. One of them hovered a few feet away. He was short and thin, with muscular arms and a slightly crooked spine that made his shoulders hunch forward toward his ears. He looked to be in his mid-50s and had apparently come to the rally alone. He cast his eyes around suspiciously, pausing to glare at the two of us; perhaps he suspected we were not true believers.

With the crowd properly whipped up, it was time for the main event. The gathering unleashed a howl as President Trump emerged from behind a curtain, walked on stage, and seized the podium with both hands.

"I'm here tonight to send a message," he began to thunderous cheers.

"It's finally time to rebuild our country, to take care of our people, and to fight for the jobs our great American workers deserve, and that's what we're doing."

Like the speakers before him, Trump offered his acolytes a script of unity and hope. "We believe that every American has the right to live with dignity," he said, reading from a scrolling teleprompter. "Respect for America demands respect for all of its people."

It didn't take long for the president to bring up Virginia.

"What happened in Charlottesville strikes at the core of America," he said, gripping the podium. "And tonight, this entire arena stands united in forceful condemnation of the thugs who perpetrate hatred and violence.

"But the very dishonest media," Trump continued, his voice rising, "those people right up there with all the cameras—"

Before Trump could finish his incantation—as he gestured toward the risers where the pale lights of the television cameras shined back— the crowd exploded. The booing was so loud it eclipsed the decibel level of the protesters outside. Chris timed it in his head, counting off slow beats: *One . . . two . . . three.* Trump didn't resume speaking for a full 30 seconds as the howls and bleats and expressions of anger filled the hall and rang in our ears.

"They don't report the facts," he continued. "Just like they don't want to report that I spoke out forcefully against hatred, bigotry, and violence and strongly condemned the neo-Nazis, the white suprema- cists, and the KKK."

He pulled from his suit pocket the transcripts of his responses and began to read them line by line. We could see the teleprompter stop scrolling from our vantage point off to the side, his words becoming more emotive and wandering.

"Here's what I said," the president promised, and he reread his denunciations, waving the papers about. Periodically Trump would return to the teleprompter and get back on message, then veer off again, often to attack his favorite target.

"Oh, that's so funny," he continued, pointing at the TV cameras. "Look back there, the live red lights. They're turning those suckers off fast out there. They're turning those lights off fast."

We were both struck by Trump's power and command of the room. The way he changed his tone—going from soft to forceful and back again—kept the audience entranced. His patter, often mocked for its disjointed effect on television, felt intimate in person. He was preach- ing to a room of believers, and he knew how to move them over and over again. Those men and women in the room, and his parishioners elsewhere, were anointed. He was their champion, and he made sure they knew it.

After nearly an hour, we made for the exit. The president was still going strong, and the crowd inside booed vigorously or let out hosannas each time he lobbed another rhetorical bomb. A peal of laughter followed us as we left the rally. Four burly Trump supporters walked ahead of us, baying loudly in the halls as they sauntered out.

We stepped out into a four-way intersection brimming with police in riot gear. Supporters and protesters lined the sidewalks, jockeying for position and crisscrossing among the police. We would later describe this as the "brackish area"—the point where Trump supporters flowed out of the rally and into the gathering outside, creating an intersection where rally-goers mixed with protesters. We found ourselves lost in the no-man's-land of the heat-soaked roadway, lodged between the police-lined fences protecting the rally-goers and the barricades corralling the protesters.

Shouts rang out behind us. We turned around to see a woman wearing a WE RESIST T-shirt. She thrust a sign high over her head with pictures of the three people killed in Charlottesville the week before— Heather Heyer, a counterprotestor, and two Virgina State Police, Berke M. M. Bates and H. Jay Cullen.

"We must condemn domestic terrorism," she declared with a stage voice. "Why won't the president condemn domestic terrorism?"

She had positioned herself in the outflow of rally-goers, as close to the exit as possible without running afoul of the riot police. She stood such that every Trump supporter had to walk by her, and many of them had already drawn around her. The lights of local news cameras swung wildly to illuminate the knot of people.

"Why won't Trump condemn neo-Nazis? Why won't he condemn the KKK?" she screamed.

"What are you yelling about?" one of the Trump supporters shouted back. He was a middle-aged man with a braided ponytail popping out from under a baseball cap. "He did condemn them. He condemned all violent groups!"

"Trump gave comfort to murderers!" she responded. "He wouldn't even say the groups' names."

"He did condemn them—by name. And he condemned all the violent groups. So why won't you condemn Antifa?"

"Antifa didn't kill anyone," she said. "Let's focus on the murderers."

A few dozen people circled tighter to watch the scene unfold. As we edged closer ourselves, a new chant went up behind us.

"Hope, not hate . . . Hope, not hate . . ."

We turned around expecting to find a new group of protestors—the woman's backup. Instead, the same four burly Trump supporters we had seen on the escalator were pumping their fists and cupping their mouths with open hands, shouting in unison.

Another animated crowd had formed across the street, and we hurried over. About 20 people were milling around next to a barricade, on the other side of which stood five policemen. In the center, we could see two African American men standing face-to-face in heated conversation with two white Trump supporters. Ten feet away, a handful of heavily armed militiamen roamed around in full battle dress—hands on their weapons and faces covered in camouflage paint. "They're loaded," Jordan said after scanning the militiamen's weapons.

We warily walked around them and approached the four men, each of them a few inches taller than us. They were making rapid-fire points back and forth with animated gestures.

"We think the language around Black Lives Matter is too divisive," said one of the Trump supporters. "It's tearing the country apart."

"But you have to understand, our kids are getting gunned down in the streets by the police," one of the other men said, "and we get no justice from the courts. The cops are killing us with impunity."

We quickly realized that, while engaged in passionate argument, none of the participants were angry. The tone was respectful. They were actually listening to each other.

"I hear you," one of the Trump supporters interjected, "but *all* lives matter, man. When you say 'Black Lives Matter,' it sounds like you're dividing Americans into camps. All lives should matter."

"You're not wrong, but we feel like our lives—black lives—have been undervalued in society," one of the men said. "When we say 'Black Lives Matter,' what we're really asking for is to be treated with the same dignity as everyone else. We just want our lives to count, too. And I appreciate that you're worried about division. But our community is in a lot of pain. We're just trying to be heard."

Throughout the conversation, television cameras were trained on the ongoing shouting match across the street. The two of us—and the armed militiamen roaming about—would be the only ones to witness this moment in the pastel orange light of a single street lamp, far from the pale LED beam of the cameras.

———————

The mood changed once the rally concluded, and the number of people outside swelled. A rush of rally-goers walked hurriedly toward the parking lots, and large crowds of protesters glommed together. Everyone seemed aware the night could explode at any moment. Loud noises made people twitch and look about. A teenager behind us started to shout; as others cooed and asked him to keep his voice down, our guards went up.

At the intersection we kept noticing the armed men. Their camouflage uniforms, woven shawls, face paint, and imposing semiautomatic rifles added to the manic energy of the night. This wasn't unexpected. Arizona, with its lax gun laws and the red hue of its politics, seemed like an apt place to find militiamen.

"Hey man, what's your deal?" Jordan asked one of them. "Who are you guys?" The man had on red face paint that came up to the roots of his combed jet-black hair.

"We're the John Brown Gun Club."

"John Brown? Like antislavery John Brown? Harpers Ferry?"

"Yup, that one. We're an anti-white-supremacy militia."

The guy handed Chris a business card, which displayed a rifle crossed with a wrench below a miner's helmet and bandanna over the words, *John Brown Gun Club: Phoenix Chapter—Putting the Red Back in Redneck.*

Trump rallies had often been portrayed as a battle between left and right—Trump resisters and Trump supporters. But on the ground it wasn't so simple. Was the woman holding the sign aloft outside the rally entrance on the same side as the two Black Lives Matter activists across the street? Were the Trump supporters dragging sleepy children behind them as they left the rally on the same "team" as the neo-Nazis? Which "side" were the police or the John Brown Gun Club on? And where did the two of us fall?

The dominant narrative of two factions battling each other was divorced from the reality we saw in Phoenix. It seemed to be an imaginary line drawn by those who didn't understand the terrain they were marking, or who didn't care enough to get it right. The majority of the people we saw that night were peaceful. Yet certain headlines coming out of events like this one made it seem as if the two "sides" were irreconcilable, defined by their fringes, and at war with each other.

Then suddenly, without warning, a deafening clap of noise caromed off the high-walled buildings on either side of the street. It shook our bones, rattled our chests, and silenced everyone around us. Some flinched and ducked. Others turned to look down the street in the direction of its origin. It had come from around the corner, where the loudest protesters had bellowed as we walked into the rally. Jordan grabbed Chris's arm and pulled him toward a barricade.

"John Brown, pull out!" one of the militiamen with a woven quilt across his camouflage jacket shouted over the crowd. As he retreated, repeating the order again and again, he grabbed another member of the gun club with long hair and a scraggly beard who was lingering too long. He took him by the collar of his uniform and roughly yanked him away. The rest of the crowd either began to scatter or, stupefied by the screaming percussion that had sent the others scampering, stared out across the police line, dumbfounded.

Everything changed after a second explosion rang out into the night. It was as if someone had fired a starter pistol. Seconds before, people were listening to one another, exchanging views and perspectives. In a flash, they were fleeing in panic.

"Let's go in," Chris said eagerly.

"But carefully," Jordan said.

"Of course—but *in!*" Chris said.

"Just remember," Jordan cautioned, "if anything gets too wild, you follow me out."

"Roger that."

We took off running up the block.

As we turned a second corner, jogging toward where the protesters were roped off, a crush of people came running up the street in the opposite direction. Some were coughing and wiping their eyes. One was saying something hysterical about the police. "They just started firing!" he said, next to tears.

Around the corner was a scene of chaos. As we came back around to the convention center, a group of masked protesters dressed in black were sprinting through a public park. Behind them, an officer was firing what looked like pellets from a long gun. Each round left the barrel with a *click*. We found refuge in a parking complex with the kind of protesters who carried signs and knew the chants but were shocked by the masked types who were currently retreating, pellets whizzing through the tree branches. As the park emptied, a stalemate emerged: the police did not advance. They held their line as the masked people disappeared into the night.

While we lingered, debating the best way to see more of the conflict, tendrils of smoke wrapped around our legs. The twin booms had been the sound of fired tear-gas canisters, and the gas was drifting in the hot evening breeze. Quickly, and again without warning, another explosion cut through the night air closer to the parking complex, sending us sprawling. We took cover behind a concrete planter box. But many around us still seemed too stunned to react.

As Chris ducked low beside Jordan, he worried about the protesters who were too dazed to understand the surrounding violence. It reminded him of a line of graffiti after an Occupy Oakland protest he had covered. *We're sorry,* someone had scrawled next to the shattered window of a coffee shop in downtown. *This does not represent us.*

"Let's go," Jordan said, and he led a reluctant Chris up the block.

As we rounded a corner, the fog thickened and Chris's throat began to burn. He coughed to clear it, but that only made the burn worse. His eyes welled up and stung. By the time his nostrils started to smart, Jordan made a noise like it had hit him, too. We ran blindly away from the tear gas. At a street corner, we stopped and bent over, spitting up what felt like a thick, ugly slime. Jordan rubbed his eyes furiously. Two others had followed us out and stopped on the same corner.

"Are you okay?" Chris asked a young woman with red hair who had pulled up her white shirt to tend to her eyes.

"Yeah, I think so," she sputtered.

A teenage boy stood to our right.

"How about you?"

The boy nodded as he spat up the gas.

We slipped behind the tall, gray walls of a hotel. A police helicopter circled above us. Its searchlight probed the streets, casting an accusatory glow over those who walked in the wide roadways. We stayed close to the wall to keep out of its beam. "Leave the vicinity," a voice boomed from above. "If you do not comply, you will be subject to arrest."

A handful of protestors hunkered down against the wall with us. An older couple held hands and wiped their eyes. Kids no older than 16, wearing black shirts and dark jeans, filtered in and out. Some came around the corner with looks of shock on their faces. Others were taking pictures and sending them off to friends somewhere in the ether. They crouched for a moment, laughing loudly with each other and swapping stories as they gathered themselves before returning gleefully into the gas-choked streets to be part of whatever was coming next.

What had metastasized into violence was now a scene not dissimilar to what one would expect outside a stadium after the last whistle of a football game or a theater after the final curtain. It was back to normal except for the beat of helicopter blades above and the thin mist of tear gas that hung in the air.

Yet the evening wouldn't end without one last spasm of violence. A boisterous Trump supporter with thick, tattooed arms and a baseball cap pulled tightly over his scalp bellowed as he passed by us. A few moments later we heard a scream down the block. As we ran over, we saw a young woman holding her face. She was next to tears and said a man had hit her. In response, her friend had screamed at a family of Trump supporters making their way out of downtown. The outburst had startled an older woman and sent her sprawling on a concrete staircase. As the enraged girl stomped away into the night, a collection of people tended to the woman. She looked bruised and painfully aware of her own frailty.

And as we walked away, shaken, someone in a passing car offered a "Sieg heil" from the obscuring darkness of the car's back seat.

As midnight neared, we found a bar with live music and an outdoor patio a few blocks from the convention center. We sat at a countertop and sipped tequila and orange juice as a fine cooling mist descended over our heads. Helicopters still circled some distance off. Protesters and Trump supporters drifted by the patio as they headed back to cars and apartments and hotel rooms. One way or another, everyone wore the tension of the night.

Ever since he was 18, writing his first articles for *The Daily Californian,* Chris had considered himself a reporter. He loved the work, and he idolized the profession's heroes. *Go to the scene,* he had been drilled for nearly a decade. *Tell it as it happened.* That night, though, had been chaotic, and he didn't envy the White House embeds and local correspondents typing for the front page just then.

It hadn't all been violence, but the headlines and leads could end up expressing as much. Chris feared an incomplete picture would emerge from the night, and not the one he had seen.

Chris also wondered if the night had given Jordan pause, if the scream of the tear-gas canisters had rattled his friend or even dredged up memories from the Corps. He wondered if the violence and anger had worried him. If so, Jordan wasn't letting on.

For his part, Jordan couldn't shake the darker signs he had seen that night. The glare of the crooked-spined man played across his imagination. How he stood apart. How he didn't speak. The menace of his aloof way. And then there was that *Sieg heil* salute; it had been offered so casually that the immense evil it conjured was nearly lost.

As the tequila numbed the adrenaline of the night, we began to compare notes.

"I gotta say," Jordan said. "Some of the people tonight were creepy."

"And terrifying," Chris added.

"And that man standing next to us in the rally . . ." Jordan trailed off. "And how about those masked people?"

Chris, still shaky, felt a surge of relief. His friend had seen the same things and was struck by the same fear about the darker elements inside and out.

"Did you see the man in the Guy Fawkes mask?" Chris asked.

Jordan shook his head.

"It was all," Jordan said, looking for the words, "disappointing."

What was clear to us through the clouds of gas and smoke was how well versed Americans were in their chosen script. The rally revealed how the gathered throngs conducted themselves when the studio lights were on, the cameras were rolling, and the drama palpable. Cameras have a way of bringing out the beast in all of us.

We also came to realize that in Phoenix there was a murmur of what we sought on the road. Even as tear-gas canisters barreled through the crowds and chaos followed, there had been fleeting dialogue. People had engaged. And while clips played out on televisions at the bar behind us of protesters felled by beanbag rounds, police officers marching toward fleeing crowds, and the president barking from the stage, we held on to this glint of something civil.

What gave us hope was that performances are not who we really are. We saw righteous, genuine anger and pain on many faces that night. We also saw people break character—stutter over their script or forget a line or two. Those intimate moments were the imprint of something altogether different than the rest of it. Performances are artificial, like the borders and lines we draw around one another. And that meant we could overcome them. Like the rock faces and valley slopes and meandering rivers that flow across the curves of our borders and roads and towns uninterrupted, there are currents to humanity that are irrepressible.

As we made our way back to the motel that night, we decided to drive north and away from these performances the next morning. We'd leave behind this borderland where nothing seemed settled, where two nations blended into one—two sides of the same desert—and where our politics compelled us to embrace ideas that left us feeling lost. The rally had shown us that there was still more we had to discover out on the road. Now we had to go find it.

Page

After leaving Phoenix, we headed north for Horseshoe Bend. There, the Colorado River whips around a cliff in the shape of a crescent. Though it's not as dramatic as the massive canyon rims just down the river, we wagered the sight was worth the four-hour drive across Arizona. Our plan was to see the bend, then make our way farther north to catch a blood-orange sunset from somewhere inside Zion National Park.

After the Trump rally the night before, Jordan craved a quiet experience. No more crowds or security guards. No more man-made barriers. Horseshoe Bend would be our respite—just the two of us and the beautiful tectonic rift he'd seen in pictures.

The road to Horseshoe Bend runs through fractured mountain ranges that border the Navajo Nation's massive 17.5-million-acre reservation. For more than 1,000 years, various tribes made their homes among the desert crags surrounding the Grand Canyon, until a severe drought rendered the area uninhabitable for a century. Over time the Paiute and Hopi tribes, and later the Navajo, moved back into the canyons as water began to flow again. Then something more devastating than a drought came down. In 1869, a one-armed Civil War soldier named John Wesley Powell led an expedition to explore the area and wrote descriptions of the exalted American landscape. Several years later, the U.S. Army forcibly removed the Native American tribes of the region from their ancestral lands.

The two of us made our way along Highway 89. Chris had volunteered to take the wheel and cautiously took us north. Jordan spent the afternoon with his feet up on the dashboard, admiring the desert in between bouts of sleep. We drove speechless for hours, watching the perpetual expanse of red sand fly by.

By midafternoon we had passed Flagstaff and were pressing on toward Lake Powell. The sun was still high above the horizon when we pulled into the parking lot for the bend. We lathered on sunscreen and ran the short trail through the dry heat of midday to reach the vista. There, alongside a handful of other tourists, we took in the rock cliffs and how they plunged into the crystalline vein of water nearly 1,000 feet below. The river glittered sapphire and emerald. The rock center of the horseshoe stood like a column topped by a painted cornice. Jordan shimmied up to the edge on his stomach, letting his head hang over the side.

"Come over!" he shouted, but Chris kept his distance.

"I'm good back here."

A small border collie sniffed its way up next to Jordan on the smooth slab of rock and hovered at the wrinkled lip of the precipice. The enormous rock formation across from the ledge looked like a great tabernacle of old Europe, its molding adorned by uneven lines of sculpted rock painted in bands of red, earthen hues.

We meandered around for half an hour before returning to the car, uplifted and free from the Trump rally.

We stood outside as the air-conditioning washed away the heat inside the car. This was becoming an Arizona ritual after every stop. The wheel scalded, and the seats burned.

"How's the Boat feel?" Chris asked as Jordan touched its faux leather.

"The Boat?"

"Doesn't that sound right?"

"It's fitting," Jordan said with a nod.

As the Boat trundled down the highway and the sun hovered in its midafternoon perch, we stopped in the town of Page. It was nothing more than a few streets dotted by a smattering of shops and three-story hotels on a high mountain mesa.

"Look," Jordan said, pointing to a broad sign above a collection of storefronts. GUNFIGHTER CANYON, it read. "We're going shooting," he declared, turning into the parking lot. "Let off some steam."

Jordan enjoyed the concentration and deep breathing he'd been trained to do before each trigger pull. The first time he ever held a gun was in the Marine Corps. In keeping with its motto—EVERY MARINE A RIFLEMAN—the Corps first teaches new officers how to shoot. Jordan's training had taken place during a freezing winter in Quantico, Virginia. It was miserable. His cohort of 300 young officers drilled for weeks until all of them became trained marksmen. Each day they steadied their shivering bodies just long enough to get a clear picture through their rifles' iron sights. And each night they waited for hours until the feeling came back to their hands and feet.

On that range, whenever one of them fired, a hot brass casing would fly out of the chamber to the right. Time and time again these casings would land on the neck of the next shooter and tumble down their shirt. But with loaded weapons on the firing line, the Marines had to grit their teeth and bear the scalding-hot metal on their skin. Jordan still has red marks on his back from a few of them.

"What do you say?"

Chris had never fired a gun before. The idea of unloading rounds at a shooting range seemed far from meditative. Growing up in the Bay Area, Chris knew guns only as instruments of tragedy.

"Come on—it will be your birthday present," Jordan insisted, getting out of the car. "And this is a trip for firsts."

Chris didn't have the will to argue. He was still weary from the night before, so he followed Jordan out of the car and back into the oppressive Arizona heat.

"But my birthday was yesterday," he mumbled.

The Gunfighter Canyon building was bare, save for a few shelves and a counter with a menu of rifle, pistol, and shotgun options hanging behind it. The percussion of high-caliber weapons muffled by thick brick walls rattled the room.

Jordan went to the kiosk to mull the choices. Chris settled in on a black leather couch facing the wall. He studied the images of the rifles—glinting and polished. Even the young men who paced the open room seemed unfamiliar and dangerous.

With his anxiety rising, Chris reached for his phone. *Hopefully this will be over soon,* he thought, and they'd make Zion National Park by sunset. Chris had dreamed of seeing the red rocks of Utah. *If we just got back in the car, if we just kept driving, we could be there in an hour-and-a-half or two.* Then Chris could stop running through the grim scenarios of deadly gun mishaps that filled his mind as he nervously scratched his stubbled chin.

"Have either of you shot a gun before?" Bob, the young man in charge of getting us set up, asked Jordan.

"Not me," Chris said from the couch.

"I have," Jordan said. "I was a Marine."

"No shit. Which unit?"

"3/1."

"Hey, Nishan," Bob shouted to a man wearing a baseball cap and a black shirt. "Hear that? This guy's a 3/1 Marine."

"No way," Nishan said, coming over. "So you were at Pendleton? I was with 3rd Tracks down in Camp Del Mar."

Nishan and Jordan were both Marine Corps captains. Bob, who listened closely, turned out to be a staff sergeant in the U.S. Army. The three of them traded names back and forth and laughed about the drab combat bases they had served at overseas. Another Marine veteran, Joey, came over as well.

Jordan often muses that the best part about being a Marine is getting to be a veteran. A strong bond unites veterans, but especially those from the same branch. As Marines, Nishan, Joey, and Jordan had gone through the same miserable training and were steeped in the same customs and lore that Marines had passed on to one another for nearly 250 years. Nishan and Joey likely had the same red brands down their backs as Jordan.

As Chris observed Jordan and the Gunfighter crew, he listened for familiar words. Words such as *platoon, gunny, Pendleton,* and *Twenty-nine Palms.* He picked up a handful, but no more. In the end, only those who belonged could fully understand. Only they could smile at the right moments and cast their eyes down just so at the sound of a particular battle or the name of a colleague lost.

"Listen, guys," Nishan said, "I'm gonna give you two extra magazines for free, and I'll throw in another gun too. It's on me. Also, I strongly suggest you shoot the MP5. We've made our own modifications, so it fires 30 rounds in less than two seconds. No kick at all."

And with that endorsement, Bob led us around the back of the building to a large cinder-block room with four shooting stations. Spent brass casings carpeted the floor.

"Impressive range," Jordan said.

"We built it ourselves from the studs up," Bob replied.

Bob was a slender man with colorful tattoos. He carried himself with a practiced confidence that masked a certain boyishness.

To Chris, the nearly barren tunnel of a room was imposing. The bricks were sandpaper to the touch. The metal shooting bays resembled stables. A shelf sat just low enough for weapons to rest at hand's reach. Many yards down a well-lit corridor, paper targets had been suspended from hooks; each target bore the outline of a human head and torso. Chris watched them flutter, blood pounding at his temples.

Bob wheeled in a cart weighed down with assault rifles, pistols, and magazines full of rounds. He checked each one and turned to Jordan. "Listen, I don't want to insult your intelligence or your experience, but I'm going to walk through all the safety procedures. Cool?"

He went on without waiting for an answer.

"Okay, I'm going to break it down 'Barney-style' for you. Let's start with the four safety rules. One: Treat every weapon as if it were loaded. Two: Never point your weapon at anything you don't intend to shoot. Three: Keep your finger straight and off the trigger until you are ready to fire. Four: Keep the weapon on *Safe* until you intend to fire."

Bob's instructions sped by.

"Okay, having said that, let's start with the pistol," Bob said.

He walked us through the basics on how to shoot the pistol, then handed it to Chris, who passed it to Jordan.

"You first."

Jordan took the gun and weighed it in his hands. In Afghanistan he had worn one on his hip at all times, day and night. He had spent eight months as a military adviser to the Afghan National Army, and one of the deadliest threats that year for Marines like him had been from "green on blue" attacks: Afghan soldiers turning their weapons on their American counterparts. Sometimes it was out of hatred. Other times the Taliban was holding their families hostage. In either case, that pistol had been Jordan's sole line of defense. Holding one again brought with it a wave of nostalgia for those days as well as a pang of relief that they were over.

Jordan slowly raised the weapon, crouched somewhat, took aim, and squeezed the trigger.

The crack of the pistol sounded through the earplugs we wore. Jordan finished a clip and lowered the gun. Now it was Chris's turn. He took the weapon gingerly, and nodded along as Bob repeated his instructions. Once his tutor stepped away, Chris leveled his arms, bent his knees, and squeezed one eye shut to better sight down the barrel. *Here goes.* He flicked the trigger and nothing happened. Too gentle. With a bit more pressure, he pulled again and the pistol unloaded with a snap. The target downrange fluttered violently, and Chris turned and grinned at Jordan before pumping out five more shots, a shorter beat of trepidation separating each one.

Chris didn't trust deadly things. Just standing there with a pistol in his hand made him feel as if he had taken on a responsibility too large and too profound. But Chris also felt the thrill, like when your guts turn after leaping from a high cliff into cold water far below.

"You want to walk him through this one, Jordan?" Bob asked. He had just shouldered the AR-15, with its long neck and protruding magazine.

"Sure," Jordan said.

Jordan was enjoying this. He felt competent and sure of himself with his old weapon, and he liked introducing Chris to his onetime craft. It was part of his history.

Jordan showed Chris how to operate the weapon, then stepped into the firing box and shot off what sounded to Chris like a dozen rounds in quick succession. Casings ricocheted off the stainless-steel walls. Jordan handed the weapon over. In Chris's hands, it felt much more unwieldy than the pistol. Chris stepped up to the shooting box again and immediately forgot where to put his hands. After a second primer, he positioned himself. He pressed the stock into his chest, paused, and pulled the trigger. The gun spat, and Chris fired and fired.

"Okay," Bob started, "it's time for this baby." He patted the modified MP5—a squat rifle that looked to Chris like a rhino, its nubby scope protruding above the muzzle like a horn.

Jordan inspected the gun, turning it over in his hands. "Is this the slide release?" he asked Bob, who nodded. Jordan inserted a magazine, stepped up to the shooting line, and unloaded the clip in one long, humming burst.

"No kick at all," Jordan said.

This time Chris stepped up and fired with relative ease. He could hold the MP5's trigger down and fire multiple rounds at once. The muzzle meandered upward powerfully with each burst, which terrified him, bringing back all his initial trepidation in one gut-turning rush. All the fearful, easily betrayed responsibility of these weapons felt enormous again. Chris put the gun down and stepped away, hoping neither Bob nor Jordan had noticed how close he had come to riddling the ceiling with bullets.

"So how'd you like it?" Nishan said with a big grin as he came out of the office to meet us. We had settled up and were headed for the door.

"Hold on," Nishan said. "You two should come back tonight. We're enlisting my cousin, Caleb, in the Army right here in the shop. It'll be a good time."

"That sounds great," Chris said.

"Yeah, maybe," Jordan added.

We left Page as the sun began to set and we drove north toward Utah. The Mormons who settled the area called it the "promised land," which led Horace Albright, director of the National Park Service, to later christen the area *Zion*. Chris had long talked about seeing it. A naturalist at heart, Chris was as comfortable in national parks as Jordan was at a shooting range. As a boy, Chris even competed in annual bird counts. It's one of Jordan's favorite mental images: eight-year-old Chris wandering around a California hillside with a notepad and binoculars. Wild lands were Chris's domain, and on our trips so far he had made sure that we stopped at Yellowstone, the Badlands, the Black Hills, and the Sawtooths. Now our plan was to watch the sunset from some crag off a trail in Zion, then continue on to Salt Lake City.

Unless we turned around.

"We have to go back," Chris said as we drove.

"I don't know," Jordan replied. "I think we should keep going."

"Why? We couldn't plan a better night."

Jordan shrugged as we sped past Lake Powell, heading west. A storm was visible off across the green Utah plains. Cracks of lightning arced out of black clouds at jagged angles. Chris had grown accustomed to Jordan's serious turns—periods when he lost himself in solemn thought, leaving his face inscrutable for long spells.

Jordan was wrestling with what it would mean to let Chris see an aspect of his life that he might not fully understand. Since leaving the Marine Corps, Jordan had kept that side of himself separate from his new civilian one. His college or law-school friends might not understand the Marine Corps's customs and traditions, its rough language and gallows humor, the things that are tolerated and those that are not. Chris might take offense at the way the Page veterans talked.

Even more, Jordan wasn't sure Chris would truly appreciate the ceremony. There are few events more humbling than witnessing someone step forward to serve his or her country, Jordan felt. Chris might view it as just a story to tell—another tale from the road rather than something hallowed. How would Jordan feel if an enlistment became fodder for cocktail parties back in New Haven?

But it wasn't just Chris's presence that caused Jordan to jam the accelerator headed north. Jordan felt disoriented. The two of us had started this trip with the aim of understanding something about America. If we went back, Jordan would, in a sense, be reporting on his Marine brothers in the same way he had reported on the Trump rally the night before. As a veteran, Jordan was one of them. Yet all of a sudden he was more like Chris. Was this breaking some unspoken code?

Every Marine swears an oath, and with it come special rules. Jordan had taken that oath seven years earlier—on December 11, 2009—after graduating from Officer Candidate School in Quantico, Virginia. That day, he had raised his right hand and sworn to defend his country. That oath is part of the foundation of Jordan's worldview. Afterward, his parents had pinned to his shoulders a new set of gold bars, signifying his rank of second lieutenant.

Rites of passage such as these are rare in American life today. We honor some of them—weddings, funerals, religious communions, graduations—but few possess the sense of sacredness that transforms their participants. Before they raise their right hand, the men and women who take the military oath are civilians endowed with rights and privileges. After, they are soldiers, sailors, Marines, and airmen with duties and responsibilities to their country and fellow service members. It is the first of many rituals that bind the military and separate them from the rest of society. And now, as we left Arizona for Utah, that separation was disappearing for Jordan.

We pulled over in a small town along the highway for gas. It was an outpost right at the intersection where the road to Zion forked off and began a steady ascent up the plains and beyond the creosote. The sun was setting and the blue of twilight was passing over the hills.

"I say we go back," Chris tried again in the quiet of the car. "Nishan obviously meant it, and what's the worst that could happen? If it's uncomfortable, we'll leave."

Jordan considered it.

"Come on, man—you were the one who said this is a trip for firsts."

Jordan knew he had just pushed Chris to do something uncomfortable by picking up a gun. Was it his turn now to do something that made him uneasy? Bringing Chris along for a night of drinking with other veterans felt like removing a piece of armor and exposing something vulnerable. Was he ready for that?

Jordan decided he was. He still felt anxious about bringing together two worlds that he had kept apart for so long. And maybe it would be a curiosity to Chris, as he feared it might. But Chris had earned some trust.

"Okay," Jordan relented. "But we need to bring a lot of booze."

"A ton," Chris said with a smile.

Gone were the blasts of rifles and the tinkle of casings. The cinder-block shooting range was transformed. An American flag, scotch-taped at its edges, adorned one wall, giving the place an altar-like feeling. Voices had dropped to a murmur. Chris stood next to a few teenagers from

Flagstaff and a middle-aged man in a polo shirt and unkempt hair—Caleb's father. Nishan, in his dress blues, stood at the front of the room. The group watched as Bob, Jordan, and Joey marched into the room, eyes straight and arms locked at their sides. Caleb, Nishan's cousin, came last. He wore a tucked-in black polo shirt and a camouflage trucker hat and walked with a practiced, deliberate pace. He stood tall, like Bob and Nishan, but he didn't seem fully comfortable with the pose. His smooth face and wide eyes were a reminder of his youth.

"Attention to orders," Nishan said, and everyone except Chris, Caleb's father, and the fidgety teens snapped upright.

"Tonight, you join the long line of Americans who have stepped forward in defense of our nation," Nishan said. "Like them, you will be called to sacrifice much in the service of a cause greater than yourself. When you recite this oath, you will go from being a civilian to a warrior, and you will take on all the obligations that this brings. This is the most important decision you have made in your life, and I could not be prouder of you."

Looking at Caleb, Jordan thought of the young protesters we had seen the night before at the Trump rally. Roughly the same age, both Caleb and the protesters believed they were defending their country—whether from a domestic threat or an as-yet-unknown foreign enemy. But there was a difference: the next morning, the young protesters would have the option of returning to their high-school or college classrooms; Caleb would have a four-year commitment that would demand much from him. He was a soldier now.

"Raise your right hand," Nishan commanded. Caleb stood face-to-face with Nishan. Both of them raised their right arms. The rest of us had formed a semicircle around them.

"Repeat after me," Nishan said. His starched collar featured the Marines' brass insignia—an eagle, globe, and anchor.

"I, Caleb Markosian...do solemnly swear...that I will support and defend the Constitution of the United States....against all enemies, foreign and domestic...that I will bear true faith...and allegiance to the same . . . and that I will obey the orders of the President of the United States . . . and the orders of the officers appointed over me . . . according to regulations . . . and the Uniform Code of Military Justice . . . so help me God."

The two men lowered their arms. And with a holler from the half-dozen men collected in the small room, Caleb and Nishan shook hands. Caleb smiled broadly. He was then, and forever would be, a soldier—part of the same fraternity that Nishan had joined a decade before.

Caleb spoke.

"I've known everyone in this room forever," Caleb said. Then, glancing at us: "Well, most of you, at least. And I appreciate you all being here tonight." The new soldier then went person-to-person, shaking their hands.

"Thanks for letting us be here," Chris said.

"Welcome," Jordan offered.

With the ceremony over, everyone filed out of the back room and into the garage, which was thrown open to the desert night.

Nishan patted Chris on the shoulder.

"I'm glad you guys came back," he said.

As we filed out into the night air and caught sight of the lights of Page flickering on the slope beyond, a feeling of elevation lingered for a moment among the group.

The three younger boys, led by Caleb, circled the alcohol like hounds. Nishan dragged the grill out from the garage and onto the sidewalk. On the way out he introduced us to Mike, his business partner. Mike was a fast-talking Minnesotan, a thick-framed man who pumped our hands hard and said theatrically, "As long as you two like cheap beer and brats, we'll be good friends."

Mike got the grill set up as Nishan supervised, arms crossed and clearly contented. He was the Gunfighter's patriarch who had collected these men on a stretch of freeway in the high desert. Nishan had envisioned this outpost in the high desert and had made it so. "All right, let's see what we've got," he said. Bob was carrying out a plastic fold-up table, which he quickly set up and layered with chips, dip, and plastic bags swimming with meat and marinade. Mike grabbed the bag and proudly started listing off the different cuts he had brought.

Caleb's dad joined us outside. Shy but friendly, he looked out from behind thin-rimmed glasses. His quiet way left him out of place in this martial group. He told us that Caleb had been making the drive from Flagstaff every afternoon and weekend so he could work at Gunfighter Canyon. He was clearly proud of his son, who watched Nishan closely all night.

"So you live in Flagstaff?" Chris asked.

"We all do," Nishan responded. "My wife and I have lived there for four years now."

"How do you like it?" Jordan asked.

"Flagstaff is the shit," Joey jumped in. "My buddies and I have a warehouse loft on a huge piece of land. Rent is $200 a person, and we can do whatever we want out there. We even built our own archery range."

Joey's azure eyes grabbed you. We sensed a pain behind them, though. Perhaps it was the slope of his eyebrows or the bags that gathered under his lids. Perhaps it was the divorce he was going through, or some other loss. Bob showed it too. So did Nishan.

"We were all working jobs we hated," Nishan continued. "After the Marines and business school, I spent two years selling medical equipment before I decided it was bullshit and struck out on my own. I wanted a sense of mission again. I met Bob and Joey out here, and after a beer, they agreed to come on board. We all wanted to work with people we liked, doing shit we enjoyed."

"There's something special about this group," Mike chimed in, as he set down a tray with the grill's latest offerings. Not only had Nishan brought together this group around a common purpose, but the group itself had taken in two complete strangers and treated us as honored guests. There was a spirit of generosity and comradeship that we had seldom seen on our travels.

The boys of Page may or may not have been religious. We never asked. But there was something almost pious about the reverence they had for Gunfighter Canyon.

As the night wore on and the temperature in the desert dropped, beers gave way to whiskey and the conversation turned to women and war stories and business partners gone rogue. The grill was left to cool as we slumped against retaining walls and sat on overturned buckets on the empty sidewalk.

Throughout the evening, we marveled at the community these men had carved out for themselves amid the Arizona desert. They each had their own lives, but everyone came together at week's end, just as a Jewish family might gather over Shabbat dinner.

Like the people we had seen in Phoenix, the Gunfighters were searching for meaning and community in an increasingly fragmented society. But while the rally-goers and protesters in Phoenix were seeking it in politics, the boys of Page were consciously removing themselves from public life. We could hear the disdain in Nishan's voice when he discussed the local regulators he had to deal with as the cost of doing business. When we told them about the Trump rally, they loved the stories about tear gas but shrugged at our political takeaways.

This wasn't the only difference between the two groups. The boys of Page had something the rally-goers and protesters did not. The common experience of serving in the armed forces gave them a base-line of trust, respect, and shared culture that made Gunfighter Canyon possible. The Trump supporters and protesters might share a common worldview, but without the network of relationships built through daily living, working, and celebrating together, their gatherings were fleeting. They did not—and could not—have the same sense of community that this group had formed.

Yet by midnight, the impression of sadness grew more palpable. The veterans spoke as if nothing would ever be as good again. They seemed consigned to living in their halcyon memories. They reminisced over war stories and riotous stopovers in foreign ports, as if these were the things that had lent meaning and color to their military life. They seemed left behind—perhaps entirely by choice.

At one point Bob came out from the garage, tapping a pack of cigarettes on his hip. He turned over a plastic pail and hunched over, his knees coming up toward his chest, and lit one of the cigarettes. He set his tumbler of whiskey down and listened to Mike talk for a moment.

"I love Flagstaff, man," he interjected and the conversation faded. "It's amazing. I mean, the things I've seen..." He trailed off for a moment, but no one said a word. "I served three tours in Afghanistan. Three. A fifteen-month tour, then another around the same, then a twelve-month tour. That's nearly four years in-country, man. That will fuck you up."

Bob shook his head and tapped some ashes out onto the sidewalk.

"I came back from one deployment and went home to my parents' house. And I had something like 30 Gs saved up from deployment. So I bought loads of alcohol, and we went crazy. Like, I remember, I was lying down on the grass, passed out, and out of nowhere, the fire pit jumped its walls and caught the pool. Of course, the damn thing popped—it was one of those plastic blow-up, above-ground pools, you know—and water went everywhere like a flood. It caught me up and fired me into my neighbor's lawn, through the hedges and shit. It just kept coming and pinned me up against their deck and tore up the wood. I saw the fire but couldn't get out of the stream of water.

"Well, my dad got the fire put out and eventually I got my ass up off the fucked-up deck, and I passed out, again. The next day I went over—this was a neighborhood, we knew each other—so I went over to apologize, and I offered to pay for the damage. You know what they said? 'Don't worry about it.' They paid to have the deck fixed and thanked me for my service.

"I found that in Flagstaff, too, man. I got this little house and I'm going out of town all the time. One time, I'm gone for weeks. Maybe two months. I was training the National Guard, getting them ready to go to Afghanistan, you know, teaching them how to run ops and shit. And when I get home, my lawn was cut. The wood I chopped that fall was stacked. The place was kept. I'm standing outside, seeing all this, and there's my neighbor on the porch waving me over. I go over and he's like: 'I see things. I keep an eye on the block, and I noticed that you go away for long periods of time—usually in uniform. So when you didn't show up for the first few weeks, I decided to take care of things until you got back.'"

"Would only get better if he had a six-pack for you," someone added.

"He did! He had beer for me," Bob said. "That's how it's fucking meant to be, man."

We left Page before the sun came up. Zion National Park was an easy drive west, and we pulled in as the first stirrings of light began to filter across the sky. We drove between the red canyon walls, wending our way deeper into the bowels of Zion's cathedral-like slopes and cliffs. Halfway through, and with the sun about to crest the horizon, we half-jogged our way up a trail cut into the rock face. At a plateau that opened onto a valley, we sat together to watch the sunrise.

We humans will likely always separate ourselves into tribes, requiring us to give up a piece of ourselves in service to the group's rules and mores. It's in our nature. It's how we stave off the dark and brutish parts of life. When we close ranks, the rituals we share do more than give us comfort: they let us experience something greater than ourselves. But we had broken through those closed ranks in Page. Jordan had shown a part of his identity to Chris, and Chris had witnessed the passage of a young man from adolescence into a clan of fighters. He watched as that young man willingly took on this mantle and embraced its hardships as well as its fruits.

Community makes us stronger, and when done right it makes us less suspicious and more noble—be it churchgoing folk gathering on a Sunday for a homily, soldiers swapping photographs in a foxhole, or protesters singing the same melodies as those who came before them. And the traditions and codes and tenets of strong groups inevitably involve an ethic of hospitality. The stories we tell one another, the parables we whisper to our children at night, and the responsibilities that form around all of this demand generosity.

Strong communities welcome the wanderer in from the cold and offer refuge for the needy. Those traits of goodwill and grace are what remain when we distill our traditions down to their elemental states. We are at our most pious then. These are the virtues that allow humankind to survive in the high desert, in our towering cities, and on the frontier where rivers bend and sunrises glint off red rocks that gleam like vermilion.

As the two of us took in Zion, we reflected on how we had changed. We had started our journey through Arizona uninitiated. We left Phoenix with an appreciation for the lengths to which we go to protect what we believe is sacred. And we departed Page with a reverence for those who open their ceremonies, pulsing with the raw power of history and tradition, to the outsider who comes head bowed and knee bent.

Mono Lake

Earlier in our friendship, on a trip from New Haven to Washington, D.C. in the spring of 2016, the two of us visited Gettysburg, where we found a low fog hanging over the fields and hills. It was late on a Sunday and the sky shed mist over the darkening gray monuments. Few people were around. We wandered for a while, pausing at a tall, aging statue to read off its panels the names of fallen soldiers. Nearby we found Lincoln's Gettysburg Address etched on a stone obelisk, and Chris read falteringly through each line as a light rain came down.

"'It is rather for us to be here dedicated to the great task remaining before us,'" Chris read, squinting to see through the gathering dew. "'That from these honored dead we take increased devotion to that cause for which they here gave the last full measure of devotion'—what's that word?"

Jordan stepped closer.

"'That we here highly resolve that these dead shall not have died in vain,'" Jordan joined in, wiping droplets from the last passage. "'That this nation, under God, shall have a new birth of freedom, and that government of the people, by the people, for the people, shall not perish from the earth.'"

Jordan led Chris around the battlefield. Up there were foxholes, he pointed out, and the Union army came up around those hills. This was a defensive position, he continued. Soldiers would aim their muskets through these notches as waves of opponents came charging up the rise.

At the top of Culp's Hill, which looked down on beige pastures with denuded trees below and green fields beyond, Jordan told Chris the story of the decades-long friendship between Union general Winfield Scott Hancock and Confederate general Lewis Armistead. A widower, Armistead had become close friends with Hancock and his wife, Almira, while the two men were stationed together in California in the 1850s.

Then came the war. Hancock stayed with the Union Army, while Armistead left for the Confederacy. Like that of many others, their loyalty to friends, family, and country was tested by the brewing conflict between North and South. They would have to choose sides, and those choices had the potential to divide them from their most cherished friends. So in 1861, Hancock and Armistead parted ways.

From opposing camps, both men fought. Between skirmishes, however, their compatriots reported how deeply and often the two men spoke of each other. At Gettysburg, the two faced off on opposite sides of the battlefield. During the ensuing melee, they were each gravely wounded. Major Henry Bingham, an officer from Hancock's staff, saw Armistead lying on the field and came to his aid. The fallen officer's first words were of concern for his old friend, so Bingham informed him of Hancock's own wounds. Armistead responded mournfully, asking Bingham to tell Hancock, "I have done him and you all a grievous injury, which I shall regret the longest day I live."

"Despite it all," Jordan said, his voice wavering. "Despite the war, and all it stood for, they remained friends. Even at the end."

At their best, friendships are resilient and capable of bearing enormous strain. But sometimes two people can be bound by something deep, and then that bond can snap with little or no warning.

Sometimes the heat of an argument will lay things so bare, and friends will hurt each other so painfully, that whatever kept the two together will be rent beyond repair.

That nearly happened to the two of us in the wastelands of Nevada. Out where valleys stretch for miles and the road doesn't bend but only rises and falls—where the only indications of humanity you will see for miles are listing wooden shacks with the promise of INDIAN JEWELRY painted across plywood signs and the glint of metal on thin blankets spread out across their length.

Out there, we almost broke apart.

It was our fifth day on the road, and we were glowing over what we had seen in such a short period—Yuma, Phoenix, the Trump rally, Horseshoe Bend, Gunfighter Canyon. At the Trump rally, we were impressed by the power of President Trump as a speaker but also leery of the strange men that roamed the fringes of the rally. Outside, we were dismayed by the theatrics and the violence. Yet as we watched the exchanges between Trump supporters and protesters, we were filled with hope.

For an instant, it felt like we had transcended partisanship.

We had left Zion in the morning free to explore the vast, untamed countryside in the heart of Nevada. From Zion to Reno the interstate highway system branched out in every direction, with no obvious route between the two. So we picked a highway that would sweep us southwest, down toward Las Vegas, then zig and zag our way north along two-lane roads until we reached the California border. From there we would trace the boundary up along the Sierra Nevada, past Lake Tahoe, and finally into Reno.

Clear skies sent sunlight over the yellow-green landscape, which stretched out into the distance toward the looming mountain ranges that flanked the road. Tumbleweeds flitted across the asphalt and steppe, pushed along by squalls of wind. With Chris at the wheel, we passed cows lounging in fields and sheep grazing disinterestedly.

There was something beguiling about agreeing, especially as neither of us had expected to see things the same way. This was what we had sought all along: an understanding about what mattered in our civic politics and a common view that reconciled our different perspectives and allowed us to see the world through one another's eyes.

"It's funny," Chris said. "The portrayal of what happens at these rallies was not at all what it was really like. If you went just by the reports, you'd think it was far more divisive than it actually was. You know?"

It was a vulnerable comment, meant as a concession, and Jordan nodded with respect. We agreed that some media were painting a simplistic and misleading picture of the complexity we had experienced.

Jordan responded in kind, complimenting the inspiring behavior of many of the protestors. Another agreement. It was only a year since we had argued so passionately over the role of activism while driving through South Dakota.

"You know," Jordan said after a lengthy pause, "it does bother me that the default assumption for so many people on the left is that Trump's supporters are 'racist, sexist homophobes.' It's not fair— especially the homophobic charge, since he supports gay marriage. Yes, he says things I would never want a president to say. But most of them aren't racist or sexist—or at least most of his supporters don't think they are. That's not what they're responding to. Yet whenever he says something, the Left and the media interpret it in the most uncharitable light, and they use that interpretation to condemn all of his supporters too."

A moment passed after Jordan said this. We had agreed on so much up until that point that we were willing to venture into territory we may have held back from in the past.

For Chris, it was a long moment. For a day or so, the intoxicating feeling of agreement had been tempered by a nagging sensation: Chris was feeling like a bad liberal. It was an odd, unfamiliar emotion. He had never been a perfect liberal, often advocating for moderation—and even the rare conservative idea here and there. But this time around, he felt a peculiar guilt. When Chris had thought to himself that Ben Carson's speech could have been delivered at an Obama rally, he enjoyed the immediate contrarian quality of the notion. Now, though, that idea stalked him. It was what he had seen and heard and concluded, but it suddenly felt wrong as it echoed around his consciousness. It tasted bitter as it aged. So did his surprise at Trump's power on stage. A small observation about Trump's rhetoric began to feel like a betrayal. And as the détente continued, this dark feeling grew until it ruptured.

"Like what?"

Chris said it with an edge.

"The *Mexican immigrants* comment," Jordan said. "He said something like, 'Mexico is sending their worst people. They're sending rapists. They're bringing drugs. And some of them are good people.' His supporters don't hear that and think, *He's racist against all Mexicans.* He isn't calling all immigrants rapists and drug dealers. He is saying that there are bad people flowing across the border—in addition to good ones, yes—but the bad ones are harming people. And we need better border security to protect Americans from them. The emphasis is on security."

"Dude, that was a racist fucking statement, on its face," Chris said. "There was so much wrong with it—the idea that they are criminals or bad. You can't just change the emphasis to suit your interpretation of it. Those words were clearly meant to stoke racism, and worst of all he's never apologized for it."

Not only did Chris feel like he had to stand up for something, but he was forgetting the language that let us disagree and debate without losing our comity. Chris had to prove to himself—and perhaps to Jordan—that he still belonged to the tribe that had raised him.

"Apologizing means accepting the Left's interpretation of his words," Jordan said. "If he didn't intend what you or the media believe he meant, he doesn't need to apologize just because you're playing a game of gotcha."

Jordan's brows arched.

We both knew something toxic had crept in.

"He didn't apologize because he was speaking to the most racist groups in our society. It was a dog whistle."

"Jesus, you guys read dog whistles into everything."

Jordan looked toward the window dismissively as he said it.

"Yes, because we should. Bad things need to be called out—now more than ever. Trump says stuff all the time that's racist and sexist."

"Like what?"

"The countless Muslim statements, for one. The *Access Hollywood* tape. And how about the Megyn Kelly *blood coming out of her you-know-what* thing? It goes on and on."

"Again, you're giving it the most uncharitable interpretation. He said, 'She had blood coming out of her eyes, blood coming out of her...wherever.' And you're reading into that something sexist. But he said 'eyes' first. Why isn't the next logical thing her *ears*?"

"Are you serious? Even if we forgive that, there's still a track record of near-constant slights and ugly statements. You can't ignore that accumulation. We know what he is saying, because it's in his policies and his words."

"No you don't! And that's my point. All of your evidence that he's 'racist, sexist, homophobic' comes from interpreting things into his words. Yes, they might be ugly and unpresidential. I already said I hate it when he does that. But you're condemning him based on your projections about his motivations, or what he 'really meant.' You might disagree with his policies, but you can't point to a single thing he's said or done that's actually racist or sexist beyond vague words."

At this, Chris snapped.

_____

The Boat had gained speed. As the tempo of our conversation quickened and our blood boiled, Chris had unwittingly let his foot sink down on the accelerator.

As Jordan made his last point, we fired up a rise, crested it, and began a rapid descent down the chest of one of Nevada's vast dales. It was one of those valleys that extended so far that the road narrowed into a spear point and was washed out by a ripple of heat. Even though the road never turned, it seemed to point into oblivion.

"That's such bullshit," Chris sputtered.

Jordan was leaning against the passenger door—as far from Chris as possible.

"Look, it comes down to this for me: Trump has said things that have made people in my life fearful for their safety," Chris said. "People I love. He has attacked the most vulnerable groups for political gain. And that's not fucking okay."

"Democrats *want* those groups to be fearful of Trump," Jordan said. "It's the best way to motivate them to vote. They're trying to create an image of Trump as an authoritarian racist. It's a conscious strategy to stoke fear. Again, I'm not saying Trump hasn't said dumb things, but Democrats bear some of the blame for the fear these groups feel right now."

"No, Democrats are protecting these groups from hateful rhetoric. The Wall and Muslim ban don't make sense except as appeals to bigotry. That's fucking racist."

"It's not racist when there is a legitimate issue to focus on. Illegal immigrants have committed crimes, including murder. People have a right to be angry about that. Trump is meeting them where they are, and raising an issue that matters to them. How's it fair to Americans that illegals commit crimes, are released back to Mexico, then come right back over the border again? Why can't he say that?"

"It's irrational."

"How?"

"It's a tiny number of incidents. You can't make policy on that. And whipping up people's anger based on a handful of cases—that's disgusting."

"He's not whipping it up. When he gets up in front of a group of people who have lost loved ones to crimes committed by illegal immigrants, that anger is justified."

"There are so many better things to focus on," Chris said, his voice straining. "More important things. It's irrational to heap all this attention on an issue that is so infinitesimally small."

"How is it any more irrational than the focus on police shootings?"

"You can't be serious."

"Do you know how many unarmed African Americans have been killed this year by cops?" Jordan said.

"If you have a point just say it," Chris retorted.

"It's 14."

"I don't trust that number. And that's not the point, anyway. Police brutality is a totally different issue because of the history of racism. It's a consequence of a whole mess of other problems."

"I'll google it for you."

"I don't need you to google it. Police brutality toward African Americans has gone on for decades. That's why it's relevant. The numbers on the other issue are insignificant in comparison."

"Chris, how is one parent's pain any more valid than another's just because it was committed by a cop rather than an illegal immigrant? Why is one group's suffering more important than another's?"

Neither of us listened. We barely let the other finish a sentence before landing our next jab. Heads were shaking furiously. Angry interruptions were mouthed. Eyes bulged. Chris's heart was pounding in his ears in a way that made him stumble over his words.

"There are decades of built-up anger toward police—justified, by the way—in the African American community," Chris repeated.

"Every time a cop shoots an unarmed black kid, it's a reminder that our country is still in the grip of real, systemic racism."

"In 2017, I think it's just as irrational," Jordan replied. "The police are not trying to kill anyone. Killing another human is the hardest thing in the world. It scars you for life. The idea that cops want to kill black kids is ridiculous. At worst, they're poorly trained."

"So explain to me why blacks are disproportionately killed by the police," Chris said. "Explain to me why they are disproportionately incarcerated."

"Explain to me how most of the cities where these shootings have happened are run by Democrats," Jordan said. "In Baltimore, the mayor and the DA were both African American. Chicago has been run by Democrats for decades, and so has Oakland. Why don't you point your anger at your own party's failed leadership?"

"It's way more complicated than that—and you know it."

"No, they're linked. You're attributing racism to police officers in a way that's totally unfair. They're doing a dangerous job, and all they want is to get back home to their kids at night. They have to make split-second decisions about when to use force or not. Trust me, it's not simple. We spent months running those kinds of scenarios. It's fucking hard to know when someone might have a weapon. Especially when your adrenaline is pounding."

"I've watched cops be racist to my friends. I've witnessed a Suburban full of kids get pulled over and only the black kid in the third row gets pulled out and asked for his driver's license. Not even the driver. I—"

"That doesn't excuse the Left from whipping up anger and hatred toward the police."

"Let me fucking finish."

"Go ahead."

Chris was trembling.

"I honestly can't believe you hold these opinions."

"What the fuck does that mean?"

Chris didn't respond as the Boat barreled down the hillside with ferocious speed.

"If you have something to say, say it!"

Chris stared straight ahead as the road rumbled beneath the car. Something had been torn, and we both knew it. The few feet between us may as well have been miles.

"I'm done with this conversation," Chris said.

––––––––––––––

Jordan stared out the window. The sun was just past its midway point. The landscape was vast and beautiful. We were nearing the ascent up the other buff wall of the valley. All this scenery, and Jordan may as well have been seeing black. His mind spun with anger and aggrievement. Every thump of the tires or growl of the engine took him away from the present.

Friends don't attack each other like that, he thought. *How could Chris be so unreasonable?*

Jordan began to question these trips and the friendship itself. *Once we get home, that's it. No more trips. I don't need this.* The feelings dragged Jordan down. Every few moments, he tried to pull himself out of the spiral. But each minute Chris didn't apologize made Jordan plunge even further into rage. And yet the two of us were just a word away from healing, Jordan knew. He could open his mouth, offer something heartfelt, and that would be it. Chris would snatch it up and offer his own. He always did. The reconciliation would begin, because it had happened 100 times before. Those words just felt too hard to say that afternoon. They were caught in his chest, and he couldn't will them out.

So instead Jordan simmered.

Chris was lost in his own fury. He felt claustrophobic and wronged. He couldn't look at Jordan—a friend he no longer recognized. Chris had always harbored the belief that Jordan didn't actually disagree with him all that much. Under a layer of conservatism, they were the same. After this exchange, Chris wasn't sure.

Both of us wanted to say something to unpoison the well, as we always did. These fights had life cycles—peaks and valleys that ended in a hair tousle, a tease, or a line of fraternal affection. But we had never fought quite like that before, over something so fundamental, and we couldn't summon the right words no matter how many times we tried.

And if we couldn't, then we would likely part ways. No more road trips, and likely no more friendship. We now lived on opposite sides of the country, after all—Chris in Connecticut and Jordan in California. With little reason to talk or see each other, we would likely drift apart.

Maybe it had all been a foolish undertaking to begin with. It was folly to think we could survive in a car for so many hours and not fight—not come face-to-face with the limits of our tolerance. Others must have tried this before, and there was a reason they hadn't told the story. Perhaps there was no story. Perhaps our differences were simply too great.

As we crested each hillock on the undulating road, shocks of yellow wildflowers spread out across the Sierra foothills like gold. We had passed around a mountain range, cutting along the granite of Nevada hills carved jagged and naked for the highways. The road leveled off from there and dropped down into an ocean of blooms which augured the coming of California.

"I love you, man," Chris said at length. "But I need some time to calm down—to find the words."

"I feel the same, Chris," Jordan said. "And I love you too."

We didn't say much more, and we were quiet for a long time after that. But we were nearly back in California. And we had broken the silence.

———————

On the other end of those empty, windswept valleys was Mono Lake. When he was growing up, Chris's mother had hung a framed black-and-white photo of the lake on a wall in their bathroom. Tufas—the great limestone towers made by the precipitation of carbonate minerals—rose on the edges of the frame. They looked like the spires of a sandcastle, doused by rain, after a child had roughly patted them into form. "It's a dying lake," Chris's mother would tell him. It had been draining for years, emptied by the decision to divert its tributaries elsewhere to quench the thirst of distant cities such as Los Angeles. As the waters receded, more of these tufas had emerged like scar tissue out of the depths. Only the work of a group of citizens who prized the lake saved it from desiccation. Chris wanted to visit, and Jordan was not going to stand in the way.

Out of the parking lot, we explored the shore. The tufas looked like the rock formations of brittle clay we had seen in the Badlands the summer before. Alkali flies parted in great black clouds ahead of our footsteps as we walked along the edge of the water, which lapped gently with the mountain breeze that cut across the lake's surface. We found a cove, removed from the groups of tourists, and sat under the tufas to avoid the heat of the sun. We loitered silently on the shore, watching the calm blue-green water lap against the finely grained, tan-colored sand.

"Can we swim in it?" Jordan asked.

"I don't think so."

"Why not?"

Chris considered it.

"I'm not sure."

"We can't leave without swimming in it," Jordan said, forcing a smile.

Chris looked out over the lake. It stretched for what looked like miles. He had no idea how expansive it was. The scene was on a scale even his adult imagination couldn't fathom. But then again, these trips had a way of adjusting the sizes of things. Mount Rushmore, once colossal in his mind's eye, seemed small—quaint, even—when we arrived at its base. The views from the peaks outside Yellowstone, or the view of Horseshoe Bend along the Grand Canyon, were infinite. The landscape below was frozen in place by the great distance.

"Look," said Jordan, showing Chris his phone, "it says right here we can."

"I guess we can."

So we took off our clothes and waded into the water in our briefs. As we swam, the salinity of the lake thickened the water and left a thin, oily layer on the surface. When we brushed our hands through its depths, a swirl of something other than water twisted in its wake. A thin slime coated our chests and legs as we paddled out farther and farther from shore. But the salinity also made us buoyant. Chris thought it must be somewhat like walking on the moon.

"There's tiny little kelp in the water!" Jordan declared.

"They're brine shrimp," Chris explained.

"Are they safe? Like, will they swim up my . . . *ahem*?" Jordan said, laughing.

We lazily swam in the water far from shore—beyond the rush of the highway, beyond the sound of people.

"Let's swim over to those rocks," Jordan said. The two of us took off paddling like dogs, and with a smile began racing toward them. We climbed up on the craggy banks and lounged in the sun, feeling the salty water dry on our skin.

"Let's go farther out," Chris said, jumping back in, and Jordan followed.

As we swam around, the water slowly washed away our lingering anger. It was like a cool salve easing our pain and healing our wounds. By the time we climbed out of the water and threw our clothes over our wet skin, we were nearly back to normal.

"I like this place," Jordan said.

And Chris smiled.

———————

Our fight had brought us right up to the edge, but we survived. The two of us had wounded one another, and the venom lingered. Yet we had begun to heal and as we walked away from the lake, our arms and faces crusted in invisible layers of salt that pulled our skin tight, we could smile again. We even shared a basket of fried food at a lakeside dive bar just up the shore, where we left wet marks on the canvas deck chairs.

Soon we were back on the road, driving along the highway grade up the face of the Sierra peak that shadowed the lake in the late afternoon.

"Look man, I really love you," Chris said, always quick with the word. "I trust you with my life. I'm sorry for getting so angry."

"I love you, too, brother," Jordan replied. "And I'm also sorry. I know I got aggressive."

"It's just that there are people in my life that really have been hurt by all of this. I care about them so much. And it pains me. So I reacted based on that. I should have been able to say that, though, rather than starting a fight."

"I'm really sorry, Chris. I didn't understand how personal it was for you, and I never would have responded that way if I did. It's personal for people in my life too."

And that was it. The words flowed off our tongues with relief.

We had found our way back to the table, to try again. Closure has its own mythology. Neither of us had convinced the other of his rightness. But friendship isn't predicated on perfect symmetry. There are greater forces at work than politics, no matter how definitional our chosen sides may feel. We had returned, because disagreement isn't anything to run from; it can be a virtue. Both of us hoped we would be able to prevent it from tearing us asunder; both of us hoped it would continue to teach us all the same. As long as we listened, we could make each other better.

Chris had been quick to dismiss Jordan's invocation of families who had lost loved ones to violence, and something about his own reaction troubled him. No matter what kind of bearing it had on policy, it upset Chris to think how callously he had dismissed someone else's pain. It wasn't the sensation of apostasy or the anger or the guilt that lingered longest.

Chris also sensed for the first time how Jordan was afraid of losing friends over his political views. He must have carried that insecurity for years. How difficult it must be to hold opinions that are not just rejected by one's peers but reviled—viewed as unworthy of discussion or even engagement. When Jordan was confronted, his armor went up not just for himself but also for all the people he cared about who shared his views—his family, many of his Marine comrades, and millions of Americans he didn't know.

How had things gone so far off the rails? In his mind, Jordan zeroed in on one moment in particular—when Chris had said that people in his life had been hurt by Trump's rhetoric. Jordan had heard those words, he recognized the emotion they carried, yet he pressed on with his argument anyway. He tried to show Chris why he was wrong. What if instead he had paused, recognized the pain his words had caused Chris, and asked to learn more? What if he had made an effort to understand that pain and to show that he understood why this mattered so much? Then things might have gone differently.

Finding common ground isn't about being right. It's about laying a foundation to argue passionately while respecting the other side. It's not about getting to agreement, but getting to the point where disagreement isn't reason to pull away.

Throughout our journeys, we would often reflect on how fragile common ground can be. Had we not been in a car together, we might have walked away. We recognized there was a limit to *how* we could argue, and it was important to understand where that line was. It showed us that our friendship was not something that could be taken lightly or for granted. We had a responsibility to each other to respect its bounds, to tend to it, and, where we could, to strengthen its resilience. That realization made it even more essential to do these trips, to solidify our friendship despite our different values and priorities.

Around seven o'clock, we pulled into Carla Medina's driveway in a mobile-home park in Sparks, just outside Reno. Carla had been Jordan's childhood babysitter. As we got out of the car in the growing twilight, Carla opened the door and gave us a big wave.

"My baby!" she shouted.

Jordan went up to give her a hug, and Chris grabbed our bags from the car.

"This is my friend Chris," Jordan said.

"You go to school together?" Carla asked, eyeing Chris's long hair.

"Yup! We're best friends."

Carla's husband, Chuck, came out to greet us too. He was a thick man with a closely buzzed head of hair. He shook our hands with a big hand tattooed with a navy anchor between his thumb and index finger. He looked like a brawler but had a peaceful temperament.

"Hope you boys are hungry," Chuck said. "I'm grilling steaks."

"And I made you tamales," Carla cut in, holding Jordan's arm. "My baby loves tamales. I taught him to eat them."

Carla led us through a tiled kitchen and into a dark living room littered with family photos, including one of Jordan in his dress blues. Carla had a stainless-steel pot of something bubbling on the stove; nearby were baskets full of tamales in big banana-leaf wraps and a bowl of freshly dressed salad. She'd been cooking all day, she told us.

Carla had taken care of Jordan from the time he was a year old. Early on, Jordan's parents had their hands full with Jenna, Jordan's older sister, so Carla had become something of a surrogate mother. The two of them had developed a special bond that had lasted for decades. She considered him one of her children.

As Jordan told it, Carla's life had been full of adventure and struggle. She achieved the American Dream, Jordan kept saying throughout the trip. Originally from Guatemala, Carla came to the U.S. and stayed for a few years before returning home with hopes of coming back. Eventually, she received a green card and brought her family with her.

In Los Angeles, Carla, her then-husband Raul, and their six children began a new life. She met the Blasheks and went to work raising Jordan and Jenna, while her husband earned his living at local restaurants. Her children went to high school, three of them went to college, one joined the Marine Corps, and each of them started their own families. Raul passed away far too early, leaving Carla alone and without enough support. Rob, Jordan's father, helped where he could with tuition, and the family persevered. Many years on, Carla was the matriarch of a growing multigenerational family. She then married Chuck, a sweet and doting man, and they had lived together ever since.

Carla kept regaling Chris with stories about Jordan as a baby. She told tales about taking him to the park, teaching him to eat new foods, and defending him from his older sister—and sometimes even his mother. Soon the conversation turned to the past few days as we told Carla and Chuck about our adventures at the Trump rally. It was our first time sharing the story with an audience and we indulged our memories. Chuck was fascinated; Carla was less impressed.

"I have no time for Trump," she declared, waving her hands as if at a fly.

What mattered was work and family, she explained. She didn't understand why everyone cared so much about what the president said or did. It was irrelevant to her daily life. Instead, she had her real estate back in Guatemala to manage, as well as a house in Las Vegas she hadn't been able to sell. And, more important, she had her grandchildren to watch over while their parents were at work. Those were the things she cared about.

"If I don't work, I don't eat," she concluded.

Mono Lake

Chris watched as Carla sat across from Jordan telling story after story. Carla looked at Jordan with maternal pride. Somewhat embarrassed, Jordan smiled and lovingly corrected some of Carla's details. They were family, somehow.

Just a few hours before, we had been in a pitched battle over immigration, and Jordan had defended Trump's rhetoric. But there we were in the home of a former undocumented immigrant whom Jordan cared deeply about, and by whom he was welcomed as family.

It all felt so complicated.

Yet in Carla and Chuck's trailer, on that evening, Jordan's conservatism was absent—as was Chris's liberalism. For at least one evening, the two of us were solely friends sharing a meal with Carla and Chuck. All else melted away. Battle lines were undrawn. Defenses were laid down. That night, the four of us told stories, spoke of life's difficulties, shared in one another's dreams, and passed around a warm meal.

We were Chris and Jordan, improbable friends once more.

PART II

PART A

Louisiana

We pulled into Morton's Travel Plaza off East Cheyenne Avenue in Las Vegas, Nevada early on a Saturday in December 2017. The stop was a few miles off the Strip, which loomed in the hazy distance. Tractor trailers of all sorts were parked at diagonals for what looked like entire city blocks.

We had flown in at dawn from New York. Both of us had finished two weeks' worth of fall exams in a weekend so we could fit in another road trip before the holidays. Jordan was back at Yale Law School for his final semester, and both of us were set to graduate in the spring. It had been four months since our last swing through California, Arizona, and Nevada.

The day before, Chris had confirmed our arrival with Peter Mylen, a 57-year-old truck driver from Daytona Beach, Florida, who would be our host for the week.

We were trying to chase down the feeling we had in Page, Arizona, and spend more time with people who might show us something we couldn't find in our daily lives.

We stood in the parking lot, blinking at the fleet before us in the morning chill. A horn blast cut through the air. It came from a blue truck with a New York Giants logo on its flank.

"Need a ride?" a man shouted down at us from an open window.

He climbed down from the cab, and there was Peter.

He was a tall, stocky man with strong forearms, dun skin, a bristling mustache, and thin eyeglasses. His presence was enormous.

"Welcome, boys," he said and shook our hands vigorously. Two prominent green-black tattoos ran up and down his forearms—one of an American flag behind an eagle, the other of a baroque cross.

"Peter," he said warmly. "Nice to meet you."

As Peter spoke, he opened his arms and revealed MAKE AMERICA GREAT AGAIN plastered across the chest of his crimson shirt.

"I wore it for you guys," Peter explained, noticing us eyeing it. "I told my wife, 'Make it red so when they start shooting at me, they'll hit their target.'" He laughed heartily—a deep, hoarse sound.

The plan for the week was simple enough. Peter had agreed to take us along for a shipment of a family's belongings from Las Vegas to Gulfport, Mississippi, a journey of 1,800 miles. Peter was a *bedbugger*—in trucker patois, someone who moves people's household belongings.

This trip would take us through Arizona and New Mexico; across the Texas Panhandle and along the state's eastern ridgelike border with Oklahoma; through Shreveport, Louisiana; and, ultimately, across the Delta and into Mississippi. We had four days to make it.

Jordan settled into the jump seat across from Peter, and Chris plopped down on the mattress of the bunk bed behind the two of them, feet dangling. Satisfied with the state of his idling rig—a gleaming Volvo VNL 780—Peter pressed the air brake. It released with a hiss that rose above the grinding turnover of the engine. Pete, as we would come to call him, put the tractor into gear.

"Here we go," he said, and with a shudder of the rig, he maneuvered us out of the parking lot, through an intersection, and out onto the open highway.

With one hand on the wheel, Pete pulled out an orange pack of Pall Malls and a red lighter. He cracked the window and lit one as the wind off the interstate between Las Vegas and Albuquerque screamed through the cab.

"I don't go anywhere unless that trailer is absolutely chock full," Pete said. When he talked, he turned his whole torso to face us.

"Because I get 55 percent," he continued, "and all the expenses come out of my pocket. The insurance, fuel, workers' comp. I'm just not one of those guys that runs a quarter-empty. On my way back from Connecticut, one time, I had mattresses strapped to the back and 2,000 pounds of cargo on my upper bunk here."

Pete's truck was already cramped. The two jump seats took up half the cab, rocking and squealing on their suspension. On the broad dash from window to window, Pete kept an assortment of items: mini-calendars, notepads and pens, sunflower seeds, trinkets hanging from the mirror, a plastic statuette of Jesus—arms outstretched—and an ever-present coffee mug. Behind the jump seats was a refrigerator, a small television, and two bunk beds. The bottom one was for Pete. The upper bunk was for his helpers—or in this case, for us.

Joining Pete for a ride-along had been Chris's idea. If we were going to get away from politics, Chris surmised, we should meet people where they lived and worked. Chris had always enjoyed reading Studs Terkel's interviews in his weathered copy of *Working,* and where better to start than with long-haul trucks? As far as Chris knew from Terkel's book, it was a gritty job—one that could teach us something not only about work but about the pockets of America we had yet to see. Jordan was intrigued by the idea. He imagined truckers shared a lot in common with the troops he knew.

Truck drivers are an integral part of American life. Each year, three million truckers transport more than $700 billion worth of goods across the branching veins of America's interstate highways. Without them, commerce would grind to a halt. Yet the industry is on the margins of society. Today, if reported on at all, trucking is most readily invoked in conversations about the supposedly imminent arrival of self-driving vehicles.

Eventually Chris found his way to Finn Murphy, a former trucker and author of *The Long Haul: A Trucker's Tales of Life on the Road,* who told us he would find someone to take us along for a ride.

A few weeks later, Finn got back to us. "I have your man," he wrote, and included a phone number.

After a 30-minute phone conversation with Pete, we decided Finn was right. Pete was loud, opinionated, and welcoming. "You don't have enough ink in your printer to get down all my thoughts," Pete had yelled over the phone with a belly laugh audible above the scream of highway air behind him.

"So," Chris said from a lawn chair Pete had jerry-rigged for us behind the two jump seats as we drove through Nevada. "How do you know Finn?"

"Finn?" Pete said. "You know, I've never met Finn."

"Really?" Jordan said.

"Yeah, don't know him from Adam."

"How'd you connect with him?" Chris asked.

"I think he knew our local dispatcher," Pete explained. "He reached out to her and said, 'Hey, I got these guys. You know any driver that might be willing to help out?' She just said, 'Hey, Pete. I think this sounds like you.'"

We were miles southeast of Las Vegas by then, gunning down a highway into the long stretch of desert between Las Vegas and Arizona with a complete stranger—a raucous, surly man with a Trump T-shirt who laughed at his own bawdy jokes and careered with speed down hills with thousands of pounds of furniture lashed to the hitch on the tractor's back end.

Just then a sedan sped onto the road from a highway entrance ramp, and its driver peered up at us as it slowly passed the cab. We looked down, fascinated by our new towering vantage. Pete noticed too, and leaned across the cab at a perilous angle. With one hand on the wheel, he pulled his shirt up and flashed a nipple, flicking it with his free hand and letting out a baritone howl, one we would come to know well.

"They love it," he said to us, shirt once again pooling at his waist, as he bounced in his jump seat over the uneven road, a cigarette still smoldering between his fingers.

———————

Pete drove hard. He whisked in and out of lanes with ease, peeling around smaller cars and lumbering trucks and swooping back into the fast lane. For such an enormous vehicle, the semi moved deftly under his hand. All told, Pete had navigated some three million miles in his more than 40 years on the road. He started as a helper, or *road dog* as they are called, sleeping in the back of tractor trailers, and for the past 33 years as the owner-operator of his own rig.

Yet this journey would be a new experience even for a veteran driver like him. A recent regulation was about to change Pete's industry. The Moving Ahead for Progress in the 21st Century Act, passed by the U.S. Congress and signed into law by President Barack Obama in 2012, required the Federal Motor Carrier Safety Administration to develop a rule mandating all truckers carry electronic logging devices, known as ELDs. The ELDs would help enforce long-standing rules limiting the number of hours a trucker could drive in a single day. Now, after years of deliberation, the new requirements were set to go into effect on December 18, 2017—three days after the start of our journey.

"I pretty much expect all hell to break loose that day," Pete said.

A poll conducted by *Fleet Owner* magazine found that only one-third of all truckers had complied with the mandate to carry an ELD. For a deadline set to affect more than three million people in a few days' time, this was a concerning number. Penalties for noncompliance could be steep, including fines and citations. By April, a noncompliant driver could be put out of service.

Pete sported an ELD on the windshield above the dash. Fitted with a GPS, ELDs are essentially tracking devices. The electronic log monitored Pete's progress to the minute, creating a precise record that the government and his dispatcher could scrutinize. Before ELDs, truckers would jot down their hours with a pen and notebook. When we first joined Pete in Las Vegas, he was filling out just such a journal.

"These logs are a pain in my ass," Pete had said before we pulled away from Morton's Travel Plaza. He was ticking away at a form with a byzantine series of lined grids on a clipboard. "I log down everything I do in this here notebook," Pete explained.

Until the deadline, Pete would still jot on the clipboard, looking back and forth from a pocket notebook full of dates and times that he used to calculate how far he had driven, the time he had started, and when he had pulled off for a nap. While not perfect, the system was tolerable because drivers could "adjust" the books to the realities of the road when regulations became too cumbersome. Pete told us how it had once taken a full 11-hour shift to load his trailer. He was exhausted and reeked. But it would have been illegal for him to drive back to the truck stop for a shower. By law, he was required to stay put and spend the night in front of the client's house. Instead, he scratched *off duty* into his logbook and made the drive to the truck stop.

"They make you lie," he said, barreling in and out of a lane to avoid a sluggish car in the wilds of Arizona. "No one who's ever trucked made these laws."

Now the ELD was set to change all that, and the anger among truckers was palpable. On our trip, the two of us would hear complaints from a dozen or so truckers we met on the road. Protests were breaking out all over the country. Three hundred trucks had driven down a highway from Sacramento to Fresno at five miles per hour to protest the new ELD mandate. In Washington, D.C., others parked along Constitution Avenue and in front of the U.S. Department of Transportation. Many threatened to quit trucking altogether.

Pete was sympathetic, but he didn't take part in the protests.

"I've got a family to support," he said. "I'm out here to run and to make my money."

It was a perspective many truckers likely shared. One recent industry poll found that 78 percent of them felt underpaid.

The weight of it all sat heavy on Pete's shoulders. He talked frequently about the pressure he felt because of the many rules on the road. It was like a boot on his neck, he explained.

"Every single day, I'm looking over my shoulder. What am I doing wrong? What are they gonna get me for? How much is that gonna cost me? And that all comes from regulation piled upon regulation just to smother us, dominate us, and break our spirit."

This resonated with Jordan, who was often skeptical of the federal government's ability to manage life in a country as large and complex as the United States. While well-intentioned, he believed, federal regulations could lead to second- and third-order consequences that often made life harder for the "little guy"—the small business owners, the owner-operators, and anyone else who couldn't hire a legion of lawyers. There is a time and place for regulation, but bureaucracy has a tendency to overreach—and when it gets in the way of honest work, it has let down the society it was meant to protect.

Chris sympathized with Pete's lament, but he also felt a twinge of disbelief. Watching Pete drive was not exactly a soothing experience. Everyone—no matter how experienced—needs rules on the road. Truckers, as a group, aren't always the safest drivers, either. In 2016, at least 4,400 semis were involved in fatal accidents on U.S. highways. Thirty-seven years prior, however, that number had been north of 6,400. The state may have been the bad guy to Pete, a man Chris had decided to trust with his life, but its dictates seemed like a necessary evil for a system responsible for keeping an eye on a fleet of millions of drivers.

"They make us feel like criminals out here," Pete concluded.

For decades, trucking represented something rough but decent in the American imagination. In the 1960s, the trucker was the marooned driver's savior and the noble of the open road. But this national fascination began to fade in the 1980s, especially after the Motor Carrier Act of 1980 deregulated the industry and opened the highways to cutthroat competition and non-union fleets.

But Pete kept on.

As afternoon subsided into night, the view was breathtaking. Arizona's red rocks and imposing valley walls were touched with sun. "This is my office," Pete said and gestured out over the landscape that stretched golden for miles and butted up against a craggy mountain range. Pete tapped at his first pack of Pall Malls and, seeing it empty, discarded it.

"I've got nothing to do but drive down the highway communing with myself and the Spirit."

Chris had settled down for a nap after seeing the exit for Page. When he awoke, the sun was down and Pete had pulled over in a dirt parking lot in Winslow, Arizona. Jordan had stepped out to check into a nearby motel. Pete was thumbing through his phone.

"Do you want a room?" Chris asked.

Pete shook his head.

"Sometimes when I'm home, I'll sleep out here," he said. "And when I'm on the road, if I can't sleep, I'll get up at two in the morning and come out and sit right here in this chair," he patted the side of the arm rest.

"Fair enough," Chris said and followed Jordan into the motel.

Morning came quickly on our second day. The two of us reluctantly climbed into the cab just after 4 a.m. We found Pete wide awake and apologetic. The ELD had yet to zero out, so we had to sit for another ten minutes until his legally mandated rest period expired.

"We don't actually have to wait," Pete said. "The mandate doesn't go into effect until tomorrow. But I'm training myself."

As we watched the clock count down, Pete laid out the rules of his craft. The Federal Motor Carrier Safety Administration allowed him to drive 11 hours in a day, but he had to do so in a 14-hour window. And within six hours of starting his drive, he had to take a 30-minute break, no matter what. He could drive a total of 70 hours in an eight-day week before having to take a few days off. The government would brook nothing less.

"I don't think astronauts go through this bullshit," Pete grumbled as we waited.

Soon enough, we made our way down a long stretch of road and pulled over at a truck stop for coffee and supplies. Truckers can stop only in certain places. Their lumbering tractors are too cumbersome to navigate most city streets. The Petro, Speedway, and Pilot Flying J truck stops that dot highway exits are concrete oases for these interstate nomads.

As Jordan and Pete perused the hot offerings inside, Chris walked the length of Pete's truck. It was white and ribbed with support beams. Blue and red markings mottled the siding. Across the back of the cab, the phrase PRAISE THE LORD was etched in Gothic letters. The gargantuan New York Giants insignia adorned a large segment of the trailer. "Gives me something to yak about with the guys," Pete had said earlier in the day. Jordan joined Chris, and Pete noticed us admiring the truck. He strode around the side and pulled open the middle door with the swipe of a hand. He patted the cardboard boxes cinched in tight from floor to ceiling and explained the finer points of fastening down the guts of a rig.

Loading a truck is complicated. You have to be thoughtful to maximize density, which maximizes tonnage, which is the only way to maximize profit. It requires finesse, a good team of labor, and experience. Know-how is the tried and true method of fitting a tricycle in snugly beside a toaster oven.

Back on the road, Pete tapped out another Pall Mall and lit it in the darkened cab, steering with his elbows as he went. We were passing through New Mexico in the fading black. Predawn was Pete's favorite time to drive. He was rested then, and there was no sun in his eyes. He had his first cup of coffee with sugar and milk, which sloshed around in his grounds-encrusted mug—one he refused to clean. It was a meditative time. The lights of the oncoming trucks and the glow of the dividers were pretty much all one could see.

"How's New Haven?" Pete asked us without the same punch to his voice. "I used to roam the New Haven Green when I was 14, 15 years old. Down there at Chapel and—"

He searched for the street name.

"Temple?" Jordan offered.

"Temple."

For a time, Pete had described himself as "born on a mountain, raised in a cave" on his Facebook page. Now it's "work hard, play hard, pray hard," a change he made after a few aunts took exception to that characterization of his childhood. Pete grew up in Milford, Connecticut, the son of an alcoholic mother who adored her children but could never take care of them. His father, Jim, was an engineer who got full custody of Pete and his sisters in the divorce. Jim was a career man, Pete said, who neglected his children and his new wife—who, in turn, terrorized her stepchildren. She fastened a padlock to the refrigerator. The house was kept locked, too, and the children were welcome inside only when she was home.

So at 15 years old, Pete ran away. Lost in southern Connecticut, he needed a place to stay and discovered a truck stop in Milford where for 25 cents a night he could get a mattress and clean sheets to throw on the floor in a cavernous room with dozens of truckers. One of them asked Pete if he wanted to help load his truck. A big teenager, Pete did it with ease. So the man took him to California. Soon Pete was a road dog, traveling in the cab and sleeping in the trailer at night with a transistor radio for company.

These days, there are almost no bunkhouses like the one in Milford. They went away in the 1970s when sleepers—trucks outfitted with bunks—became more common on the market, changing the industry forever.

Pete may have found his calling early, but his youth wasn't serene. His troubles started with groups of friends at the *Rocky Horror Picture Show*, passing around flasks of brown liquor and hand-rolled cigarettes. Later, when he wasn't working, he and a pack of like-minded guys would follow the Grateful Dead up and down the East Coast. He lived in the back of a pickup truck, sleeping on lawns and washing himself in creeks and gullies. On the night Jerry Garcia died, Pete attended a candlelight vigil on the New Haven Green.

He had children, and they became estranged. He worked and eventually got his own truck, but he wasn't clean. There were vices on the road, and Pete was not immune to them. From time to time, when it all became too much, he tried moving to other parts of Connecticut to escape the dealers and friends. It didn't work. They always found him again. And the substances took their toll.

Until one day, he got sober.

Chris was incredulous.

"You just stopped?"

"Sure did," Pete said. And he's been sober ever since.

As we drove, Pete told us how he recently met his first son, Pete Jr., after decades apart. His son had called him, drunk, in the middle of the night, and Pete had told him they should get a meal.

"I know you are mad," Pete said to his son when they met. "You're mad about my absence. Mad that I was away."

Pete offered his son one swing.

"I'll keep my hands behind my back, and you can hit me across the face," Pete had said. Pete Jr. asked if he could bank it, but his old man said no. It was an expiring offer, and Pete Jr. chose not to take it. It was the start of their reconciliation.

Pete began to cry as he told us the story. Pete often cried when we discussed family or faith. For years now he had styled himself a good family man—the kind of father and husband who emerges only after years spent ruing a family's absence.

At one point we passed a young man with his thumb up walking down the side of the highway. He wore dirty clothing and his hair was long and matted. Pete normally would have picked him up, he said, but with the two of us in the cab there was no space. As a stray once himself, Pete often tried to help lost kids on the road. His wife calls these hitchhikers his "special charity cases."

Pete's wife was omnipresent in the cab. She was his fourth. The life of a trucker can be rough on a relationship. Pete was on the road 28 days of every month. It takes a unique kind of spouse to put up with that sort of life.

"Each wife who I was married to I was madly in love with," he said. "I'm still good friends with every one of them. I let each of them know that the time they were a part of my life was a huge blessing to me. And I hope that I was a blessing to them. Now, okay, the blessings have ended. We gotta go our separate ways and hopefully you'll have blessings with someone else. But the time I had with each one of them was wonderful."

Yet to hear Pete tell it, his current wife was something special.

"I love my wife so much," he repeated over and over. They had been together for 15 years, and Pete claimed there hadn't been a single day of anger.

"Like I tell her, I'm the best husband in the world," he laughed. "I come home once every month. You cook me a steak, do one load of laundry, then I'm out of here. Okay? And then you get 2,000 dollars a week for that. So, really, how bad can it be being married to me?"

"This one of yours?"

Pete held up a small lime-green pocket Bible after a coffee break. It was just after seven in the morning on our second full day, and sleep still weighted our eyes as the dawn light entered the cab.

"It's mine," Chris said.

It was a new possession for Chris. A man on the street had handed it to him. Chris had put it in a pouch designed for water bottles on the side of his backpack, and it must have slipped out onto the thin mattress in the back of Pete's 18-wheeler.

"A man of God?"

Chris shook his head.

"I was born skeptical but not faithless," Chris said. "At this point, I just haven't had something to believe in yet."

Seeing the disappointment in Pete's face, Chris mentioned his Saint Christopher's pendant. His mother gave it to him when he turned 21, and the saint's story had resonated with him. He told Pete and Jordan how, like Saint Christopher, if he were ever to find faith it would be in service to this world, not the next.

Pete, though, was practically brimming with faith. It was in his greetings, his hopes and dreams, his politics. He saw God on the road, in the sunset and the landscape ahead of him. God was why he picked up hitchhikers and called his family every night and sought their forgiveness when he did wrong. Everything is a blessing, Pete told us, and God, well, God is love and his word is love.

We spent an hour digesting how the Bible instructed him to love all mankind and, at the same time, prohibited same-sex relationships, including both his sister's and stepdaughter's. He was conflicted over this, racked by the gravity of what he had to do: disobey one commandment in service to another. But ultimately Pete came around to the conclusion that if God was love, how could a loving relationship be wrong? It hurt him to reject a passage of the Bible, but he found a greater cause in supporting his sister and stepdaughter in their relationships, even if it might leave him damned one day.

Pete's faith was in the runaways he took in, too. "With young people who I see out here traveling the road, struggling," Pete told us, "I really think that God is gonna give me the words to say what they need to hear, you know what I mean?" Pete was an evangelist for compassion. Over and over, he told us how all he wanted was to love and to help the people in his life, as Christ did for him when he was locked out of his childhood home or when the liquor left him all-consumed or when his children needed his advice.

Pete picked up a camouflage pocket Bible from the dash, where cigarette boxes were stacked alongside his wallet. He opened it at random. "Would you read it at some point?" Chris asked. Pete tried then and there, but couldn't focus on the words while driving. So he handed it over to Chris, who put his finger on the jostled pages and read aloud.

"'Am I not free? Am I not an apostle? Have I not seen Jesus our Lord?'" Chris read. "'Are you not the result of my work in the Lord? Even though I may not be an apostle to others, surely I am to you. This is my defense to those who scrutinize me. Have we no right to food and to drink?'"

Jordan put his hand on Chris's shoulder.

"Isn't that Pete in a nutshell?"

"I was thinking the exact same thing."

"Tell me what that doesn't say about right now, right here, our discussion that we're having," Pete said, "to randomly open that book, and you tell me the Lord doesn't exist or doesn't intervene on our behalf in situations right now? That shit don't happen by accident. Thank you, Jesus."

We didn't know Pete well, but it all felt fitting. Pete was no saint. He was rough around the edges and seemed to take pride in his vulgarity. But Pete was a servant of the God he knew, and to the people he met. In his impiety was a deep piety.

Pete quietly teared up as the light of the sun took over the world in front of us. The clouds were pink, and the mountains were still purple.

The golden sawgrass along the highway divider practically glowed in the brilliant dawn.

The ELD had become Kafkaesque since crossing into Texas. It spat out numbers that made little sense. The mandated break came too late, and the device had seemingly shaved three hours off his total drive time. Pete waved aloft a 50-page manual that showed how to use the ELD only with an Android phone, not an inset device like the one he had.

"This doesn't work for inbred truckers," Pete growled. "That's what you get for 700 bucks."

Conversations with Pete were a meandering experience. One moment the topic would be quantum mechanics. The next it would be politics, or football, or the Dead Sea Scrolls. Music—especially the 1970s rock he listened to on the radio—was another kind of education. Character, Pete said, was built by music.

We were in the Texas Panhandle now, and bound for Louisiana and Mississippi.

As we drove, Pete confessed to us that he had prayed that morning for God to give him the words to say something insightful. He prayed every day, and his humble ask as he sat in the dark waiting for us to emerge was to say something that would enrich us. He prayed for it three times before the sun came up.

Pete was self-conscious about the two of us being in his rig, he admitted. Perhaps our presence was some sort of test. A way to prove the merits of an autodidact's highway scholastics. His education had come to an end after eighth grade, but with countless hours to kill on the road he had turned to educating himself. He read. He watched the History Channel. Dr. Phil was a source of inspiration. He had days on end to think as he trucked, and he tried it all on as we spoke.

We came to know Pete as an enigmatic thinker, and no more so than in the realm of politics. Trump inevitably came up in conversation, and we were surprised by Pete's opening statement.

"You know," he said, his MAKE AMERICA GREAT AGAIN shirt still stretched across his chest and belly, "my biggest problem with him is that he doesn't acknowledge climate change."

The diesel engine roared as Pete gunned past a doddering car that was skittishly attempting to merge onto the road.

Pete went on to lament Trump's sexism. He unloaded on the inequity of white privilege. He told us how he regretted what Trump had said about immigrants and Muslims, both on the campaign trail and since.

Two days after the 9/11 attacks, Pete recalled, he was inching down the New Jersey Turnpike in his rig. Pete had arrayed his dashboard with miniature American flags, as many other drivers had. As he approached a ticket booth, headed for New York City, he noticed a man waving at him from the next lane. The driver was Muslim, Pete said, and he told Pete he feared going into New York without a flag.

"He was afraid for his life," Pete said. "So I gave him a handful of flags. Must have had 30 or so on my dashboard. He'd worked his whole life in Brooklyn or something, and now he had to fear for his life."

Pete voted for Trump nonetheless.

"I really don't think he gives a shit about anything," Pete said—and he meant it as something to admire. "He says what pops into his head. He's not a trained politician."

Pete was upset about how the FBI was trying to undermine the president. He thought Hillary Clinton should have been charged with a crime. He thought disability and welfare created incentives not to work—that they bred a sense of entitlement that kept people out of the workforce. He lamented that Americans were losing their sense of responsibility and liberty, that they weren't providing for themselves through hard work. But he believed that affordable health care should be a right. It was just too important. Most of all, he bemoaned the lack of a moral education among the next generation.

"The kids are lost," he said. There is so much political correctness, he continued, that we don't say the right things as well as the wrong things. It meant we were losing the bearings that would keep the country going in the right direction.

"The kind of nation that our forefathers envisioned for us has been corrupted," he said.

But no matter what complaints he had, Pete was proud of his country. His criticisms were those of someone who felt passionately about the subject matter. "I love America," Pete would say over and over again without a hint of irony or self-consciousness. He said it like John Wayne would have: entirely sure of its rightness. He was unwavering in his faith that this mantra, and the patriotism it represented, would never fail him. That if tested, it would never falter. That his faith in his nation—in the idea of America as he knew it—would never be misplaced.

It was a pillar of his life—a north star. "God and country," he said at one point. "The two things I care most about, other than my wife and kids."

Later that day we were on I-40 East, driving through the Texas Panhandle on the way to Amarillo. Amarillo is trucker friendly, Pete explained. There are scores of places to park, and a steakhouse that offered a free 72-ounce slab of meat to any trucker who could finish it. We saw a faded sign for it emerge from a cotton field as we drove.

"This machine is struggling to stay alive," Pete said. He was checking the ELD. "I powered it on and off in hopes that it would reset, you know."

"Are you in trouble if it's not working?" Chris asked.

"I hope I'm not in trouble," Pete said after a moment, lighting another cigarette. "I have a paper backup and that's what the law says."

He seemed stressed.

"Well, it's not going to work," Pete said, giving up again and tossing it aside.

———————

At one point, Pete had called truckers the "last of the cowboys." They lived for the freedom of the open road. That's who they were in the 1970s, before deregulation and cutthroat competition stripped the industry of its frontier ethos. Now men like Pete felt yoked. Regulations, state troopers, and "four-wheelers" all haunted their tracks, hassling them on their journeys down the highways.

"Pete, what does the American Dream mean to you?" Jordan asked.

"It's hard for me to describe the American Dream in less than half a book," he said.

"We've got time," Chris said.

"I want the American Dream to be the freedom to choose your course in life. To be free from the tyranny of the government. I think that people can rule themselves 90 percent of the time. Do we need guidelines? Yes. But you have to let people live their lives."

"Do you think you've achieved it?" Jordan asked again.

"Not *my* American Dream, no," Pete said.

Pete lamented the regulations that made it difficult to generate a profit and the taxes that siphoned off his pay. He admitted to having little money tucked away for retirement. "When I'm laying in bed at night and thinking about how things are gonna pan out in my later years, it's sad to say my main concern is my wife. What happens to her if I go down? Is she gonna be taken care of?"

The American Dream is different for everyone, Pete concluded. "But who draws the line and says, *Now you're a success*? My line is when I've made sure that everybody around me—my family, my friends—when they know I love them, when they know I have taken care of them."

Pete then turned the question back on us. He wanted to know our conclusions about it based on our travels.

"Chris and I come at it differently," Jordan said, "which I think is reflected in the Marine versus the journalist. My mission is more active. I want people to believe in the American Dream. I want people to see the best of America. Dreams are aspirational—they're never guaranteed. But you have to believe that they are possible. I think Chris's mission is more exploratory than mine. His approach is to say, *Let's see what we find and lay it out, so that people can decide for themselves based on what we see. Even if that means showing that it no longer exists.*"

It was a distinction the two of us had discussed at length. Jordan believed we would find positive signs for America wherever we went. He believed the dream was alive and well. In the Marines, he had served with men and women of every different race, ethnicity, religion, and class. Most of them were 18 or 19 years old, and many of them got into trouble more often than not. But when faced with the most difficult challenges, they performed selflessly and heroically. They didn't always get along, but they united when it mattered. That spirit, Jordan believed, was uniquely American, and he expected to find it everywhere among the people we met.

Chris was far less confident than Jordan. From afar he saw fractures and inequities that cast a pall over the country, and braced himself to see them manifest at every stop. Chris worried about the structural reasons why too many Americans—based on nothing more than an accident of birth—were excluded from the country's riches and how that affected what felt like an unbridgeable chasm that stood between so many Americans. As we made our way across the country, Chris worried we would witness America's dissolution in real time—a tragedy with no salvation.

"I guess I've achieved some semblance of the American Dream," Pete concluded on second thought. He had struggled, yes, but he also had a wonderful wife, and they had a home together in Daytona. Work was plentiful. He was often on the road, but he could support his children. He was scraping by, but overall things were good. And they were good because he loved trucking.

Chris asked him how long he wanted to keep doing it.

"Until I'm 70," he said. "Or until I die on the road."

By late afternoon we had driven deep into Texas and were approaching the Louisiana border. The ELD was still on the fritz, and Pete was getting frustrated. So when we pulled into a truck stop the two of us decided to give him a wide berth. We sat in silence, watching Pete busy himself with one of a hundred undone tasks. Finally, Pete looked over at us.

"So, who wants to drive this thing?"

We looked at each other.

"You first," Chris said.

Jordan and Pete switched seats.

"Get your camera out here, Chris," Pete said, "because you don't know what the hell will happen when we do this stuff."

Pete gave instructions. Jordan adjusted the seat and looked at the pedals and buttons in front of him.

"Should I not be pressing the brake right now?" Jordan said with concern as the truck wheezed.

"It's pretty foolproof," Pete said. "Not that you're a fool."

"I wish I had a seat belt," Chris said from the back.

Jordan pressed the air brake, which released with a hiss.

"Oh boy," Chris murmured.

"You're freestyling now," Pete said.

Jordan tentatively touched the accelerator, and the truck lurched forward with a roar.

"Gun it, baby!" Pete said.

Jordan crawled out into the lot with two hands on the enormous wheel.

"Hang her left," Pete said, and Jordan did as he was told. We sailed out across the parking lot, wet with fog, and among the trucks—to the amusement of the few men sipping coffee under the eaves of the convenience store.

"Why don't you come around and give it a big U-turn so you can get a sense for the angle of the dangle?" Pete said.

"Around that way?"

"Tell you what, go up there," Pete said. "Steer toward me until the last minute. Now straighten her out. Good. There, that's good. Now put her in reverse."

Jordan looked at him.

"Let's back her into that big hole back there next to that green truck."

Jordan slowly worked the rig backward. The tractor would knife out at severe angles with each twist of the wheel, and Jordan would correct. A few minutes later and we were in the spot—only somewhat askew.

"Again, man!"

Jordan pulled the rig back out into the open lot, then backed it into the space between two trucks again, this time with more ease.

Pete made Chris follow.

"Throw it into Drive," Pete said. "Do it, baby."

Chris trundled out into the lot.

"Cut through this hole," Pete said, and Chris slashed between two trucks parked in a line. He slalomed back through the two parked trucks and swung around them into the same space Jordan had backed into. Pete made Chris back in twice. As Chris took his second stab, this time a little faster, a little more confident, Pete answered his phone as it rang.

"Oh, you know," he said, "I got these two Yalies driving my rig. Nearly destroyed a Peterbilt."

"Today the world is supposed to end," Pete posted in a trucker's group on Facebook. It was our third morning on the road, and we had awoken again before dawn. The ELD mandate had gone into effect at midnight. And the day truckers had dreaded was here.

"It will be a big clusterfuck," Pete had said the night before. "We'll wing it tomorrow."

The day wasn't off to a promising start. Pete walloped the ELD. Still no sign of life.

"I should be okay," Pete said. "I have the paper log as a backup."

It seemed like he was rehearsing an excuse.

The fog was thick in Louisiana. Highway signs came up out of the ether with less than a truck's length of warning. The air was cold.

"Doesn't it smell different down here? Can you smell the bogs?" Pete asked.

"Yeah," Jordan said.

"Me too."

We cut through bayous and groves of piney trees.

Now that we were within striking distance of our destination, Pete began making preparations. Movers often outpace their clients, so they will leave a load with a storage company—called a destination agent—that makes the final delivery once the client is settled. Finding help to unload can be difficult, though, and Pete started making calls to workers. Chris would dial off a spreadsheet from the jump seat and hand Pete the phone. By then, the two of us felt like honest-to-god road dogs.

Pete's ELD was back working, at least partially: the screen showed the truck moving down the highway, but the log was still bum. Pete didn't seem to mind, though. Earlier that day, we had approached the notorious Shreveport weigh station in tense silence. Pete had a transponder above his dash. When an inspection site required him to stop, it would flash red. Green meant a bypass had been granted. The three of us watched it. When it flashed green, we took a collective breath in unison. Salvation. We had passed the scales and evaded the state. The road was mercifully free, at least for now.

But Pete had other issues. After crossing into Louisiana, he had called ahead to the destination agent's warehouse in Gulfport, Mississippi, only to find out it was full. So Pete called the firm that booked his dispatcher and asked for a new drop point. We were told to head for Slidell, Louisiana, 40 minutes northeast of New Orleans, and we updated the GPS. Just 100 more miles to go.

"We're going to slide into Slidell with some '70s music," Pete said, twisting the radio knob. Creedence Clearwater Revival's "Heard It Through the Grapevine" had come on.

"You know," Chris said, "these guys, Creedence, they sound like they're from down here. But they grew up just a few blocks from my childhood home in El Cerrito. Went to school across the street from where I did."

"Really?" Pete said, incredulously. "Hoy-erd it through the grape-vine?"

Night fell as we drove the last 100 miles of straight highway, which passed through swamps coated in a layer of fog that lingered over the mud beaches and canal berms. There was traffic through Baton Rouge. The eerie first notes of "Children of the Sun" vibrated through the cab, lit red by the brake lights of the freight tractor ahead of us.

Around nightfall each day, Pete would start making phone calls. Our conversations would lull—the day fully chewed over—and he'd drape his headset over his scalp and start dialing. It was a common pastime for a trucker with nothing but time on his hands.

One night he called a nephew. "I love you, buddy," he said loudly into a voice-mail box.

"Call Kit-Kat," he told his phone next and checked in with Katie, presumably a cousin or daughter or granddaughter. "Thinking about you," he said.

No one answered for a spell, until he called his wife around 7 p.m. It was their evening ritual. Every night at the same time, he would speak to her in hushed tones, smoking a cigarette.

"How was your day, baby? Good? Do you mean it?"

Only one more morning before we reached Slidell.

———————

The warehouse was in a commercial district on a small street flanked by muddy ditches and pines draped with moss. As we arrived the next morning, the rumble of a train sounded not far off. The air was wet and thick and the pines along the frontage road practically dripped with condensation from the feverish mist that haunted the branches and colored the sky a sickly gray.

Pete exchanged paperwork with a woman at the front desk, then sat down at a round table where we joined him. All three of us slumped low, weary from the jostled drive. We sat wordlessly for a moment in that sterile room off the warehouse, which resembled a portable housing unit squeezed into an airplane hangar. Pete opened his phone and set a timer for two hours.

"Everyone's got me on the clock down to the minute," he said. "Might as well put them on it too. And when it zeroes out? That's when I start screaming and making all kinds of gestures."

The office seemed designed to remind drivers of their second-class status. The walls were covered with instructions and dire warnings: THIS COMPANY TOLERATES NO ALCOHOL OR DRUG USE. NO LUNCH BREAKS AFTER TWO O'CLOCK. ALL DRIVERS MUST OBEY FOG RULES. The driver's bathroom was outside the office, in the hangar. The door stuck and peeled away from the jam. Its lock was a thick, aging rubber band that one could wrap around a foot and pull tight while sitting down.

Pete stood up.

"I'm going to see if I can get around these office people and get to the real working-class folk. You'd be amazed what $20 can get you."

And he set off.

Soon enough, Pete was marshaling the effort to unload his truck. Six men were working it, scuttling in and out of the warehouse. They balanced mattresses above their heads and rugs like scales across their shoulders. A ramp descended from the open back of the truck to an impromptu staging area. Two men were carrying furniture and cardboard boxes between the truck and the warehouse, where four other laborers would take command and stack items in wooden boxes along walls of exposed insulation.

In the warehouse the workers cackled and chatted. Outside, they dodged Pete's glare and worked silently, save for the occasional mumbled question or two about what goes where.

"Hey, hey, driver," the foreman said from the sloping lawn next to the warehouse door. His name was Craig, and he was taking a smoke break.

"Yeah?" Pete said.

"I'ma get a big New Orleans fleur-de-lis and paste it right over that there helmet," he said, gesturing at the blue Giants helmet on Pete's rig.

"Do it and I'll drive my rig right through your building."

The work motored on, but Pete was no longer the only driver on site. Others had begun to collect around the warehouse, mingling like gulls perched on the gunwale of a fishing boat.

One driver with a long scraggly beard limped over to us. He wore a Trump hat, black jeans, and work boots smeared with muck. He was rangy, nearly toothless, and tall.

"Been to the Chinese place up the road?" he asked Pete.

"Nope," Pete said. "Good stuff?"

"Yeah, steak actually tastes like steak," the man said. He seemed intent on a conversation, no matter how busy Pete made himself with the unload.

"What you running?" Pete asked offhandedly.

"Eight loads or so. Wouldn't believe it. This one woman has 20 bookshelves. Had to break it all down."

Pete grumbled a note of commiseration and kept folding mats.

"Man, I'm way over my hours," the other trucker continued. "I'm trying to cheat my logbook, man. I'm still running paper."

"You don't have an ELD?"

"Naw, not yet. They really start fucking with us in April. My man said he'd get me one next week, and I'm like, 'You ain't gonna see me 'til April.'"

The driver's dog, a Blue Heeler with mangy hair, stalked the ground beside us and settled on its side in a wet patch of grass, where it panted uncontrollably. The driver's helper, a man with a large paunch, wandered about with the now-familiar joy of a man who had occupied the cramped cab of a truck too long. He stood across the street, near their rig, unsure of what to do with his hands.

"You know, my brother tried to drive for you up there," the driver said, noticing the company logo on Pete's truck. "Filled out an application and everything."

"What happened?"

"They saw his driving record."

"Giants fans, huh?" a second driver said loudly, noticing the Giants logo just as the foreman had.

"We all Saints down here," he said to Pete, his *here* sounding more like *he-ah*.

"Yeah," Pete quipped, "you sure look like Saints."

The second driver, the one ribbing Pete, had wet hair, matted and thin. His eyes were sunken from the "barroom," as he put it, the night before.

"Practically have halos over your heads," Pete said.

The driver with the long beard talked incessantly. He picked up steam as he spoke, as if it had been days—weeks—of total silence on the road, as if this was his last opportunity to tell his story.

"You shown them anything fun? Any girls? Drugs?" he asked Pete, who tried his best to ignore him.

The man hooted with the thought. Then he told us how he had fooled around with the wife of a friend and sawed off her state-issued ankle tracker, only to abandon her at a truck stop after she found naked photos of herself on his phone and had stolen his keys and a wad of money. Then came tales of delinquent fatherhood and kids scattered across the country.

As the work wound down, we realized we'd soon be leaving Pete. The two of us were ready to be free of the cigarette smoke and the long, brutal days. But our affection for Pete had solidified over days spent together in that cabin.

Pete came over. We made small talk, trying to avoid the inevitable goodbyes. Jordan asked Pete if he was itching to get home. He would be there for Christmas after all. "I'm excited," he said. "Then, after a few days, I'll be excited to leave."

We were huddled on the far side of the truck, away from the truckers and the labor. It was quiet on that side—just the three of us again, as if we were back on the road. Pete looked at us. "I had to walk away," he said, and we knew what he meant. "Now you see the whole thing. We have the family-orientated guys, the business types, and—" he paused. "Even the riffraff. Like anywhere else."

Pete was from a different world than us, but he was now a friend— a man we both felt deep affection for, like some distant relative rediscovered.

"You know," Pete said. "You were always worried about being an imposition on me, but you weren't." He was tearing up just as he had when we spoke about God and blessings, runaways, and his wife.

"Drive safe out there," said Pete, his lip quivering.

We took an Uber from Slidell over Lake Pontchartrain and into New Orleans that afternoon. The same dense fog hung tight over the placid waters, and by the time we burst into East New Orleans it had only just begun to burn off under the winter sun. As we rode, we both thought about Pete.

Chris's thoughts returned to our last meal together, the night before.

The three of us had sat together at a truck-stop diner in Hammond, Louisiana. Pete, ever energetic, had pushed his phone across the orange table toward the two of us, who were sick with fatigue.

"Look at this," he said and played a video.

The dinner was practically a gourmet affair compared with our earlier meals at nearly empty fast-food joints across the Southwest. We had stopped at the palatial Petro station because it was Pete's favorite. It was abuzz with the sounds of truckers catching up and stretching creaky joints while dozens of engines grumbled in neutral in the parking lot.

Pete gestured down at the video.

"Look, look," he said.

It was a series of clips from a magistrate court in Providence, Rhode Island. The judge, Frank Caprio, heard a number of cases involving parking tickets, delinquent court payments, and other petty crimes, citations, and misdemeanors.

As the video played, the judge presided with verve.

At one point, Caprio faced a single mother practically swimming in parking tickets. "How much can you pay?" he asked. "Not much," she responded.

"Okay," the judge said. "I order you to pay not too much for eight weeks."

In the video, Caprio scolded a high-school basketball player who had run a red light and told him to stay in school. He threw out a parking ticket issued a minute before parking was permitted. He invited young children up to the bench to set the fee for their parents' citations. And he refused to take a young woman's last five dollars.

Pete chortled with happiness as each courtroom exchange played out. There was something about the judge that Pete found irresistible. He was wise, a hero. But his dripping Rhodie accent and dry wit made him an everyman, too. Most of all, the judge was empathetic. He was a man clothed in power who also possessed grace.

"He's like Solomon," Pete had said as our food arrived.

The freedom of the highways could be seen as an escapist fantasy for men who can't be socialized or don't want to be. Yet a truck is no hermitage. Pete served the very society in which he seemed so ill at ease. He may have slept fitfully while at home and often sought the comfort of his rig on nights that others might rather have spent in their own beds. He may have preferred the diners and the array of tiled showers of truck stops to the higher pressure of the pipes at home, but he served home, community, and country all the same.

In the end, Pete's presence had enriched us, just as he had prayed it would.

Mexico

Highway 2—the Mexican thoroughfare that shadows the U.S. border—took a wide, arcing turn north and east through the small town of Janos. As the sun set in brilliant purples and oranges behind the mountains at our backs, the road leveled out and finally pointed due east.

The two of us were in the Boat, along with our friend Richie. As Jordan jammed on the accelerator and looked down at the navigation, our conversation was terse. Out of the radio's static emerged a country-rock station from El Paso, and we knew we were close.

Chris turned around and looked out the dusty rear window toward a mountain range. The sun glanced off its face, golden and brown like marbling. He furrowed his brow—*not good*.

The day before at a cigar shop in Tombstone, Arizona, Richie had told a man with a white ponytail and red Indianapolis 500 shirt that we had driven from Tijuana to Mexicali on the Mexican side of the border the day before.

"Really?" he said. "And you didn't have any trouble?"

"None at all," Richie said.

"And we're driving to Agua Prieta today," Chris added.

The man's eyebrows shot up.

It was a common reaction. *Don't end up in Ciudad Juárez at night,* we had often heard. It was a warning we likely didn't need to hear more than once.

It was August 2018, and after departing on our latest road trip we had decided to drive south to the border. Our plan was to weave in and out of the crossings at Mexicali and Naco and Antelope Wells— passing from the United States into Mexico and back again—to meet those who made their lives on one side or the other. The trip would take us from San Diego to El Paso, exploring border towns along the way and leading us straight toward Juárez.

All we knew of Juárez was its violent reputation and the pace at which its journalists wound up dead. Chris had a distinct memory of one story. In 2010, after one of its photographers was killed, *El Diario,* a Juárez-based newspaper, had published an open letter to the cartels— a chilling assignment for any writer.

"You are, at present, the de facto authorities in this city," it read, "because the legal institutions have not been able to keep our colleagues from dying. Tell us, therefore, what is expected of us."

In Bisbee, Arizona, later that morning, before crossing back over once more, the three of us huddled outside a coffee shop.

"What we're about to do might be dangerous," Jordan said.

The concern among the three of us was palpable.

"So if you feel uncomfortable," Jordan continued, "speak up."

Chris and Richie nodded, and we drove on.

But things hadn't gone to plan by the time we reached Janos. We were many miles past Agua Prieta and even the next crossing at Antelope Wells. At that moment, we were banking toward Juárez.

"Sun's setting," Chris said.

And the engine roared a little louder as Jordan pressed down on the pedal and the Boat lurched into the purple of the Juárez twilight.

———————

We had met up two days earlier in a Glendale parking lot, where Chris had found Jordan waiting in the sweltering heat next to the Boat. Eight months had passed since our drive with Pete, so we embraced and caught up in the windward sweep of the San Gabriel Mountains. After graduating, Jordan had taken the California bar exam and Chris had returned to Berkeley to carve out a writer's life. We were both looking toward the future, but first we would use what little vacation time we had to get out in the Boat for as long as we could before our funds ran low and our lives beckoned.

We planned to be on the road for at least five weeks, and Richie, a law-school friend, had asked if he could join us for a few days. Our plan had been to head northeast toward Denver, but Richie was flying into Huntington Beach, so we drove south through Orange County to meet him.

On the way, Jordan spoke up.

"I have a thought," Jordan said as we drove south on I-5. "What if we go to Mexico instead?"

Jordan's fascination with the country ran deep. Growing up, he and his father had bonded over annual fishing trips in the waters off Baja California. He loved Mexican culture, especially its food and music, and he was something of a Latin dance devotee, having spent a few years in a dance company in college. More recently, he had visited Mexico City, Oaxaca, and Guanajuato as part of a business-school trip.

Chris scrunched up his nose. The way Jordan had proposed it made Chris think his friend might harbor his own reservations. Cartels and coyotes must pass over those same highways on the other side of the border. But the two of us had long talked about exploring Mexico's northern states, and this was our best opportunity yet.

"We could start in Tijuana," Jordan continued, "and just pop out at the next border crossing if it doesn't feel right."

Chris tapped the windowsill.

"And Richie speaks Spanish, too," Jordan said.

"Okay, yeah, let's try it," Chris said.

So we picked up Richie and set off for Tijuana, where we found a cheap hotel. It was our second August in a row in the city, and we were somewhat familiar with its boulevards and landmarks. There was the sprawling, divided Avenida Revolución, lined with bars and tiled coffee shops, brewpubs, and dance halls that, on clement evenings, pulsated with amplified music. On our first visit, we had driven through timid and unadventurous: we explored the Avenida, then scurried back into the United States in time to reach Phoenix the next evening.

This second time would be different. Not only had we been to Tijuana once before, which was enough to make us somewhat more intrepid, but we had been on the road taking in new places regularly by then. We were generally more gregarious. So with Richie, the three of us picked our way over tilted sidewalks, sidestepped exposed rebar, and watched the headlights of cars approach, fly past, and recede into purple eddies of smoke and smog.

We were headed for Avenida Revolución, which we knew was well-patrolled by masked police officers, the *federales,* when Jordan noticed something else.

"Look," he said, "what's that?"

Chris followed his gaze.

Down an alleyway were white string lights adorning what looked like a courtyard. Laughter filtered out. Chris inspected it from afar until he noticed Jordan already disappearing through the vestibule and into the oasis.

Beyond the wall was a luxurious courtyard lined with ferns and succulents, dozens of food carts, and a sea of white-tiled tables. It was late, perhaps eleven o'clock, and the entire place was awash in conversation.

We ordered *carne* and *pescado* tacos and drank local beers. A shy young woman in a red shirt and white jeans cleared the table, and when Chris asked what the place was called, she answered in Spanish.

I don't speak English, she seemed to imply.

Richie, a barrel-chested man from Missouri, stepped in. The waitress and Richie went back and forth, one sentence flowing into the other.

As she walked off, Chris looked at Richie expectantly.

"Well? What did she say?"

"She's not Mexican," Richie said. "She's Colombian. This courtyard is sponsored by a local company—Telefonica—and the carts are run by young people trying to get a foothold in the food industry. If they do well here, they can get a brick-and-mortar place."

The scene was more reminiscent of Brooklyn than whatever half-baked expectations about border towns we may have still carried with us.

"The clientele is mixed," Richie translated.

"Americans and Mexicans?"

"And others from across Central and South America."

Once ravenous, then sated, we strolled through downtown and the red-light district just past the city's iconic arch, which resembled a pinched version of the one on the Mississippi in St. Louis. We hailed a cab back to the hotel and rode through the streets with the thump of American heavy metal pumping through the car. Our driver whisked us past street vendors and churches with doors locked tight, the electric crosses above their doors doused.

At the hotel, even though it was deep into early morning, no one was ready to turn in. So we gingerly sipped tall shots of Don Julio tequila at the hotel bar while a round woman with a thin fuzz of dyed blond hair sang karaoke at full lung.

"Okay," Chris said. "Tomorrow. What's the play, gents?"

"I say we drive as much of it in Mexico as we can," Jordan replied.

"Agreed."

"Those are pretty heavy cartel routes," Richie said, and we all nodded gravely.

Assessing the safety of driving across Baja, Sonora, and Chihuahua by car was beyond the three of us. Chris was drawn to the risk of it all, yet his mother's voice always played across his mind at moments like this: *Stay safe, be smart.*

"And we don't want to meet a crooked cop," Richie added.

"I say we drive as far as we feel comfortable," Chris said.

"That's doable," Jordan said, looking down at his phone.

As the only one with military training, Jordan felt responsible for the safety of the group. He wanted to balance Chris's newfound adventurism with Richie's caution. Jordan felt comfortable driving through Mexico during the day, but nighttime was different.

"There are crossings at Naco," Jordan said, reading off his phone, "and Antelope Wells, and, well, Juárez of course."

We all paused.

"We'll drive and cross before sunset," he said.

"Of course—nothing past sunset."

"That's right."

"So there it is," Chris said. "Juárez by sundown."

"Juárez *before* sundown."

A recorded trumpet wailed and the woman reached for a soaring note to meet it.

Chris shot his tequila and Jordan and Richie pushed their drinks away as the woman wrapped the final note and took an exhausted bow to a smattering of applause from the strung-out hangers-on who remained.

The sun came up in a blaze over the city. Before we drove east, we had one stop to make: Desayunador Salesiano Padre Chava, a service center for the scores of South and Central American migrants who gathered in Tijuana each year. Visiting the center was our reason for coming to Tijuana.

The *desayunador,* or "breakfast counter," was part of a larger Catholic organization that provided services for those without. Much like soup kitchens in the United States, it was run by volunteers who arrived before dawn and worked until well past noon in order to provide a meal to more than 1,000 people each day.

Much of the news that year had focused on those who had crossed the border and found themselves trapped in detention centers outside cities such as El Paso, San Diego, or Laredo. They were *migrants, asylum seekers,* and some combination of *undocumented* or *illegal* immigrants, depending on who was talking. There in Mexico, however, the people who came through the doors of the *desayunador* carried none of our labels—at least not yet.

We turned down a road in the shadow of the border and parked the car in the sparse shade. Outside was a long, unruly line of 100 or so people. A man holding a black-and-white photo pleaded with the guard at the glass doors.

"He's looking for a loved one who he lost," Richie whispered.

After a moment, the guard at the door turned to us.

"*Hola,*" Richie said, poised to explain our presence.

Before he could, however, the guard piped up in fast Spanish.

"*Sí, sí,*" Richie said, then beckoned us past and into the room.

"What did he say?" Chris asked as we walked into a cafeteria.

"'Are you here to serve?'"

All around us, tables were set with plastic tablecloths. As the line outside hummed, the volunteers inside said a prayer and burst into a flurry of activity.

Nelson, a short Salvadoran with a goatee and a gray Dodgers hat worn backward, would show us our morning task: washing dishes. He led us back into the bowels of the kitchen, where we passed crates teeming with peppers, vats of simmering stews, and enormous insulated coolers of rice wafting with steam. With the doors thrown open, men in aprons spooned each out onto plates with practiced speed. People of all ages accepted theirs with nods and ate at long tables.

Every morning, hundreds of migrants and locals—the deported and the hopeful, the homeless and the otherwise down-and-out—walked through the center's door to have a meal, make a phone call, get a haircut or a new coat, receive legal advice, or get a medical checkup. Some found work through the program. Others, like Nelson, got a bed in exchange for volunteer hours, working in the kitchen for weeks if not months.

In the back the three of us were handed aprons and directed toward large industrial sinks. Jordan started scrubbing dirty chipped plates yellowed with age and clear plastic cups with Sharpie numbers on their bases—they came in by the dozen—while Richie and Chris began drying them with threadbare towels.

Nelson directed our work with mute hand instructions as heavy Spanish-language music played over a stereo.

"Ask him if they ever play," Chris hazarded, gesturing outside to a dusty soccer pitch in the back.

"He's afraid to go outside," Richie said, translating Nelson's quiet words in halting phrases. "He doesn't leave the center often. He's too afraid of being deported."

Nelson smiled at our simple, muttered attempts at Spanish. He took two cups and swirled soapy water in both before shaking them together like a cocktail.

"You gotta watch out," someone said behind Jordan. "A dog took a bite out of my hand out there once."

Jordan turned around to find a young man washing pots the size of blow-up pools in a deep sink. He had short-cropped hair, a pencil mustache, and tattoos up and down his thin arms.

"You guys speak Spanish?"

"Only him," Jordan said, nodding at Richie.

"You need a Tijuana girlfriend," the man said. "They'll teach you."

Jordan laughed.

Josh was a gregarious twentysomething who had grown up in Indiana. His family had settled there after crossing the border from Mexico when he was a young child, he explained. His father had joined the Marines and was stationed in Italy. Even so, Josh had been deported after getting a speeding ticket. He volunteered at the *desayunador* during the day, then worked nights as a waiter at the Hong Kong, a night club in the red-light district.

"All my friends are strippers," he said, pulling out his phone to flick through photos and selfies. "Man, they work all day and make tons."

Josh was headed back to the States soon, he explained. He'd had enough of Tijuana. Precisely when he would move back, though, was a detail he hadn't yet figured out, he said, spraying charred bits off the bottom of a pot.

While Josh and Jordan spoke, Nelson began opening up to Richie— who, in turn, was translating for Chris.

"What I want is not for me," Richie said, listening to Nelson speak as he worked, his eyes on the sink the whole time. "My dream is not about me."

"When I was growing up in El Salvador, it was a hard life," he continued. "We didn't have enough. I was raised by my mom. My dad was in Los Angeles, but he died of an illness. Because we didn't have our own house, we moved a lot. My sister and I would go to the market during the rainy season when we couldn't sell water, and we'd take tomatoes, green peppers, and onions out of the trash to eat."

Nelson seemed to be at confession.

"Do you want your own family?" Richie asked.

"Of course," he said, drying his hands. "I left a girlfriend in El Salvador. She was crying. 'When are you going to give me a child, Nelson?' she said. I don't have a place to stay. I don't have work. How can I bring a kid into this world?"

So Nelson went north and lived in fear of being sent back to El Salvador.

"The first time I traveled here, to Mexico, was 2015," he said. "I was 22 years old. But I didn't make it far into Mexico before they deported me."

This happened half a dozen times, leaving him exhausted. But he kept at it, hoping one day to cross into the U.S. He kept making the trek north—back to Tijuana.

"If they arrest me they'd deport me back to El Salvador," Nelson said, "and I wouldn't try again. I would have wasted so much time trying to get to the U.S., I couldn't do it again. I'm still in a hurry, I really want to get there, but I've gotten used to life here, so I can wait to go when it's right."

A friend of his had tried, he told us. He died in Arizona, and his body was never found. Nelson fell quiet for a moment. Sunlight slanted through the window as it heated the city outside.

"Now I'll tell you my dream," Nelson said.

He had started off bashful but was soon vulnerable and open.

"My dream is to go to the United States. I don't want to live my life there—just 10 or 15 years. I want to buy a house for my mom wherever she wants to live. And I want to buy a house for myself."

Jordan turned around to listen. Regardless of his position on border enforcement, he found himself rooting for Nelson.

"I have to work hard," Nelson continued. "Money is not happiness. Happiness is being with your family. Now that I'm here, I feel so alone. I'm missing out on the care of my mom, and time with her. She always took care of me and fought for me when I was younger. Now it's my turn to fight for her."

Creedence Clearwater Revival came on over the speakers. First it was "Have You Ever Seen the Rain?" The rest of the album, *Pendulum,* followed track after track.

"I've lived more than an old person," he said. "So many things have happened to me. But I don't want to forget any of it. That keeps me going. That reminds me of why I'm doing this, why I keep going, why I'm fighting. My mom—she's why I keep going. That's why I don't go to the club, or drink; I don't want to lose these thoughts. I don't want to forget my family. I can't forget them."

"Why do you wait?" Chris asked.

"I'm waiting for when it's really foggy," he said. "So they can't see me when I cross. If it gets foggy, I'll do it immediately."

The day had started out overcast, but the gray only skirted the mountains and did not descend into the streets, so Nelson stayed put that morning as it burned off.

Chris's heart ached for him, and he knew Jordan's did too as his friend wiped his eyes.

"I'm not telling you this for pity," Nelson concluded. "It's just my story."

Afterward, we ate breakfast. *Nopales,* chicken, rice, and peppers with beans—the same food they'd served the migrants and wayward folk minutes before.

"Will you join us?" Jordan asked Nelson before we sat down.

"No, no," he said. And with that, Nelson went through a doorway and disappeared.

After leaving the *desayunador,* we drove east. All day the border fence rose and fell along the slope of the mountain like a layer of rust on beige-colored sand. It was the same fence we had seen a year earlier from the other side when we drove to Phoenix. We passed whole communities cut out of hillsides. Around noon, the three of us huddled over a bench alongside scores of sweating travelers in a Mexicali taqueria and ate tortillas piled high with charred meats.

The roads were clear as we took the crossing at Calexico and stopped for the night outside Tucson at a motel with cheap chenille blankets.

We spent the next morning driving toward coffee in Tombstone, Arizona. From there we would head south and pass back into Mexico at Naco, entering the Sonoran Desert—a major thoroughfare for smuggling into the United States. Back on the Mexican side of the border, we would head east toward Juárez, then make it back to American soil by nightfall.

When we stopped for gas just outside Bisbee, the last town before the crossing at Naco, Jordan asked a bearded attendant if it was safe to drive to Naco and beyond.

"In Mexico?"

"Yes."

"I hear they have terrible roads."

"In what way?"

"Just bad."

"Like get shot up bad?" Jordan said.

The man laughed.

"No, man—potholes and stuff."

At the border crossing, we followed a trickle of pickup trucks through a maze of concrete blast walls and inscrutable signs. As we tried to navigate the labyrinth, a man in a combat vest on the Mexican side of the border stepped forward and beckoned us over to an inspection station. He had a round face and cheeks smeared white with sunscreen. His colleague in a flak jacket slipped on gloves, while the first man opened the driver's door and began flicking through our bags, asking questions in Spanish.

We clustered around a metal inspection table with the white-cheeked man, who hauled over our bags and poked through them. His bearded partner asked us to open our trunk and hood.

"He wants to know what we're doing and why we were going from Naco to Agua Prieta," Richie said. "And he asked if there was anything in our car."

Jordan and Chris exchanged a knowing glance. It felt like we were back in Idaho, being interrogated by the trooper, except now Chris was calm and performing his best Jordan impression.

Our conversation, clipped at first, became more natural once introductions were made. The man with white cheeks was Ivan. The other was Noel. They were Mexican customs agents.

"What are they saying?" Chris ventured, but Richie pushed on until Ivan muttered something and they both laughed.

"He said you look like Kurt Cobain."

Everyone looked at Chris. His tousled auburn hair pooled in locks around his shoulders. He had on a T-shirt and skinny jeans, and his cheeks were unshaven. This had become his road-trip uniform—more disheveled than rock star.

"What?" Chris asked, looking down at himself.

Ivan kept speaking to Richie.

"Oh, no, no," Richie said as Ivan made a pistol with his finger.

"Military guys come down here with guns all the time," Ivan said in English. "They forget their guns are in the car. Were you in the military?"

"No," Richie said. *"Pero el era,"* he said and pointed at Jordan.

Ivan glared at Jordan, and after a moment made a circle with his finger around his ear.

"Crazy," he said. "All crazy."

Jordan smiled at him, but the customs agent didn't return the look. Chris laughed nervously.

A moment later, the two agents completed their inspection. Noel stuck around to talk while Ivan retreated into the shade of their outpost, where a radio crackled.

"Americans don't like immigrants, right?" Noel asked. "They're pretty racist?"

Richie explained that it isn't like that. Not for most people, at least.

A few feet away, Jordan bristled. Just because many Americans—especially Republicans—wanted increased border security didn't make them racist.

Noel, for his part, admitted that his only interaction with Americans was with the daily grocery shoppers from Arizona who crossed the border to buy cheap products on the Mexico side. Every once in a while, a group of boisterous young men or military folk would come through the area.

We asked him if they ever interacted with the U.S. Border Patrol or American customs agents, who had an office just a stone's throw away.

"No," Noel explained. "Never."

Odd, Jordan thought. *They work so close to each other but they're complete strangers.*

Some of them are good guys, Noel said, but some are shady. So they stayed away.

"That's true of any group," Jordan retorted, and Noel nodded.

"I hate Americans," Ivan said, wandering back over. "Why would I like anyone that treats my people so badly? Why?"

Chris smiled weakly.

"Even us?"

Chris wanted to find a connection, some sign that the gap between us could be bridged, but Ivan nodded and made the crazy sign by his ear again, nodding toward Jordan.

"*Todo.*"

Noel wasn't quite as adamant as Ivan. He didn't think all Americans were bad. He had family around Los Angeles and San Diego. The *antiguo* Americans—the older generation—might be racist, he explained. They thought the two of them, customs agents, would try to rob them or hurt them. But the younger generation was better.

Ivan nodded reluctantly.

"How are the migrants viewed by the locals here?" Richie asked.

"We don't have problems with migrants," Noel said. "We see them as people."

Southern Mexico was a different story, though, he admitted: They are less tolerant and try to keep Central Americans out. But in the north, they help the migrants. They offer them food and shelter—and treat them like humans, he said.

"Do you ever have issues at the crossing? Do you stop migrants?"

"No," Noel replied.

"We don't stop migrants," Ivan cut in. "Mexico doesn't judge people like that. They are humans, and we see them as humans. Americans don't."

The word *racismo* peppered their opinions.

It pained Chris to hear that Americans were viewed this way, but Jordan was less sympathetic. Noel had just admitted that Mexico was doing the exact same thing to migrants on its southern border. Couldn't they see the hypocrisy?

As we chatted, Mexicans drove through with a wave, and a drug-sniffing dog barked somewhere nearby on the U.S. side of the fence.

"So do the young people give you hope for America?" Chris asked.

Noel nodded.

"Yes, a little hope for America," Richie translated.

But Ivan shook his head.

"Why would I be hopeful?"

He looked away from us. The distance between him and Jordan seemed even larger as he left to inspect a white Cadillac that had pulled in. The driver wore a black shirt with CUBA printed across the chest. He looked at us askance.

"How do you choose who to pull over?" Chris asked.

"It's random," Noel responded. "But if someone looks suspicious, then we don't care. We pull them over."

"Suspicious like us," Chris said.

"*Sí,*" Ivan shouted over. Noel smiled—and laughed a little too much.

We parted ways with handshakes. Noel took his hand out of his glove and smiled broadly. Ivan remained distant and reserved—his smile wan.

"So you like rock?" Chris asked as Ivan rounded the car alongside him. "Kurt Cobain?"

The officer nodded.

"You like the Black Keys?"

Another nod.

"Yes, yes."

The two of them lingered by the passenger door.

"What do you think of Slipknot?" Ivan asked, and Chris laughed.

"So you really *do* like rock."

Ivan nodded again. Perhaps it was the same as the *desayunador*: a genuine exchange could bridge any divide—even an exchange involving Slipknot.

As Richie and Jordan were saying their goodbyes with Noel across the way, Ivan placed his hand on the Boat's open door.

"Want to come along?" Chris tried.

And Ivan's officialdom snapped back. A familiar stern mien came across his features.

"You sure?" Chris said dryly. "We got room."

"No, no," he said. "He'll kill me."

And he pointed at Jordan and made the "crazy" hand gesture one last time before mumbling a *Safe travels* in Spanish and disappearing into the shadowed eaves of their office.

———

The streets of Naco were empty as we passed through, so we took off down the highway and began to climb through the rolling foothills and up through the mountains that sprang up out of the Sonoran expanse. Horses grazed the hillsides, and *capillas*—roadside chapels—offered a simple shrine every few miles or so. Their cracked plaster was adorned with graffiti. On each roof was a cross bent at strange angles, telling the course of prairie winds over countless seasons like a weather vane.

Our interaction with Noel and Ivan had made us more confident. Whether we understood one another or not, the conversation had been civil.

As we drove on, the desert stretched out before us. We stopped at a vista point and gawked at the sheer size of the valley below. Across it arched the border wall, a thin ochre ribbon like an unspooled line of yarn. Thousands of miles of open expanse and the only man-made mark on the entire landscape was nothing more than a strand of steel, cleaving the terra-cotta valleys of the Sonora in two.

Mexico

We descended the mountains, down wicked hairpin turns and along smooth roads. *So much for potholed streets,* Chris thought as we glided across mile after mile of level lanes of asphalt.

As we took one long banking turn out of the Sonoran mountains, we came across something that took us all back. Chris drew a sharp breath, Jordan groaned, and Richie shook his head.

On the shoulder, in a shallow gully below a sheer wall of umber rock, was the ashen wreck of a big rig. It must have lost control on the last switchback and tipped in a fiery swoon, its brakes locked or severed, and crashed in a long, arching slide into the margin. There— shunted off to the side—it had smoldered, turning a sickly and twisted gray-black under the flames of its own engine.

Jordan hit the brakes and reduced our speed as we passed and took it in like a wake: the hull was scarred black. The cab was crumpled in on itself. Glass was flung everywhere in a savage halo.

"Landed square on the cab," Jordan said.

"Driver's side," Chris added.

Perhaps it was the smell of burned steel coming off the midden, but the odor of Pete's Pall Malls occurred to both of us as we solemnly passed the remains.

The beige hills became green ones along the highway, and fields of peppers lined the floor of the deep, long vale we found ourselves in as we left the Sonoran mountains. The sun was slipping down behind us. Feeling confident, we had jetted past the border crossing at Agua Prieta. Mexico was too enticing to leave. There was another crossing at Antelope Wells about two hours east, and the sun was still high. We felt a rush to each mile, as if we were surviving a road we had no business driving. The border closed at 4 p.m., we had learned, and it was now a little past 1.

We pulled over at a truck stop for a late lunch and ordered plates of

138

carne and glass-bottled Cokes. The tables were covered in blue-and-white plastic tablecloths, and our feet settled on concrete floors. The men in the room looked and talked and acted like many of the men we had met with Pete—gregarious and unassuming.

American, European, and Japanese cars crawled the highways just as they did in the U.S. It was a thoroughfare with unfamiliar signs but the same badges of industry and advertisement. The highway was not the outlaw den we had been told fables about. It was just a highway, same as those across the Arizona desert to the north.

We talked about how foolish it was for us to be worried about this side of the border. We talked about how distance, and the obscured nature of the place, bred outsize fears. We laughed at ourselves for being so naive. As we merged back onto the highway, we were even becoming a bit cavalier about it all.

Until Jordan twitched.

"Shit."

"What?"

"The time change."

"What do you mean?"

"We're in Mountain Time," Jordan said.

"And?"

"And it's an hour later."

"Holy hell," Chris said, putting it together. "Antelope Wells will be closed."

A familiar, chastened silence fell over the Boat once more. We would have to drive to Juárez to get back over the border.

Jordan checked his phone. We would make the crossing in Juárez just after 7 p.m., around twilight.

"We're doing this?" Richie asked.

"We don't have a choice," Chris said.

Outside Juárez, Jordan knifed down the highway through the descending darkness. Feeling uneasy, the three of us feigned calm. It felt like the time we ran out of coolant on that Dakota highway, when the rush of each passing semi had rattled the Boat. Whenever we found ourselves where we hadn't intended to be, it felt like something menacing was following us.

The night went from pink to purple, and the mountains behind El Paso merged with the sky as we reached the outskirts of Juárez. Teenagers loitered on street corners. Drivers idling at traffic lights peered over the lip of cracked windows at us, and we stared back through grime-touched glass.

As we drove down narrow highways, Chris searched for Juárez on his phone, clicked on a U.S. State Department website, and read a recent travel warning: "The consulate reported that there were 179 registered homicides in the month of June, making it the deadliest 30-day period so far this year."

He kept searching.

That weekend, gunmen had raided a house party and killed eight men and three women on grass-lined Oasis de Egipto Street in Juárez. The killers were reportedly settling scores in a simmering feud between crystal meth and heroin dealers. The bodies were found bound and tortured. The week before, 35 homicides had occurred from Friday to Sunday. *El Diario* reported that 200 people had been killed in July, and more than 700 since January.

The violence, some said, was reminiscent of the drug wars around the turn of the decade—a conflict that left more than 10,000 people dead.

Chris lowered his phone and closed his eyes. The border loomed, illuminated by the lights of the customs stations in the gathering darkness.

We pulled into the traffic lanes leading to the Bridge of the Americas. The squeal of brake pads and the groan of idling engines engulfed us. As we inched forward, our fear began to release. Around us, older men and women peddled trinkets, sun visors, and bottles of water with torn and flapping wrappers. U.S. Border Patrol agents in green fatigues answered frantic questions in Spanish and stopped the shiftiest of would-be crossers. Families, troupes of young men, and truck drivers in cowboy hats waited in the sluggish lines. All were bathed in the sickly rouge cast by the universe of flickering rear lights.

Jordan listened to the rush of wind as we spun into El Paso and took Highway 10 along a ridgeback overlooking the lights of Juárez. The Boat passed over the undulating hills of Texas, which descended toward the border and gave way to Mexico beyond the imposing fence.

Perhaps it didn't feel like bedding down after humping through Afghanistan, but a familiar relief flooded Jordan's senses. He had learned to manage fear and uncertainty—through training, the tales of heroism that inspired him to join the military, and, of course, his responsibility for the men and women who relied on him to conquer it. But Jordan had been a civilian now for nearly as long as he'd been an active Marine, and Afghanistan, the Horn of Africa, and Officer Candidate School in Quantico were feeling more distant by the day. As fear crept back into his bones, it reminded him how far away it all was.

Around midnight, we piled into a pizza place in El Paso for a meal and a drink to soothe our aching adrenal glands. Jefferson Airplane played in the background, and a liquor rep named Lindsay passed around tequila shots in high-rimmed shooters.

When Chris heard the first plaintive notes of "Comin' Back to Me," a favorite, he finally let the tension of the day go. He zoned out and realized how much he loved the travel, the camaraderie, the happenstance. There at the bar, his earlier feelings seemed foolish. His spasms of fear out on the highway had felt like a matter of great import simply because the territory was unknown. Ivan's circling hand motion played across his imagination—maybe Jordan wasn't the only crazy one in the Boat.

All of us felt humbled to have seen Juárez instead of just hearing the stories people carried back. We may always fear people, places, and ideas that we don't understand. But that fear shouldn't stymie curiosity. We had to see a thing to begin to know it, and in doing so, we opened our aperture just a little bit more. Fear, for us, had led to misunderstanding.

Jordan shot his tequila. Richie considered it. Chris muddled a lime on the lip of his, dropped it in to sip, and kept taking in the music.

———————

We crossed back into Juárez at sunrise to see what we had passed through the night before. We drove past the headquarters of *El Diario* and took in La Equis, a giant steel *X* painted red and visible from El Paso. The monolith is said to represent Mexico's merging of two cultures, the indigenous and the Spanish. It was a symbol of welcome for travelers. Downtown, we walked around a bustling central square and stared up at the cupola of a cathedral.

Juárez was a city, same as any other.

The night before, we had spoken at length with Mark, a bartender, and Lindsay, the liquor rep, at the pizza parlor. El Paso and Juárez were sister cities, they explained. They blend into each other. Americans in El Paso crossed over to get cavities filled and crowns installed by Juárez dentists. American teenagers walked across the bridge for wild afternoons free from their parents' dictates and even their country's laws. Residents of Juárez crossed for work inside El Paso malls and for courses at the University of Texas at El Paso or to visit emigrated family. The two cities merged at their edges.

At various points throughout our journey, we had marveled at how two cultures could be physically so close yet so far away on other fronts. *Less than 100 feet separate them but it might as well be 100 miles,* Jordan had thought at the border crossing in Naco. But even at a remove, we can see and harbor profound truths about one another.

Stepping outside the U.S., we were struck by the lasting quality of a peculiar dream. Despite what Ivan and Noel believed about

America, something still drew people north. Migrants from all over the continent make for Tijuana and elsewhere, because the United States still represents something. Less and less the promise of wealth and more so the opportunity for a modest life—though a modest life is its own form of wealth when set to the lilt of Nelson's Spanish. This dream remains a powerful lure, a spring of optimism so enticing that people pool like leaves at places like the *desayunador* in the lee of the border wall just to be close to it—just to feel like they are in concert with those who made it up the road to Los Angeles, El Paso, and more distant places.

This dream is complicated, much like the people who fashioned its myth and who redefine what it means every day. At its best, it is a vision for how life can be better for all people. It's the raw material of the American conscience. And somehow, during our time in Mexico, we saw evidence of that dream along the way. We weren't sure whether it would prove lasting, or if it was just the afterglow of something long since passed. But we had witnessed it being refashioned and newly articulated in an industrial kitchen, the smell of bleach and lard in the air, by a man who perhaps knew it as a *sueño.* A man who believed in it so much he would hazard everything for it.

With a last look, we set our sights north to drive back through El Paso and on toward Santa Fe. Chris squinted up into the sun and wondered what the weather was like in Tijuana. Had the sun risen bright and clear that morning, or had the city awoken to a day shrouded in that unseasonal mist? Chris thought back to those lonely, unbroken stretches of highway the three of us had just driven across. Had the fog crept down over the hills? Had Nelson served breakfast that morning? Or was he perhaps somewhere out in that vast wash, trudging north, with only his dreams to keep him company?

Lorain

We pulled the car over in Denver at dawn. The night before, we had driven north on I-25 through the sand and scrub of New Mexico and into the evergreen forests along the alpine shelf of Colorado. We had just parked outside the house of a friend, who had agreed to take us in for a few days of rest after we dropped Richie off at the airport.

Jordan killed the engine, and we sat. We sat for a long time, listening to the muffled tuning of the new day around us. For the first time in a week, the two of us were alone, and we were exhausted. The trip through Mexico had taken its toll. But there was something else. Before we rested, we had some healing to do.

"Chris," Jordan began, "I'm really sorry about Carlsbad."

A car went by, its tires noisy on slick streets.

"Me too," Chris said. "I thought we would've been able to handle that kind of thing better by now."

A few days before, on our way from Los Angeles to Tijuana, we had stopped in Carlsbad, a town 35 miles north of San Diego, to see another old classmate. The four of us hadn't seen one another in months. We found a bar along the Strand, ordered wings and fries, and settled in, trading bar-exam stories and ruminating about what lay ahead. As the night stretched on, the conversation turned to politics and things grew more and more charged until someone—neither of us can remember who of the four—said something about how Republicans are just much better at stealing elections than Democrats.

Chris glanced at Jordan.

"That's ridiculous," Jordan said, bristling. "Every Republican says the same thing about Democrats."

"Well, at a minimum I'd say Republicans are just better at it," someone said. "Democrats are way too disorganized to be effective."

Jordan noticed Chris tense up, but pressed on anyway.

"That's a silly generalization," Jordan said. "Both sides are trying to win, and they're both good at it."

"Yeah, but only Republicans push policies that systematically disenfranchise people."

"Like what?"

"Gerrymandering."

"Gerrymandering is bipartisan. Both parties have done it for 200 years."

"What about voter ID laws?"

"ID requirements don't disenfranchise people. Electoral integrity is a legitimate concern. It's completely reasonable."

"Republican officials have been caught on camera saying those laws are designed to suppress minority votes."

"Bullshit."

"I can pull it up for you."

"I don't care what some idiot somewhere said. I can pull up any number of dumb quotes from Democrats. My point is that there are legitimate reasons why Republicans believe it's important to have at least some kind of identification before voting."

Contentions ricocheted across the table.

"Plenty of academic studies have shown no evidence of widespread voter fraud," Chris said.

"And there is clear evidence that voter ID laws suppress the votes of low-income people, especially minorities," someone else added.

"It doesn't need to be widespread to be a problem," Jordan replied. "Even a couple of hundred votes can swing an election. And every election, there are reports of dead people registering to vote. How do you explain that?"

"Even assuming that's true, which is the greater harm? You're describing a handful of cases, and voter ID laws prevent thousands of legitimate votes each cycle. This is a cost-benefit analysis."

"Voter fraud is a crime; having an ID is a basic feature of society," Jordan replied. "Most states provide them for free anyway. Again, my point here is that Republicans have legitimate reasons for supporting voter ID laws that are not just Machiavellian."

"No, they really don't."

"So you think Republicans are just ill-willed on this? And Democrats are pure?"

"Yes."

"You don't think Democrats, even a few of them, have ulterior motives in getting rid of ID requirements?"

"Democrats want more eligible voters to participate, and that's a good thing."

"But Republicans have only bad motives?"

"Yes!"

Chris saw Jordan's jaw muscle clench.

"Look, I'm just trying to understand, but you haven't said anything that justifies the Republican position," someone said.

"Yeah, because nothing I say can get through your partisan filter. If you truly believe that Republicans are just malicious, then nothing I say matters."

"Show me statistics—then I'll believe you."

"Great, I'll write you a fucking report."

"I don't need a report, just tell me."

"But," Chris interjected, "what about—"

"—what about what?" Jordan snapped.

"Why are you so mad?"

"Say what you were going to say."

Chris glared.

"I'm done with this conversation," Jordan said, got up, and left.

An hour later the three of us were back on the road, heading for San Diego. We began talking again at the border with Mexico well after dark, but a bitterness lingered for the rest of the trip. And it still hung over the car as the two of us idled in the thin air of Denver in the early morning days later.

"Well, I love you, dude," Chris said. "I'm sorry things ended up where they did."

"I love you too, man."

Healing, by this point on our journeys, was relatively easy for us. But the tenor of this fight, and its lingering wounds, weighed on our minds. What did it mean that we couldn't extend our civil dialogue beyond the two of us? It felt like through long and excruciating hours of fights, debates, confessions, and reconciliations we had earned something—the ability to trust each other so that somehow, despite our differences, we had forged a common language. But our friends didn't seem to share that language, and in their presence we felt incapable of passing it along or abiding by it.

"I feel like we aren't able to speak as ourselves sometimes," Chris said outside that house in Denver. "I feel like we become standard-bearers for our parties—even when we don't want to be."

Jordan nodded. He squeezed Chris's shoulder, got out of the car, and walked up the steps and into the house.

Chris lingered for a moment, looking up among the trees and feeling the rising sun on his face. Our dialogue felt fragile again—as it had been just before the saline waters of Mono Lake washed it all away almost two years before.

Lorain

Over the next few days, we explored Denver. In the mornings we took long walks through the northwest corner of the city, stopping for coffee and perusing the shelves of local bookstores. At night we enjoyed the food and craft-beer scene under the guidance of our host, Colin. Much to Chris's delight, we even chased down My Brother's Bar, supposedly one of Jack Kerouac's favorite haunts in town.

Our conversations became long and voluble again. Our thoughts returned to what we had seen and felt in northern Mexico, and what we hoped to see on the rest of the trip. Only a week had gone by since we left Los Angeles, which meant we had a month to go. Chris was anxious to see Detroit, where his godfather had been raised, and Jordan wanted to stop off in Nashville, where one of his translators from Afghanistan had just become a new father.

"How about a county fair?" Jordan asked as we paced the streets of Denver.

"Why not?" Chris responded. "Can't say I've ever been to one."

We decided to attend the Lorain County Fair in Ohio—an annual event that Jordan had found on a "Best of" site a few links down a Google search page.

One evening before we left, Colin told us he had extra tickets to a Leon Bridges concert at Red Rocks Amphitheatre.

"We have to go," Chris said to Jordan.

Bridges had a soulful voice and sang the kind of music that conjured up the records Chris's mother had played for him back in Berkeley—Bruce Springsteen, Waylon Jennings, Buffalo Springfield.

"You'll love him," Chris said excitedly. "He's got this crooner's voice, and he puts out these crackly records like the Black Keys or something."

"I bet, man," Jordan said with a smile.

"It'll be like going to a Sam Cooke concert—like hearing Richie Havens at Woodstock."

Chris was caught up in one of his flights of zeal, something Jordan had seen often by then.

That night we enjoyed cured meats, cheese, and beer with Colin and his friends on a knoll just outside the open-air theater in Denver Mountain Park before descending into the columns of giant red-rock outcroppings that give the place its name. The Beatles, Jimi Hendrix, and the Grateful Dead had all played in that space chipped out of the hills of Colorado. A familiar roar of human voices—that singular outpouring of deep anticipation—filled the air as Leon took the stage, and the place came alive as the first melody echoed up the canyon.

Jordan looked over at Chris. A joyous, carefree spirit came out of him at gatherings like this. Jordan felt the opposite among crowds. Once, as a teenager going to concerts in Los Angeles, he had let go, same as Chris. But it felt like a long time since then. He had been drilled to be wary of large groups, and his vigilance never quite went away. As Leon strutted and sang, Jordan breathed deeply and tried to unwind.

For years by then, Jordan had grown weary of hearing Republicans described as ugly racists, or something just short. When faced with those kinds of accusations—especially when leveled against broad swaths of people, people he knew and loved—Jordan would defend the party even when he didn't agree with it. Those feelings had rushed out of him in a snap back in Carlsbad, and they still tangled his thoughts as Leon launched into his latest.

Yet song by song, the music and Chris's enthusiasm began to soften the knots in Jordan's shoulders. Whatever toxicity remained from that fight was leaving him.

Chris was less distracted. He glanced up behind us at the sea of people, swinging, humming, laying an arm over a friend or partner. It was a soothing tableau—an unfathomably large and ecstatic gathering of people—and Chris was entranced. The howling battles of the road and the innumerable troubles of a country left him, at least for a moment or two.

"He's damn good," Jordan said, as Chris turned back around.

"He really is."

———————

We left Denver before daybreak the next morning. Jordan took the wheel, and Chris kept talking to keep both of us alert. We drove through the cornfields and meadows of Kansas and passed onward into Oklahoma and Arkansas. In Memphis, Tennessee, we paused to pay homage at the Civil Rights Museum, standing on the spot where five decades earlier a sniper's bullet had cut down Martin Luther King Jr. on a balcony of the Lorraine Motel.

Then, somewhere out past Memphis, the voice of Malcolm X passed through a pair of headphones we were sharing.

"It's got to be the ballot or the bullet. The ballot or the bullet. If you're afraid to use an expression like that, you should get on out of the country," the great orator railed.

"I like the *empowerment must come before reconciliation* point," Jordan said, speaking over the recording.

"If this is a country of freedom, let it be a country of freedom; and if it's not a country of freedom, change it."

Jordan found him mesmerizing. Malcolm X was acerbic, direct, powerful. His was a call to action.

"Whose speech do you think was more effective?" Jordan asked. Before Malcolm X we had listened to King's "I Have a Dream" address.

"I think you'd have to say MLK, based on how we remember it," Chris said. "Besides, it's a master class in how to give a speech."

Chris, like many, was often drawn back to the reverend's words. They offered something timeless. King preached love in the face of insurmountable danger, and while his courage stirred the two of us in that Volvo all those years later, his poetry was nearly as affecting.

"You know he almost didn't say those words?" Chris said.

"Which?"

"'I have a dream.' King had said it so often, he almost didn't use it again. Someone had to encourage him to say it."

Jordan nodded as he absorbed it all. Harmony, understanding, reconciliation—it all flowed out from the words of a leader who would give everything to persuade the country of his vision.

"I wonder if 'Ballot or the Bullet' might've had a broader reception today," Jordan said.

"Maybe," Chris responded. "But if they'd both lived, they would have seemed a lot closer in message."

"How so?"

"Malcolm had started to change after coming back from Mecca. He was softening his tone. Before—"

Chris didn't finish the thought.

As the Boat drifted north toward Cleveland, we fell silent.

Chris bit his nails. King's and Malcolm's words weren't just beautiful; they were certain. A good speech has conviction, purpose, and moral clarity. Yet all Chris saw around him was complexity. Since we set out on the road, we had experienced challenges to what we thought we knew. All we could do was acknowledge how humbling it was and keep at it. We could talk to people. We could learn from them. And in the process we could cross a few lines together that, perhaps, we weren't supposed to cross under other circumstances.

"About Carlsbad..." Chris ventured. "I understand your point."

"Oh, yeah?" Jordan said.

"About electoral integrity."

As the silence deepened, Chris's thoughts had returned to our fight. Chris had disagreed with Jordan, but the conversation shouldn't have gone that way. Pummeling one another wasn't conducive for friends to listen or learn.

"Just look at how Russia was able to affect voters in 2016 with Facebook," Chris continued. "It could've been much worse if they'd directly hacked voting booths."

Jordan heard a cautiousness in Chris's voice. We were venturing back into what could be turbulent seas, and Chris was testing the waters.

"And when you really think about it, it doesn't have to be an either-or choice," Chris said. "One can be for election security *and* for expanding the franchise."

Jordan looked over.

"We may never see eye to eye on voter ID laws in places like the Carolinas or Wisconsin," Chris continued. "But I understand there's a defensible value behind the concept, at least when the two of us are talking about it."

Since Carlsbad, Chris had often wondered if he could have reduced the tension by admitting what he saw as reasonable in Jordan's perspective. A single word or two might have expanded the conversation. There is a grace in acknowledging the virtue in someone else's views, and Chris hadn't summoned it.

"Sure," Jordan said. "And I get the concern around these laws, especially if political actors are shown to have bad intentions."

Chris nodded.

"No matter what," Jordan continued, "the negative effects of voter ID laws should be mitigated, and there are bipartisan ways to do that—like longer windows for voting and free identification cards for low-income residents."

We sat in silence for a moment.

"I feel like we can often get here," Chris said. "To a place where we agree."

Jordan considered it.

"I think on most issues, we're actually debating policies that reflect two values we both share. The difference is how we choose to prioritize them."

"That makes sense," Chris said. "The problem is when politicians or policymakers trot out those values as a defense for something more nefarious that only *looks* like one of those values."

Chris glanced over at Jordan.

"That's right," Jordan said.

We were engaging, again, on things that mattered.

"The challenge," Jordan continued, "is that we live in a world of uncertainty. We don't have perfect information. Not just about the scale of the problems, like voter suppression or electoral fraud, but also about the motives of the people emphasizing one priority or the other."

Jordan paused.

"So the question is, how do we reconcile our different priorities when we don't trust each other's numbers and we don't trust each other's intentions?"

"Have some humility, I guess," Chris replied.

Jordan nodded.

"I think just recognizing that there are competing values goes a long way," Chris said. "Even if leaders never actually agree on certain policies, that's still a basis for understanding."

Two years earlier, we had nearly torn our friendship apart in Nevada. That fight had revealed real differences between us—differences that would persist. Our friendship would have to navigate them from there on out, and that was okay; they weren't a reason to pull away from each other. Now, as we sped for the belly of the Midwest, we were realizing something else: the road was humbling us.

The people we were meeting—and the fuller picture of one another—were complex. Yet in our weaker moments we sometimes overlooked that complexity. We might generalize or rely on symbols to understand each other, knowing full well that those things often obscure what matters most. Sometimes we fell prey to our prejudices and expectations. It was the easy thing to do. But then, when we calmed down, something else could take hold. We could remain open-minded. Good faith and compassion could take root.

Wide river valleys with low green prairies replaced the fields of corn where homesteads rose up along their slight hills like sentinels—some long ago abandoned.

As we pulled up to a toll booth, we were met by a pungent rush of air.

"Whoa," a toll-taker with glasses that made her eyes small and colorless said.

A truck sagging low with cows pulled out of the next booth.

"Pigs smell the worst," she said.

As the window went back up, the gentle words of a stranger seemed harsh and foreign. When left to our own thoughts, the same nagging worry returned: Could we find a way to talk like this with others? Or would we splinter as soon as we left the Boat?

We reached Lorain by late afternoon, finding the county fair at the end of a dusty parking lot bisected by a railroad line. Inside was row after row of farm-equipment stands. Retirees in turquoise T-shirts square-danced, and thin men, blue around the eyes, cajoled us to shoot air guns at feathery paper targets.

We meandered through the maze of booths.

We were prone to amble like that after a long drive. The fatigue of the road would slowly slough off us as we walked—whether in Memphis, Yellowstone, or there in Lorain. We passed through the junior barns, where teenagers showed off prized cattle, sheep, and pigs. Young boys and girls with white-collared shirts tucked into dark, belted jeans presented fidgety chickens to admiring parents and onlookers, who took photos and rhapsodized over the quality of each fowl.

The Lorain County Fair was a simple picture of untroubled Ohio life. The grounds felt safe and serene. Everything moved at a slackened pace that suited the road-weary like us—until we stumbled across a more raucous affair.

Outside a large tent, men and women dressed in red getups talked jovially among themselves and passed out American flags. The booth practically teemed with the middle-aged, and election placards along the walls made it clear this was a Republican tent.

Lorain, with its largely white working-class population, had long been a Democratic stronghold. But on election night 2016, Donald Trump took Lorain County by just 388 votes, the first time a Republican had won there since Ronald Reagan. A revision later handed the county to Clinton by the slimmest of margins—121 votes—but the sea change was evident. Four years earlier, President Barack Obama had carried 57.8 percent of the vote, trouncing Mitt Romney by 16 percentage points. Two years after Trump's election, the Republicans filling the tent seemed ascendant.

We passed by and ducked into another tent, where a television reporter and a cameraman lingered a step or two outside. They eyed us as we walked under the flap and out of the din.

Inside looked like a makeshift storefront on Bourbon Street or Times Square. Hats, T-shirts, flags, and vanity items lined the tarpaulin walls. Then Chris stopped, tapped Jordan on the shoulder, and nodded upward.

Jordan followed Chris's gaze up the wall and spied a large Confederate flag hanging next to an assortment of other standards.

"Hey, fellas," said a stout man with a pimply chin. "Anything catch your eye?"

"Just browsing."

"Lots of good stuff here," he said.

"Sure is."

The reporter and cameraman outside made more sense. It seemed as if we had stepped squarely into a heated political debate at the county fair, of all places. Reading up on our phones, we learned that shops at the fair had sold the Confederate flag for close to eight years. But other sites in Ohio—including the larger Ohio State Fair—had banned its sale, and pressure was mounting on Lorain to follow suit. Three billboards on the outskirts of the grounds demanded a ban on the "Stars and Bars," and someone had draped the Confederate standard over one of those signs just as we arrived.

We exited the tent from the other side and found ourselves in another row of booths. Politics had not been on either of our minds when we reached the fair. We had recently escaped it, only to be thrown back in unprepared.

Soon after, we came across the stall of a group of Democrats with election signs in robin's-egg blue. All four of the gray-haired women there that day held miniature American flags. One of them had a whole handful.

"Love the flags," Jordan said as we walked by.

"Where are you from?" one asked.

"California—by way of Connecticut."

"You two are a long way from home."

"Things are a little more subdued over here," Chris said. "There's a Republican tent up the way, you know."

"The Democrats have sort of pulled out of Lorain," one of the women said. "We're here as volunteers—to protest, I guess. But more to be here to represent our community. A lot of people in Lorain and Wellington think like us, and we want to make sure they're heard."

The other women nodded.

"Here," one of the women with glasses said, pushing a small American flag into Jordan's hands.

The fabric was frayed at the end. The glue showed on the splintered dowel. Such a small, delicate thing it was, yet Jordan had gone to war under that flag—and some of his comrades had perished for it.

Jordan grasped it and looked at the woman.

"Thank you," he said, and we made our way down the rows of booths.

———

As the sun dipped low, the Lorain fairgrounds were emptying. Those who were left kept to the long shadows below the farm equipment and the trees. We ate alligator served by a Florida couple who drove up and down the Eastern Seaboard every year, working fair after fair all season long.

"Which stop is your favorite?" Jordan asked.

"They start to blend after a while," said the red-faced man with a ratty baseball hat, turning away from a fryer bubbling with alligator fat.

We gnawed on bratwursts with sauerkraut and grainy mustard dished out by the descendants of German immigrants who owned a family restaurant in nearby Cleveland. We even perused a few RVs for sale, kicking their hitches and mumbling about the monthly payments.

"It's astounding," Chris said as we passed another row of booths. "No one seems all that concerned with the flag."

"Looks that way."

The flag's presence might have been a news story, but Lorain, on balance, seemed more concerned with the judging of a goat, a dance step or two, and the specs on a tractor engine than a flag hanging in a tent down the way.

We settled in along the siding of a corral with dozens of other onlookers, then watched as handlers with sticks and tucked-in polo shirts chased prancing horses with braided tails and manes. An official-looking man with a purple tie and short sleeves gave hand-gesture orders and inspected each horse, which, to a stallion, pounded their hooves and flicked their tails upon his stern touch.

The day was waning as we made for the parking lot, and Jordan kept glancing down at the small American flag in his hand. He felt something stir as he turned the fabric over, rolling its dowel back and forth between his fingers.

The night before, we had shared a meal with Jordan's Afghan translator, Zabiullah Mazari—Zee, to Jordan—at his home outside Nashville. Jordan and Zee had spent many evenings together in 2013, talking late into the night. Zee dreamed of a life in the United States, and before leaving the country Jordan had sponsored Zee's special immigrant visa. Five years later, Zee ushered the two of us into his apartment, and Jordan saw how those conversations had come to life. Zee's wife brought out their newborn boy, whom she placed in Jordan's arms. We drank tea and talked over a spread of Afghani and Somali cuisine.

Not long before, Zee had worn the American flag on his own uniform, just as Jordan had. Back then it had been only an idea for Zee—and a gamble of an idea at that: he could have been killed for displaying it, and so could his family.

But now the flag was his, too.

In Lorain, these emotions welled up in Jordan. America was generous. America was good, and able to transcend whatever that other flag meant. That logic shaped Jordan's worldview. It was why he was proud to wear that flag overseas, and proud to make the case for its people wherever he went.

With that same shred of dyed fabric twirling in his hand, and an after-image of the Confederate flag still in his mind, Jordan looked over at Chris.

Things were probably more complicated for his friend. The flag meant something different for Chris, and for the longest time Jordan resisted that notion. Yet faced with the complexity of the road, Jordan had come to terms with how the flag could mean one thing to himself, another to Chris, and yet another to Zee.

In Lorain, volunteers in red and others in blue—standing only 100 yards away from one another—handed out American flags to passersby. The "Stars and Stripes" was theirs in equal measure, and even to those who might disavow it. We may not always agree on which values it embodies, and even when we do, we might prioritize those values differently. But that flag, and the weighty ideas it carries, belongs to all of us. Maybe that's enough for it all to still matter.

With the exit gate in sight, Jordan stopped short.

He turned to two girls no older than 12, who had walked by holding hands.

"Hey," Jordan said. "Here."

He handed the little flag to the nearer of the two. She took it in both hands and scampered off into the crowds beyond.

Detroit

A hard rain fell on Detroit the afternoon we arrived. Chris's family friend had agreed to let us stay in her home in Grosse Pointe for the week. Its decor evoked the 1950s—the city's heyday. Grosse Pointe, a suburb to the northeast, is a relic of that time.

"Like Gatsby," Jordan said as we drove down the wide lakeshore boulevard into the city the next morning. The lawns were manicured and deep green. Warm lamps lit cobbled driveways and patios. Not a slab of sidewalk concrete was off-kilter. Along the lake the houses were terrific and gargantuan, yet it all felt out of time; its grandeur was ancient.

That day, we took in the city. We stood in the foyer of the Guardian Building, its art deco ceilings painted like peacock plumage. We gawked at *The Spirit of Detroit*—a glorious bronze statue—and its inscription, a passage from Corinthians: "and where the spirit of the lord is, there is liberty." Jordan wondered what Pete might make of such a passage. We stood in the shadow of the Renaissance Center, where we marveled at the black metal fist of the Joe Louis memorial. These were monuments to a halcyon era. Yet we were some of the only people on downtown boulevards built for a parade. A foreboding filled the Boat as we drove from neighborhood to neighborhood. Thick air hung over abandoned lots and crumbling brick buildings.

On our first afternoon, we left downtown for a coffee shop in Lathrup Village, a suburb north of Eight Mile, just outside the city limits. We were scheduled to meet with Satori Shakoor, a performer and storyteller who had agreed to tell us about Detroit. Jordan had reached out to her after seeing a video of her speech online.

Satori was elegant. She had her hair in locks, wore a colorful dress, and spoke with a raspy, poetic voice. We listened intently as she told us about community farms springing up out of empty lots, how the tap water was tainted, and the ways gentrification seized the few blocks still occupied after the latest exodus.

"Detroit is an amusement park for wealthy people," she said.

But it was still her city. Eastern Market, newly reopened, brimmed with produce and the fare of local artisans. Jack White's Third Man Records cut new Detroit albums on vinyl. The Detroit Institute of Arts was home to Diego Rivera's famed frescoes of the working man and working woman. Satori also told us about a downtown bar where district attorneys, criminal-defense types, and a coterie of judges in fancy suits held court and sipped martinis. She told us about the 36th District Court, the largest district court in Michigan and one of the busiest in the country.

"You can learn a lot about Detroit's criminal justice system just by hanging around there," Satori said.

We were particularly interested in these legal haunts, because we had come to Detroit for a specific purpose: to better understand what redemption means in today's America. The two of us had often discussed this ideal, and it was one issue over which we found little disagreement. Everyone should have a second chance, we both believed. We debated the role of institutions and personal responsibility in the struggle, but when it came down to it, both of us shared the view that those who paid their dues, atoned for their wrongdoing, and worked to become better people deserved a second or even third act. We agreed it was among the most fundamental of American values.

Satori knew all about second chances. She had lost her mother to ovarian cancer, then her son to an automobile accident. Her life became a "joyless chore," as she tells it.

"Wounds can be inherited," Satori told us over the purr of air-conditioning in the coffee shop. "You might not feel slavery or loss directly, but it's there. It's in your bones. Children feel their parents' wounds, and parents feel their own parents'."

Then she had the opportunity to tell her story on stage to an audience that grieved with her. In that moment, she found something: telling stories heals, and that was what Satori wanted to give back to Detroit.

"Stories," Satori said as we gathered our belongings and stepped out into the heat of the day, "are just one way of exorcising that pain."

Many in Detroit have certainly known pain. The city gave birth to the automobile, transforming the 20th century and creating nearly unfathomable wealth. Marble museums, mile-long factories, and multistory mansions went up as testaments to the city's gilded age. Then it all fell apart. As the scions of car fortunes left for Dearborn and Grosse Pointe, the population cratered and median household income in the city plummeted. Soon nearly 40 percent of the population lived in poverty, including over half of the city's children. Almost half of all adults were functionally illiterate; over a quarter were unemployed. Detroit had one of the highest murder rates in the country, behind only Baltimore and St. Louis. As the wounds of poverty and limited opportunity got passed down from one generation to the next, feeding the downward spiral, more burdens piled up. In 2013, the city filed for bankruptcy and went into receivership.

Recently, however, a new narrative about Detroit had emerged. Sports stadiums and music venues had sprouted up downtown. Skyscrapers, once abandoned, were refurbished. A new light-rail network circled the business district. In Midtown, art installations and trendy restaurants cropped up like wildflowers. Young people, attracted by cheap housing, made their way to the city. And a downtown renaissance was celebrated. People were fixing things.

Chris's godfather, Dan—a man who in many ways was a father to Chris—grew up in Detroit and had told Chris countless stories about his Motor City childhood. Over the years, at meals and on afternoon walks through the hills behind Berkeley, Dan told Chris about the Motown concerts he stole away to on weekends as a teenager, getaways up the peninsula to Leland, and football games on Fridays. Chris had often visited him at their family cottage north of Traverse City, but it was Detroit where Dan's father had worked his way up the hierarchy of the automotive business. Detroit, carved out of the shores of Lake St. Clair and the Detroit River, was a city of opportunity, history, and great artistic movements. Chris knew the Detroit of Dan's youth was gone or disappearing, but the stirrings of this renaissance were visible. Perhaps Detroit had reached its nadir and had only up to go.

Yet as we drove back down into the city from Lathrup Village—past Eight Mile and through Highland Park—it was hard to fully imagine this rebirth. Back in the city, we turned the Boat off the highway and found ourselves in an abandoned field. Vines grew thick and wooly up chain-link fences. Most blocks were empty save for a single house with shattered windows and inscrutable graffiti. In the distance stood a solitary Gothic skyscraper.

"It's like watching Rome go to seed," Chris said, watching the decrepit scene out the window as we passed block after block of fallow land and empty foundations.

———————

Two days later, we rang the doorbell of a two-story cinder-block building on the corner of a strip mall a few blocks off Eight Mile Road. It was a sweltering midmorning. We were there to meet a group of former inmates from the Women's Huron Valley Correctional Facility—three women who made handbags for a living at a nonprofit called Bags to Butterflies. Michelle, the director of the program, led us upstairs.

"Welcome, welcome," she said. "Come in. The women are very excited to meet you."

Michelle opened the door into a workshop, where three women in aprons sat around a small table, tinkering with wood panels dyed various colors. Along the walls, completed wood purses were lined up next to hot-glue guns, shiny metallic clasps, and other crafting equipment. Michelle introduced the women, calling them each *Ms.* There was Ms. Charlene, a short woman full of wild energy who introduced herself first. And Ms. Brenda, who sat at the table, shook our hands with a gentle smile, and offered us a proper "How do you do?" And finally Ms. Tonya, who towered over us from her perch on a stool not quite sized for the table. She was quiet, more reserved.

We settled onto stools around the table while the women worked. Things were hushed at first. It was a workshop, after all, and we were intruding on their lunch hour. And for a moment, we were aware of how out of place we were: two white men in a room of black women who had served many years in prison.

"You don't remember how to do it?" Michelle asked Brenda, who was planning how to paint the side of a half-completed bag.

"The ladies haven't learned this technique yet," Michelle said. "I'm actually learning it myself, and now I can show them."

After 25 years in corporate communications at Ford, Michelle had founded the program to help newly released women—known as *returning citizens*. After an interview, if the women accepted an offer to join the workshop, the bags became the heart of their reintegration. Around that table on the second floor of an office park, they would build each handbag. It was the beginnings of a livelihood. Charlene, for one, had made six or seven bags and sold a couple of them online.

At the same time, the women were slowly acclimating back to society. Michelle helped with bus tickets, housing, and career counseling. When women came to her, Michelle would ask what they wanted in their next phase of life. Charlene wanted to sing, so they found her a vocal coach. Brenda wanted to serve her church. And Tonya wanted to drive, so Michelle took her to the DMV.

"Of course, a few times the instructor, he told me, 'You gotta keep up, now—you gotta speed up,'" Tonya said. "I didn't want to go too far too fast, you know."

"You had fun?" Chris asked.

"Oh yes," Tonya said. "He said I did great when it comes to stopping. Old people when they go to a stop sign or a red light, they, well, people jump, and I was smooth. I was proud of that."

"A natural," Jordan said.

"Oh yeah."

"I think it's important for them to have a voice in their future," Michelle said. "I don't want to dictate what they should do. They know what their desires are, so if they share that, then we can get them connected to the right people who can help them on their journey to success."

"I went in as a singer," Charlene said with a warble, "and I came out as a singer."

She was irrepressible.

"What do you sing?" Jordan asked.

"Any and everything," she said, and the other women hummed and clucked. "Aretha Franklin was my idol, so mostly her songs. 'Respect' was one of my favorites. So when she passed away, the only thing that I could think of was how she inspired me. She made me want to be who I wanted to be. And I wish I could go to her funeral."

She trailed off for a moment. Franklin had passed away on August 16, just a few days prior, and a public viewing was held at Detroit's Charles H. Wright Museum of African American History.

"And if I could be like her—" Charlene said, still deep in thought.

"No, I'm gonna be me, and I'm gonna make my *own* name. I'm gonna be somebody—and y'all gonna be in the front row when I do!"

"There she go," said Michelle, chuckling, as she helped fasten a shoulder strap to Brenda's bag.

"Brenda," Jordan asked, "what do you want to do?"

"Oh, just relax," she said, and the other women tutted her short answer.

Brenda served three years—a short sentence by comparison with Tonya and Charlene's nearly half-centuries. She was a godly woman who mentioned her pastor time and again.

"I enjoy people," she said. "And I know that everyone is put on this earth for a purpose. And I have the gift of help, and I just enjoy doing things and helping people."

Brenda told us she had worked with the Ronald McDonald House and had been a trustee of her church.

"I hear God, and I listen," Brenda said of her time in prison. "I was walking the grounds, and I said, 'God, I know you gave me an assignment and I will be obedient, but you didn't have to put me here to show me; I believe you.' So when I was there I did a lot of advocacy for the women because our conditions were deplorable."

At the Women's Huron Valley Correctional Facility in Pittsfield Township, where all three of them did their time, storage closets had been converted into cells. Scabies outbreaks went undiagnosed and untreated. Leaks and mold were common, kitchens understaffed, medical care scant. Around the time we visited the city, inmates in Michigan prisons had been dying at a rate unseen in a quarter century.

Brenda, horrified by the decay and neglect, wrote to the NAACP and the American Friends Service Committee.

"The women," Brenda said, "I always promised them, 'When I get home I'm gonna do something,' and they told me, 'Don't forget us, don't forget us.'"

But Brenda could barely get her own life in order. When released from prison, most Americans face a series of interlocking barriers that often lead them right back to prison. Many returning citizens don't have an identification card or a driver's license, which prevents them from accessing basic services. "Ex-cons" are often discriminated against in employment and housing. Desperation can set in, and a single wrong step while on probation—even missing a meeting because of car trouble—could land a former inmate back in prison. Almost one out of every three people who complete their sentences will find themselves right back in prison in a matter of months.

Brenda's trials began anew when she couldn't find an apartment. Landlords turned her down over and over again. Her pastor told her, "God's got something better for you," and as Brenda tells it, "Within an hour, I got a call back: 'You have the place.' And I started running, I started shouting, and the cat thought I was crazy. But those are the things that I can share with the women, because as long as we have hope, anything is possible."

As we spoke, the women revealed great concern for those left behind, yet parolees were prohibited from contacting those still in prison; it was a violation. So those women, some of whom Tonya and Charlene had presumably known for decades, were just out of reach, separated from their friends by the state.

"I never gave up," Charlene said, echoing Brenda. "I kept telling myself, *I'm not dying in here. I'm not gonna die here. God has a plan for me. I'm gonna get out.* And each year I kept saying, 'This is my year— this is my year.' And in 2017 it was my year."

Chris hadn't retained a whole lot from his class on criminal law, but he did remember the accepted reasons for punishment—notions like retribution, deterrence, incapacitation, rehabilitation, restitution, and restoration. For society to send these women to prison and, upon release, brand them with an invisible iron as untouchables— a caste unworthy of shelter or work—was unjust. What purpose did it serve?

We had been told a few days prior that it was not good form to ask about a returning citizen's crimes, and so we didn't. But it wasn't hard to find the *Michigan Chronicle* pieces explaining how Tonya had been convicted of murder and Charlene of conspiring to commit murder.

Charlene offered up her own impression, though.

"No sin is greater than another," Charlene said matter-of-factly. "And if you don't do nothing but pick up an ink pen from work, you committed a sin. It's just that you didn't go to prison."

Remorse is a prerequisite for parolees. It means that one has taken responsibility—or so our system says. Charlene was back in her home, and she was singing. She was taking responsibility for her freedom, but it wasn't clear to us whether the same was true of her crimes. How many years was enough to free her from those sins? Would she ever be totally free?

"I went in at the age of 20, and now I'm 62," Charlene said. "So I'm still learning. I get scared sometimes, getting lost, 'cause I don't know nothing about where things are."

Her words hit Jordan in the solar plexus—40 years in prison. Forty years was unfathomable—the balance of a lifetime. *Sent away for so long,* Jordan told himself, aching at the mere thought. Among the three of them, Charlene, Brenda, and Tonya had served more than 85 years in prison.

"The city must look very different," Chris said.

"Oh yes, it's just devastating," Tonya said. "I couldn't find nowhere. Everywhere I lived—" she trailed off thinking about it. "I've been lost about four or five times. I don't recognize the place, you know?"

Tonya had two children, she told us—a boy and a girl. She also had five brothers and two sisters, but two of the brothers had died last year just a month apart. Charlene also had two children, but her story was less uplifting. Neither her son, 45, nor her daughter, 43, would allow her back into their lives, she said. They'd been toddlers when Charlene went away, and now she had five grandkids and three great-grandkids.

"They say I owe them 41 years," she said. "They won't accept me right now, but I can't worry about them. I have to worry about me. I have to find me.

"They'll come around," said Charlene, the two of us reduced to silence in the face of more heartbreak. "Once they see me on stage and say, 'That's Momma,' then they gonna come around."

In that room, it felt cruel that these women had to relive their crimes at every turn. Since then, we've both thought about that word—*cruel*—and whether it was the right one for the situation. But in that moment, the word felt justified. We weren't thinking about victims or how justice is served. Instead, we saw the pain of these women and the way their horizons had been narrowed.

Charlene, Brenda, and Tonya were focused on betterment, on reentering society. They had paid some form of dues—heavy or less so—and were sent back into a seemingly foreign land, where they were citizens again. What else mattered?

"That's what I'd like to do right now. I'd like to be skilled at making these bags," Brenda said, testing a strap with a tug. "Because I just hope that I can move forward and be something, and I'm going to do that. I'm going to be a butterfly."

———————

Over the next few days, we visited Detroit's renaissance. We spent afternoons in Grosse Pointe, ate breakfast at diners, known as Coney Islands, and ran along the waterfront. We drove through Mexicantown and sampled tacos after briefly walking around an art exhibit built into an abandoned block called the Heidelberg Project.

But it was hard to know what to believe. When we crossed Alter Road leaving downtown, we experienced Detroit's split personality. We'd see the new Detroit, crowned with refurbished Gothic sky-scrapers, public art, and posh eateries. Then, a few blocks later, we'd descend back into the city's troubles as we passed empty blocks where lot after lot had gone to seed. Back in Grosse Pointe, Old Detroit reemerged unchanged. Brick homes—lantern lights flickering on broad porches—dotted the streets. They glistened gently on summer nights from behind long, tree-lined lawns.

The renaissance, it seemed, was block to block. It was an imperfect narrative that was both under- and overinclusive. But then again, stories always are. We tell them to make sense of our surroundings, and oftentimes that means reducing the world to something we can appreciate. Stories are our best estimation—a way of guessing at the forces that leave us where we are, where we're headed, and where we've been. Detroit and its mythology seemed no different. The renaissance was a story, and a good one; it made sense.

But stories don't always conform to archetype. Detroit in the 21st century is complicated, its story imperfect. The tale of the renaissance was told alongside the tragedy, and perhaps knowing which story was most explanatory—which was "right"—was its own fool's errand.

We spent one of our last afternoons walking along the flanks of the ancient Packard Automotive Plant—a ruin of Detroit's golden age. We walked a small stretch of its half-mile length, where thousands of assembly-line workers had once bolted together cast-iron Packards (and, in wartime, P-51 Mustang fighter-plane engines). Now an investor planned to restore it.

When we arrived, cicadas bleated and nothing much moved. Cement walls were blistered with graffiti. A sapling managed to grow from the roof. Its eight feet of frail bark and stem gave an account of the decades like the rings of a redwood. The sidings were splintered, and decay showed through the empty gape of the windows. We walked until we realized how long the facility stretched through wooded, grassy lots. Rather than stroll its full length, we settled under a crumbling awning to avoid the sun.

Here was a catacomb—a mausoleum for a deceased part of Detroit. The Packard plant might have been in the process of being redeveloped—a symbol of latent progress—but something about it seemed irredeemably dead. Jordan found it impossible to peer into its rotted innards and not wonder what could possibly survive or reemerge out of such depths.

Dissonance is unsettling. That's all we could think about that night. We took a drink at Cliff Bell's, a jazz bar Satori Shakoor had recommended, as throngs of Detroit Tigers fans meandered the streets under the ballpark lights not far off. As we listened from stiff red-velvet stools, Chris was lost in thought.

"Forty-one years in prison—can you imagine?" Chris said to Jordan as we watched a man play a saxophone on stage while another plucked a bass and a third splashed a cymbal and drum set behind.

"It's unbelievable," Jordan said.

The next morning we were scheduled to visit Parnall Correctional Facility in Jackson, Michigan, some 80 miles west of Detroit. Jordan had found a woman, Frannie, who ran a program for inmates there. Usually it took weeks to get into the minimum-security prison, but the slapdash visitor applications we had submitted were approved. We would drive through Dearborn on Michigan Avenue—the same long road that connects Detroit to Chicago—and make our way past the concertina wire and through security at Parnall. And there we would see a group of inmates perform Shakespeare.

———

Gabriel—a young Hispanic man with glassy eyes, a pencil mustache, and thick tattoos running up his neck and face—rose to his feet with a copy of *King Lear* in his hand and began to read aloud.

"'Yet better thus,'" he said, enunciating each of Shakespeare's words carefully, "'and known to be contemned, than still contemned and flattered.'"

Gabriel was playing Edgar, the disinherited son of the Earl of Gloucester, who was hiding naked in a bush just as his blind, grieving father, led by an old man, mused about throwing himself from a cliff.

In the stark prison classroom, two other men, Reggie and Dominic, held their copies of the play and followed along.

"'But who comes here?'" Gabriel said. "'My father, poorly led? World, world, O world! But that thy strange mutations make us hate thee, life would not yield to age.'"

All three men circled one another.

"'O, my good lord,'" Reggie, a stocky African American man, read. He was playing the old man. "'I have been your tenant and your father's tenant these fourscore years.'"

"'Away, get thee away. Good friend, be gone,'" Dominic read falteringly. Gabriel and Reggie whispered words in his ear as he paused and considered the most obscure. "'Thy comforts can do me no good at all. Thee they may hurt.'"

The two of us looked on from plastic chairs flanked by dozens of inmates wearing black wristbands, blue and orange jumpsuits, and white tennis shoes. We were in a classroom with a red carpet, fluorescent lights, and a coughing AC unit. There were perhaps 30 of us in that room at Parnall Correctional Facility, yet only four of us—Chris, Jordan, Frannie, and Frannie's assistant, Catherine—would be free to pass out of the prison gates later that afternoon.

The men around us were part of a program called Shakespeare in Prison, which brings the 16th-century British playwright's work to inmates. Frannie, a young mother and theater professional with wavy hair and thick glasses, was helping the inmates rehearse for their next performance.

"'And worse I may be yet,'" Gabriel said, walking away from the other two, his character Edgar brooding. "'The worst is not so long as we can say, "This is the worst."'"

"'He has some reason, else he could not beg,'" Dominic said, sounding out odd spellings and arcane words. "'In last night's storm I such a fellow saw, which made me think a man a worm. My son came then into my mind, and yet my mind was then scarce friends with

him. I have heard more since. As flies to wanton boys are we to th'
gods. They kill us for their sport.'"

A few minutes earlier, Gabriel had led us in a warm-up in which we
formed a circle and raised our arms as if lifting a heavy burden from
the floor to the ceiling, all in tandem. It felt like we should hold hands,
but Frannie had told us we were not allowed to touch the inmates
except for handshakes, high fives, or fist bumps. To enforce the rule,
a correctional officer walked through the middle of the circle every
10 minutes.

Dominic looked at Gabriel with arched eyebrows and furrowed brow.

"'Know'st thou the way to Dover?'"

"'Both stile and gate, horseway and footpath. Poor Tom hath been
scared out of his good wits,'" Gabriel read, and the ruse was set. The
earl was unknowingly speaking to his own son.

The three gamely worked through the scene and its dialogue.
When the scene ended, the three men looked up as the room burst
into applause.

"So," Frannie asked as the din came down, "what's that scene about?"

"It's sad," Gabriel offered.

"It's rough," another man added. "He's talking to his son and doesn't
know it."

"Edgar is greatly pained by his father's malady," Gabriel continued.
"I can only imagine how I would feel."

"Good, good," Frannie said.

"It's about the stripping away of illusions," Gabriel continued,
following the thought. "He's better off being known than otherwise."
Gabriel quoted the first line of the scene again: "'Yet better thus, and
known to be contemned, than still contemned and flattered.'"

"Better to know the truth than not," Reggie added. A few voices
around the room murmured agreement.

"But why is this guy naked in a bush?" a larger, ursine man in a wheelchair asked, and the room exploded with laughter and theories.

"Orange! Orange!" Frannie shouted, and a few of the men took up the call. The group had been looking for a word to say *Shut the fuck up* in a nice way, one of the men explained to us. Suggestions were aplenty.

"What about *apple*?" someone said from the sidelines. The group talked over one another and Frannie tutted.

"It's too hard. *Apple* will get caught in your throat."

"What about *red*?"

"Oh, I love it," Frannie said.

"But we already have a Red."

A man in the back with a long red beard raised his hand sheepishly.

"We'll find it, guys," Frannie said, attempting to refocus the group. "What about this?" She opened her copy and read aloud. "'As flies to wanton boys are we to th' gods. They kill us for their sport.'"

"I agree with that," said Van, a lanky man next to Jordan.

"We are worthless in their eyes," a man with little eyes said curtly. "That's what he's saying."

"That's right, though," Van said. "The Bible says, 'No man can know the mind of God.'"

"The earl, he's talking about his son," Gabriel said, his voice rising above the fray. "That's important here. He's sad about his lost son. He's remorseful."

A contemplative quiet gathered. Chris noticed two tattoos under Gabriel's eye. One was a teardrop, and a cross was needled into his flesh beneath it.

"He's stating his father's thoughts," Gabriel continued. "So really what we're talking about here is how easily we cast people aside when they don't meet our expectations. Like wanton boys do to flies. It feels like now that he's blind, well, he wants to see."

There was a profundity to what Gabriel had stumbled upon and, as before, the room fell still, as if struck by the gravity of the insight. Gabriel's unguarded words about *King Lear* seemed to have cut somewhere deep for a few of these men. Edgar's plight, the earl's pain—it all touched their lives in a place they had perhaps cauterized with time and disinterest or anger or disgust or indignation—anything to push off the discomfort of it. But the silence pooled around more than those tender scars. In that moment, they seemed to mull over opportunities held and lost, lives touched and dashed, and, somehow, still the existence and presence of salvation. That silence seemed to be a recognition that lives change, and how deeply beautiful and magnificent and terrifying a changed heart can really be. They were there out of a yearning for clarity, no matter how painful what emerged might be.

"Is that right?" Van said, turning to look at Frannie.

"There is no right," Frannie said.

It was the man in the wheelchair who spoke up next. "But there's more here, right?" The earl was saying he thought of his son in his last moments and that he didn't hate him, the man explained. He had discarded him like the wanton boys discard flies, but he too was regretful. "He's looking back on his life," the man said. "He's thinking about his mistakes, right? Like you do before you die."

"Ain't it strange," Red said, "how everyone who talks about suicide thinks it will make anything better?"

"It does," Van retorted.

His words took Red by surprise.

"No it doesn't."

"Yes it does," Van said. "It gets rid of the pain."

"No it doesn't, because it also cuts off the ability to make it right."

"Sometimes when people have a heavy weight," added a man with a ponytail, "they want to put it down."

"It's selfish!" Red practically screamed.

The room came alive with thoughts and shouts.

"It's not just for you," Van said loudly. "I mean, I was there. I was in the hole, and I had it right here."

He gestured as if he had a razor just above the artery on his wrist and dragged it up his forearm.

"I thought about it. I wasn't learning, and I thought of my family. I thought, *Okay, they won't have to do this anymore.* I wasn't doing it for me—I was doing it for them. And I sucked at it, thankfully. But when you're in that moment, you aren't thinking about yourself."

"I know," Red said. "I never tried it, but I have journals full of plans in my storage locker back home. But what you're going through is doing away with your life's potential."

The crackle of a guard's intercom emanated from outside.

Matt, a man with a brain tattooed on the side of his head, spoke up. "Maybe he's looking for, I don't know, redemption." He meant the earl. "Atonement, maybe? What's the word?"

"I like that perspective, Matt," Gabriel said, nodding and looking across the room.

"That's common with people at that point," another man said. "They're looking for closure."

As the session wrapped up, Frannie turned things over to us. "Prepare a few questions," Frannie had told us two days earlier. The men wanted to share their stories with us.

"We're curious," Chris started. "What has this program meant to you?"

"In here we're not groups," the man in the wheelchair said. "We're not stereotypes. We don't divide people."

"This is a safe space to be oneself," Red said. "We accept. It's what we're here for. The energy in here is not usually found out there." He gestured toward the prison yard.

Acting brought more than just camaraderie, though. The program was about "risking," "daring," "braving," they said. They took "flak" and "razzing" for joining the troupe. But the ones willing to suffer the slings and arrows from their fellow inmates ended up growing, and it had transformed them.

"It's helped me be more human," a man named John said. "I'm more accepting of people."

The emotional tenor to the room was another draw.

"It's about finding the common ground," Gabriel said. "We can all relate to sorrow. We can all relate to anger."

Then James piped up. He was a severe man who sat in the back and hadn't reacted except to sneer or laugh. "I'm learning to be friendly, understanding—to not take offense so easily. I don't want to be rude when I get out. I gotta learn, and this class helps. It teaches me to be patient—to listen."

A common sentiment went around the room: there was nowhere to learn these skills in the "real" world. No one would let them practice. But with Frannie, they could—safely. More than once the room was called a "safe space." A place of self-exploration.

"Shakespeare is a catalyst to learn about ourselves and what we couldn't get outside," said the ponytailed man. "It's how we explore what got us here in the first place."

Something about Shakespeare made emotion feel less transgressive, less uncouth. They all rendered themselves vulnerable together, and the plays allowed for a measure of self-reflection.

Then Chris looked at Jordan, who posed the question we had come to Detroit to ask.

"We want to know," Jordan said, "what *a second chance* means to all of you."

"I have to rebuild myself," said Eric, a tall, angular man. "I can't show love if I can't understand it. I can't show empathy if I don't understand it."

"It's about self-worth," someone echoed. "I can't love if I don't know love."

"To me," one man said, "redemption is about continuing. It's not about undoing what I've done—it's about moving past it. Not burying it, but moving forward and saying, 'That's what I've done, and I'm never gonna do it again.'"

He considered his own words.

"It's not up and out; it's through."

There was an unavoidable knowledge of wrongdoing in their words, and that meant change. "You have to eliminate yourself," Eric had said, and it matched what many of his fellow inmates expressed. Some would hazard to destroy the self and rebuild it. Like the women at Bags to Butterflies, they were picking up the pieces and creating something new.

One voice, a prominent one, chimed in.

"I call it *the aha factor*," Gabriel said at last. "It's that moment when you realize you gotta do something different with your life."

For some men, Gabriel explained, that came when they were asked to write themselves a letter from the perspective of their victims. For others it was something wholly different but with the same outcome: they knew they needed to change. Frannie had told the two of us that many of these men would get out of prison someday soon. They had served nearly all their time and had behaved well enough to wind up in a minimum-security facility on the verge of freedom, prompting them to reckon with that coming day.

A shadow passed over Gabriel's face—the same expression as the one from his reading. He was Edgar again—the cast-out son, the fallen man.

"In order for me to have redemption, I have to do things exactly the opposite from the way I've usually done them," Gabriel observed. "I have to step outside myself. Something has gone so drastically awry that I have to try something new.

"I'm a crystal-meth junkie," he continued. "I've been here too many times. And my stepdad, the man who raised me, he is out there on the yard."

"Really?" someone barked.

"Yeah, right out there. Forty-eight years old. He's always been on the same stuff as me. He raised me. And he wants me to be like him, but I need to do something new. I need to break free. I don't want to be like that when I'm 48 years old. That's not what I want to be."

Gabriel leaned forward to peer around the room at the men sitting next to him, and Jordan saw him anew—his tattoos, one of which read "To the light"; his glassy emerald eyes; the rasp in his voice. There was a clarity to his words. His life had been a tragedy thus far, and he knew it. He had a chance to set things right. He had the conviction to change, and he knew what he could become if he didn't act. In fact, he faced it daily. But only God knew whether he would transcend it all.

"There's got to be a lot of 'want to' in you. Drive, you know?" Gabriel said. "You have to come to a point where you're not okay in your misery."

We drove away from Parnall and turned northeast. We had planned to travel through Canada, along the banks of Lake Ontario, on our way to upstate New York. Detroit was soon to be far behind us, yet we had a feeling it would have a hold on us for a long time to come.

We cut east, following the crooked highway as it pinched in toward Port Huron to make the Blue Water Bridge crossing at the border with Canada. Chris turned to Jordan.

"It doesn't seem right."

"What?"

"Well, that we get to just drive off, and they're still there."

It was hard to know what story to tell about Detroit. Acts pile up one after another. What we had seen, though, seemed to lead toward a reckoning with what had transpired and hope about what could follow. Satori's entreaty—to tell stories to heal—seemed ever-present, and stories were righting unmoored lives from Parnall to that workshop just off sweltering Eight Mile.

We had almost reached Ann Arbor when Jordan perked up.

"Smell that?" he said, looking in the rearview mirror.

Chris, who had his feet up on the dash, took a whiff.

"No—what is it?"

"Shit," Jordan said, fixing his eyes on something in the mirror. "We're on fire."

Within a moment, the car was engulfed in acrid smoke. Jordan pulled off onto a long exit ramp and eased the Boat to the shoulder. We hopped out and found the left rear tire smoldering and leaking ugly rubber smoke into the Michigan twilight. We had both been so lost in thought that neither of us had noticed. The silver edge of the wheel— perfect and polished from the heat—had cut through the tire.

We sat down and waited three hours for a tow truck, then watched as the driver cranked off each rusted lug nut and replaced the mangled tire with a temporary spare. As the sun disappeared and night turned the world purple and fuzzy, we gingerly steered the Boat down the road to a mechanic who could replace the tire in Milan, just off a railway track snarled with ivy.

"Well, I guess you were right," Jordan said.

"Huh?"

"It wasn't fair that we got to just drive away."

Portland

The harbormaster's boat cut a slender wake as it moved away from the docks and out into Casco Bay off the coast of Portland, Maine. The two of us had boarded along with Charlie, a 68-year-old deputy harbormaster, only moments before. We threw on life jackets and with the engine purring took off to patrol the bay.

Out on the water, we crawled past the docks. Not long ago, these piers teemed with fishing boats. Now they were largely empty—save for a Royal Caribbean ocean liner the size of a few city blocks. It towered above the water like an imperial man-of-war. Tourists bustled up and down Commercial Street in the Old Port as we pulled out into open water.

Charlie lazily steered the boat. Jordan stood at Charlie's side and Chris balanced behind, one hand on the pilothouse roof. It was a stagnant day that languished with dry heat from shore. On the water, though, a breeze lifted off the Atlantic and cut through the riggings and across the bow. As we went, we slipped in and out of fishing grounds, lobster buoys, pleasure-boat wakes, listing sailboats, and the wharves that dot the hundreds of miles of craggy shoreline of the Calendar Islands in southern Maine.

Portland

As we left the harbor's mouth, a wood-sided motorboat steamed by at a fast clip. Charlie, from behind dark sunglasses, waved his arm. *Slow*, his gesture said, and the painted colors on the harbormaster's hull prompted a slight downshift in the offending craft.

"We're not law enforcement," Charlie said. "If they don't want to listen to me, then I'll call the Coast Guard."

Some boats yielded to his authority. Others simply ignored us.

"Cop on the sea?" Captain Kevin Battle, the harbormaster, had said to us onshore before we boarded Charlie's ship.

"We're more like mall security," he joked.

We had come to the harbormaster in hopes of exploring Maine's storied lobstering industry. Chris had just taken a class on property law and had read about the industry in a famous book, *The Lobster Gangs of Maine* by James M. Acheson. Lobstering was an ancient profession. Native Americans used lobster for bait and fertilizer for centuries. Englishmen in Popham Colony fished the crustaceans out of the shallows as early as 1607. Once canning began in the 1840s, lobster reached markets more distant than Boston and New York. But this also led to a precipitous decline as "snappers"—small, still-growing lobsters—were caught and sold at market. Laws followed, including one prohibiting the snaring of pregnant females, and the population stabilized.

In response to this volatility, and through time, lobstermen—the term applies not just to men but to women as well—formed social groups and mores to regulate themselves. They formed harbor gangs and developed their own ways of drawing territories and resolving disputes. Old forms of vigilante justice were doled out to offenders of these codes, and lobstermen found a way to get along and make money despite their competing economic interests.

But this equilibrium was often challenged.

Lobstering had just taken a direct blow from a new tariff regime imposed not long before we arrived in Portland. That summer, President Trump had touched off a trade war with China. In June, the United States levied a slew of tariffs on more than $34 billion worth of

Chinese goods, including 6,000 items ranging from nuclear reactors to chicken incubators. China responded by slapping a 25 percent customs fee on American-made products, including Maine lobsters. Prices cratered as the burgeoning Chinese market turned toward Canada and other providers to sate its appetite.

All this and we couldn't find a single lobsterman.

"Good luck," Captain Battle had said from behind his desk. "They won't talk to you. They just won't trust you."

So we had cajoled him into sending us out on the water with Charlie instead. We had met Charlie on a wharf strewn with the chalky shells of oysters and clams, cracked into jagged pieces by the intruding beaks of harbor gulls. Charlie was a quiet man—a New England Protestant. He shook our hands and introduced himself politely as we jumped the gunwale and came aboard.

"Who's the first mate?" Jordan asked.

A small, panting dog in a life vest snaked in and out of the gear on the deck.

"I call him Dog," Charlie said dryly. "It works for him."

As we motored out toward the Calendar Islands, Dog scampered about the small craft—up and over buoys and coiled lines—often pacing his favorite lookout at the crest of the bow.

"Hey," Charlie yelled out as the wake of a Windermere sailboat came at us. Dog leaped down off the bow, then scurried along the gunwale and onto Charlie's foam seat in the pilothouse.

"The lobster boats slow down," he said, gesturing at Dog, who had returned to a balanced crouch on the bow. "They don't wanna dunk the dog."

Charlie seemed as skeptical of our purpose as Captain Battle had. "Did you ever see *Route 66*?" he asked after we mentioned our search. In an episode of the 1960s television show, Charlie said, two men went out on a lobster boat and came back with one of them bleeding and sprawled over the side of the vessel—the victim of some quarrel out on the water.

From afar, the lobster industry appeared to share some of its heritage with bootlegging and other backwoods enterprises. Blood feuds rivaling that of the Hatfields and McCoys broke out over grounds, permits, and slights real or imagined.

But violence was far from our minds that afternoon on Casco Bay. Sailboats rocked over gentle white crests of tidewater, and rolling green-golden hills hugged the bay tightly.

"Hold on, Dog," Charlie said as we plowed through another wake— our nose pointed back to harbor.

A few days before arriving in Maine, the two of us had driven from upstate New York to Vermont, where a friend of Chris's let us stay. The house was down a dirt road cut out of a leafy forest outside Peru. A wide pond gurgled behind the house. The curve of the misty Green Mountains stretched for miles just over a rise in the road no more than a couple of hundred yards beyond.

None of this registered upon our arrival. Chris simply pointed Jordan to his bedroom, then the two of us closed the doors to our respective rooms and did not emerge until well past sundown.

Not for another month or two did Chris identify what was weighing on him: Detroit had left him grieving. He woke in the morning exhausted. His outlook on life dimmed. Other mornings he would wake up rejuvenated, only to find his energy sapped moments into the day. There was a responsibility to what we had experienced. We had been entrusted with life stories—tragedies, mainly, with moments of small, incomplete redemptions—and that weight sat heavy on Chris.

Jordan also felt drained. For him, these trips had always been an opportunity to see the best of our country. Detroit revealed a more dismal side, one that he had always known was there but had never experienced. In the stories of the people we had met, he saw the distance between principles and practice in American life, and that gap was a challenge. America, he felt, was built on second chances. But too many of the people we had met in Detroit hadn't been given one.

A few days after leaving, Frannie had sent us a poem Gabriel wanted to share with us. It was titled "My State Blues," and he had scribbled on the side, "To Frannie, here's something to remind you of the people you give hope to."

"Lost my mind in far-off reverie," he wrote. "It now resides in a place where wild things grow . . . anchored to reality by headstones, row after row . . ."

It was written in rhyme.

"Focused on that elusive place 'home' that I claimed to once know . . . in My State Blues. Oblivious to common sense, facts . . . What gets us sent back? It's insanity, things done time and time again expecting that to warrant a change of events.

"Walking out on family and friends just to be caged-in, again and again."

We carried that weight to Portland. It made Chris crabby, and left a noticeable pall over Jordan as well. We had become a monosyllabic pair, save for the few times one of us mustered the energy to remind the other that our spells of silence were nothing personal. We were tangling with something larger, something fearful and nameless that careened around each of our thoughts and left us unsure what to do except to turn it over in our heads while we drove, mile after mile.

Captain Battle's pessimism didn't help things. Exhaustion had set in, and the thought that we might never find a lobsterman was deflating. Jordan still sent out emails—even turning to LinkedIn to search "lobster" and "Portland ME." He typed away even as we disembarked from Charlie's patrol boat that afternoon and returned to the muggy heat of the Portland waterfront.

Frustrated in our search and stained pink and red by the sun, we dawdled in the parking lot of a local bank off Commercial Street. The murmurs of the Old Port wafted above the hum of the straining air-conditioner, but none of it was loud enough to drown out our own internal dialogues. We hunched over a late lunch—lobster rolls and fries from a local shack on the water.

"I'm not sure I like lobster," Chris said.

"It's not for everyone," Jordan responded.

Come morning, we found the piers along Commercial Street adorned with the dried tails of fish snagged long ago. The sun had tanned them gray. The alleys were wet with offal and the spray of leaking hoses. Men in waders, dragging vats of ice, slipped in and out of clapboard doors and into dark rooms where tubs of water churned. It was our second day in Portland, and we were still looking for a lobsterman. But that day we were looking for one in particular—a man named Willis Spear.

The night before, Jordan had finally heard back from one of the lobstermen he had contacted.

"I called a couple of friends who are lifelong lobstermen," the man had written. "One of them said he would be willing to talk with you."

Jordan called the number, and a voice on the other end told us to meet him at the docks around 10 a.m.

Willis, a resident of nearby Yarmouth, had a reputation on the docks. He was something of an activist. When the city council proposed easing zoning laws so that pleasure yachts could moor where lobster schooners had tied off for decades, he took to the water, according to local news sources. Calling other boats over his VHF radio, he carried a petition across the bay on his own 35-foot rig, collecting nearly 70 signatures to halt the change. The new zoning ordinance would have made the moorings prohibitively expensive. As far as Willis was concerned, it threatened lobstering as a way of life.

It was the first salvo in what seemed like a battle for the future of the waterfront. Custom House Wharf, where more than $150 million in seafood was hauled ashore each year, was up for redevelopment. Real estate firms had proposed condominiums, hotels, and parking garages. The lobstermen feared they would be pushed out of their berths—and for good reason. They were already losing wages because tourism traffic was blocking their perishable shipments from getting to market. Worst of all, their voices were being ignored.

Jordan showed Chris a photo of Willis from a news article. He stood next to a sign about ensuring fishermen had access to parking along the wharf. He had broad shoulders, a thatch of wild white hair, thin glasses, and long, ill-fitting jeans. This was our man—if we could find him.

We stopped first at the Porthole, a local bar along the wharf, and found a waitress with blond hair pulled back in a ponytail.

"Pretty sure Willis was just here," she said. But he was out on the water now. We were too late.

The waitress directed us to the working side of the dock, and we made our way over. The restaurant side boasted live music every night and smelled of Clorox and other cleaning fluids; this side stank of fish guts. Metal parts lay rusted and warped with salt and sun and time. A woman in an apron threw fish heads to cackling gulls. Lobster traps tangled with vascular rope lines were stacked along the docks below the piers. This was the famous working waterfront. The lobsterman's narrow domain.

We walked up and down the dock in search of Willis's boat, the *Providence,* and found it along a placid stretch of wharf near the mouth of the channel.

"Guess we're not too late," Jordan said, but Willis was nowhere to be found.

At a loss, Jordan turned to two men in knee-high boots—one young and one old—huddled over something he couldn't make out. They had been eyeing the two of us as we pointed at the *Providence* and stood, puzzled, beside the dock's splintered pylons. As Jordan approached, he found the younger of the two rolling a cigarette.

"Willis?" the older man said. "I heard he was in the hospital."

"But we spoke to him this morning."

"Oh," the man said, watching the other pinch the cigarette and lick its length. "Well, that's good news. You might try the Porthole, then—see if he's having a pint."

Things felt dire again.

"It's only 10:30 in the morning," Chris said to Jordan as we surveyed pink salmon flanks, gray shrimp, and purple tuna at the Harbor Fish Market. "And already we've heard this guy might be dying—or tying one on."

We returned to the Porthole and sat at the brass bar. Leon Bridges played on the stereo. Gulls yapped wildly from roof spines. The Old Port looked like a Colonial relic, all narrow alleyways and tightly packed buildings. Indeed, Portland had been burned down and reborn over and over again throughout its 400-year history. Each turn added a layer of worn history to the cobblestone paths winding along the harbor.

After loafing by the bar for a few minutes, we tried the *Providence* again—and there stood Captain Spear.

"Come on board," Willis said, and the two of us climbed a yellow ladder down to the deck below. Willis, 67, was an imposing man with a jutting jaw and a thick chest. His face was wrinkled, his lips chapped. He kept a worn hat snug to his ears. Willis was a workingman, and he carried himself tall.

After brief introductions, Willis confessed this was a workday for him—he couldn't stop for us. He had bait to fetch and repairs to make. But he agreed to bring us along for an hour or so.

With Willis at the helm, the *Providence* motored down the dock to where an ancient man in an oiler waited with black plastic boxes of rotting haddock and herring, gray sole, scrod, and other groundfish.

"Now I don't want you touching this stuff," Willis said to us with fatherly care. "Once you touch it, you can't get it off you." The man in the oiler nodded.

Willis, grunting, took aboard one heavy crate of fish after another. Each sloshed with rank liquid as he bent under the weight. Like Charlie, Willis was a soft-spoken, humble man. He tried to wave away a check the bait man offered, accepting it only after the man quietly insisted with adamant, excited words.

We pulled back up to the dock, lashed the *Providence* to a berth, and chatted under the eve of the pilothouse. Willis was intent on installing a cleat on the side of the boat. A stabilizer sail flapped in the wind while he examined the hull and planned his repairs. We pleaded with him to let us help, but he refused. Within minutes, he was drenched in sweat. His joints flexed deliberately with age and use.

Slowly, Willis let us pitch in. We could move a crate of fish here, then stack another atop that one there—snugly, of course. Before long we were bent over, helping to measure and mark for Willis's drill. We spent the rest of the day outfitting the ship. There were lobster boxes to lug aboard and stack tall. The bait needed to be shifted up-deck. We toiled away at all the small labors required to make the *Providence* sea-ready.

"First day back in a while," Willis said, sitting up, sweat on his cheeks. As he recovered, he tapped at his chest. Heart attack two weeks ago, he explained.

"It was a warning. I'm glad I listened."

After a stent was put in his chest, he had been laid up in his family cottage on Long Island in Casco Bay for the past four days.

"Should you be working?" Chris asked.

"Oh yeah—I'm fine."

And with that, he mustered a deep reserve of energy for the final fastening of the cleat to the fiberglass hull of the *Providence*. Willis got up, painfully, and tied off the sail.

"Where you from?" he asked us. He twisted the line up and over the pegs of the cleat, grimacing with the effort.

"Los Angeles," Jordan said.

"I'm from the Bay Area," Chris added. "Berkeley."

"Berkeley, huh?" Willis said. "My pop was born in Stockton. Grandparents worked for Del Monte Food farther south around the Depression."

"Yeah, not that far."

"You know that author—what's his name—Steinbeck?"

"John Steinbeck."

"Yeah, that's him. I love *Cannery Row*. You know it? What's that bay down there?"

"Monterey."

"Monterey, that's right."

Willis uncoiled himself and stood at his full height.

"You know my favorite line? What is it? From *Cannery Row.*"

He pushed his glasses up his nose to wipe his eyes and consider it.

"*A troubled glass of misunderstood virtue,*" he said. "I love that line. It about describes my life."

———————

His work complete and the sun setting below its meridian, Willis had turned to us. "So," he had said, any hint of distrust long since evaporated into the heat of the harbor, "what do you want to know?"

Willis was a fisherman, and fishermen are dock people. They tie up at the wharf, mend traps, drink liquor and watery beer, avoid their spouses, and kvetch about the small tragedies of a working way of life. The docks are their domain. A fiefdom for pilots and captains and deckhands alike. Although, in Portland those days, there was often another presence: the tourists.

"They're so desperate to see the real America," Willis said. "I mean we're running out of it. That's what they're looking for."

He told us about the tragedy unfolding on the docks in Portland, as he saw it. Each year, tourists flooded into the city to experience the vibrancy of an endangered working waterfront. "I mean I'm not bad with tourists," Willis explained. "I can live with them, but there are times when I can't get to my boat. The wharf is full of cars—four or five deep—and they don't give a shit. They might be in the Porthole restaurant, having a burger and a glass of wine. I'll go in there and say, 'Look, I gotta get out on the water.' And it's like talking to the dog, you know? So then I'll say, 'I'm gonna tow.' And then I get their attention that way.

"Everybody wants to be here," he continued. "Because this is the last of the Wild West. You guys are down here with the last of the cowboys, or whatever."

Willis had already reminded us a bit of Pete Mylen, the trucker who ferried us from Las Vegas to Louisiana. They both had solidity and wisdom after decades of labor in hard professions. And they had used the same phrase—*the last of the cowboys*—nearly word for word. Pete and Willis were lenses into the worlds of the men and women who laid the foundations for the present, good and bad. They were a reminder of something about our past, and perhaps a harbinger of our future too.

"You feel like you're a monkey in a cage," Willis said, his words snapping. "And the tourists, they just stare at you and they'll literally tear the boards off these buildings to get a look."

He shook his head. A pang of guilt washed over us. Were we so different from the vulturine tourists? We too had wanted to experience the lobster industry. We had hustled our way into it, calling and pestering a number of people until we found Willis.

"Are the waterfronts being sold?"

"It's been discovered. Like all waterfronts in America," Willis said. "This place right here, right now as we speak, is one of the most sought-after places in America."

Waterfronts were becoming the battleground for competing forces: traditional industries and ways of life on one hand, development and tourist demand on the other. And with each passing day, that conflict felt more existential for the less-monied fishermen and trappers of the docks.

"The city is kind of giving away the crown jewels," Willis said. "The history of it and how important it is for the next generation and for people..." His voice trailed off. "The heritage," Willis said. "It's the heritage that's being taken away."

"It's good of you to stick around to lend a hand," Willis had said to us earlier in the day. We had long ago finished the repairs on the *Providence*. "Most of the time people will come down and talk and then—"

He gestured out with his arms like waves disappearing over a far-off horizon.

"I think you've earned a trip around the bay," he said. "Come on, I'll take you with me to Long Island."

We may not have been able to go out fishing for lobsters, but at least we were getting to sail across the bay with a lobsterman. We helped Willis stow his tools, and with everything set we untied the moorings holding the *Providence* fast and set a course out into the harbor. Willis stood at the helm and the two of us leaned against the wooden lobster tank beside him.

Along the way, Willis began to call out different landmarks on the coastline. He pointed to a gun emplacement on a large hill overlooking the bay. It was a cannon from the U.S.S. *Maine,* the famous ship whose sinking launched the Spanish-American War in 1898.

"And that over there is Willard Beach," he pointed. "That's where I took my wife on our first date."

It was also where Willis's father taught him to mend a line and bait a trap. He had grown up on Casco Bay, and as a boy he had learned all about its shores. Willard Beach was where they would spend nights and dry fish. But now the beach was peppered with million-dollar homes, he explained.

"When I was a boy, I learned from these guys on Long Island," Willis said. "The same island that my wife's got this little house on. They taught me how to fish. I would row and haul traps in a small wooden rowboat when I was 12 or 13. I just loved it. And as I got older I got a boat with an outboard motor. I'd lobster with guys during the day. We'd get in at dinnertime. I wouldn't go home to eat. I'd go out in my little boat and haul like 25 more traps or something. Just loved it."

Back then, the Maine fisheries were plentiful. "If you read anything about the history, the reason this place was settled is because of the fish. And all the early explorers, from like the very early 1600s, said they never saw anything like it. The quantity and quality of the fish that were just out here. And we got a chance to see the tail end of it, before they just disappeared. I started fishing in '76, and by '86 they were gone. Within 10 years they were all gone."

Willis and his fellow fishermen had been pulling too many fish out of the water. Getting rich off the ancient fisheries, they thought little about what was to come. Willis saw it happening and sounded the alarm. He tried to tell people what would happen if they kept taking small fish and pregnant fish and even adults without temperance, but no one seemed to listen. He joined councils and commissions, and even became president of the Fishermen Co-op, but no one would take heed.

"I still fished because everybody else did," Willis said. "But I'd go to meetings and I'd say, 'Hey, we ought to stop.' I got laughed out of the room."

In the early 1980s, fishermen across New England hauled 100 million pounds of fish out of the water each year. By 2016, that number was a meager 3.2 million. With the cod fisheries collapsing, Willis swallowed his pride and began shrimping in the winter and lobstering when the weather changed. The money wasn't as good, but he loved it. In the meantime, his children were getting bigger and becoming men in their own right. A few of them were attracted to the same industry as their father.

He tried to persuade the government and the fishing industry to close down certain areas for a while so the fish could spawn, or to try a new method of fishing instead of towing nets.

"I was trying to do something for the next generation," he said. "Not for me, just for the next generation."

The federal government eventually imposed quotas, and fishermen became versed in the language of conservation, but their Damascus road moment may have come too late. Northeast cod fishing in 2018 was the least valuable in half a century. And some experts project lobster populations will plummet by another 40 to 60 percent in the next 30 years.

Willis didn't believe such dire predictions, however. There are stirrings of life in the old fisheries. The quota for 2018 was bumped up ever so slightly, and Willis has heard tell of massive schools of fish, ripe with eggs.

"It was a hoot," Willis said. "Never thought I'd see them again in my lifetime."

Around sundown, we pulled into a quiet harbor on Long Island, where several boats rocked in their berths to the rhythms of the soft tide. Rusting lobster traps lined the shore, and the white wooden planks of the dock creaked under our feet as we made our way to land.

"Come on," Willis said. "I'll give you a tour of the island."

It was a 15-minute walk to Willis's house on the opposite shore. We cut across a junkyard filled with old maritime equipment, making our way onto a road that wound up and away from the bay.

Willis's house was a warm, wood-sided home with a chimney running through the center. His wife, Christine, greeted us with a gruff hello. There was suspicion in her tone, and she put us to work immediately, moving two-by-fours into their basement.

Time passed, and Willis and Christine invited us to have dinner with them. We ate pizza and salad with olives and grilled chicken with a few beers and a bottle of pinot noir that Jordan had brought.

The two of them spoke charmingly about their early years together—Christine's life as a fisherman's daughter and now as a fisherman's wife, and the years when the sea provided a small fortune. But their life together had not been without its own dramas. Willis had a boat and a slip, and so did his sons. But they also once owned large shares of entire wharfs and shipped fish and lobster all over the East Coast. There were ebbs and flows to the Spear family's fortunes. The ocean could be fickle, and so could fate. Fourteen years ago, Willis and Christine lost one of their sons to cancer on Christmas Eve.

"I had four sons," Willis had said on the ride over. "Now," his voice trailing off as he held up three fingers.

After dinner, Willis took us on a tour of the island, telling us sagas of money, betrayal, and marriages somehow constantly on the rocks. He carried with him generations of stories, and he told them as if that history were a part of him and ever-present. They were elements of his identity and his sense of place in the world. Earlier that morning, Willis had told us a story about his ancestor, one of the first settlers in Maine, and how he had nearly died in the 1600s on an expedition near the Finger Lakes. Various other Spears littered the history of Maine. Willis carried their memories, which connected him to his past and thrust him into the future through all the generations of Spears to come. Like the needle on a compass, these stories coalesced to give him a true north—one tethered to the rocky coastline and the shifting waters that carved it.

Eventually, Willis drove us to the port to await the 7 p.m. ferry back to Portland. He parked his truck and we watched the sun set over the water. The sky was painted pink and red and orange as a cold wind passed through the windows of Willis's pickup. A distant peak shimmered on the far-off horizon like an earthen jewel.

On the ferry back to shore, the two of us started to open up again.

The tension of Detroit was easing. The evening had also given us a deeper understanding of the precariousness of Willis's life. He and Christine were getting by, but their financial situation was touch-and-go. Christine went back to work as a nurse to help pay their bills. Willis's fortunes were tied to his daily hauls, which seemed to bring in less and less each year, and were now imperiled by his heart attack. It was a lot for one family to bear.

Yet Willis projected comfort, even safety—a kind of rootedness. Perhaps it came from his sense of history and his place in it. His stories were of a particular heritage, one handed down from generation to generation and embedded in his memory and identity. Even through struggle, they allowed him to make sense of the world.

———————

The morning was purple over Casco Bay, and the docks were cast in gray. They reminded us of the wharfs off San Francisco, where crabs are hauled in by the thousands and sea lions bark their displeasure at passersby. When we arrived, the *Providence*'s engine was already purring as the mirage of the sunrise spread across a low bank of white clouds. Gulls cawed overhead—a pelagic symphony above the docks of New England.

"Don't get on until we lay bait, okay?" Willis said to us as we approached, laden with coffee and sunscreen. He and his sternman, Tim, were already hard at work.

The night before, as we awaited the ferry, Chris had delicately asked if we could join Willis for the lobster hunt the next day.

"Well," Willis equivocated.

"We'd bring coffee," Chris said.

"And we'd stay out of your way," Jordan added.

"You'd have to be there real early."

"What time?"

"Five-thirty."

"We'd be there at five," Chris said.

Willis watched the surf as the ferry churned toward the dock, alight with deck lamps.

"I take mine with two sugars," Willis relented. "And Tim does a triple-triple."

So we were back—back on the dock, cupping coffee, under the flinty morning light on a day begun before the sun heralded its start.

"We might spill some bait and wash it off," Willis continued. "And you can get fish poisoning if you get it in a cut. It can go septic." A thick hose was put upon the stack of flesh, and Tim started picking through the bait. He tossed fish one by one with a finger in one of their gills. The soiled water leaked about the boat.

"Thought this was going to stink a lot worse, Captain," Tim said as Willis slipped on white gloves and joined Tim in picking through the vat of rot. Box after box of fish went into a large plastic vat that sat at the center of the deck like some gory altar. They sprayed and picked through each group, looking over the decomposition, seeking the ripest for the lobster below.

"The lobster where we're going don't like cod," Willis said. "The rest is herring." And lobster did enjoy herring, we learned.

The sorting complete, it was time to hose down the deck. Tim, a volunteer firefighter on Long Island, wielded the hose deftly.

"Come aboard," Willis said at last. "You're safe now."

Tim set about preparing the bait by spearing the fish and slipping them into mesh bags, while Willis assumed his position behind the steering wheel.

As we motored out to the islands, Willis regaled the two of us with stories of ocean gold. How the English once dried fish with a pinch of salt on island beaches and hauled them to Boston for market. How the sardines in Canada made millionaires of their mongers when the region was finally connected to New York City. How the English and French killed each other over herring in battle after battle.

Tim smoked a cigarette as he worked. The two of them had laid the traps two weeks ago, before Willis's heart had stopped. Traps are typically pulled back up after three to five days; any longer than that and the lobsters can slip away to freedom. There was no telling how many crustaceans were left. Willis's mortgage, his license, his bait and repair costs, and Tim's paycheck all depended on whether the lobsters had settled into the traps or had found their way out. Tim, puffing away, stole a moment of serenity as the sun rose and we charged into the bay.

The first buoy—which signaled a line of eight traps below—was hauled aboard with gusto. Willis steamed up to it and hooked the schooner around, flicking out a boat hook and looping the line into a winch. The engine roared and the line began to coil, helped along by the gentle touch of Willis's gloved hand. Seawater spun off it, and then the first cage came up out of the depths. Tim hauled up a dozen boxes, one at a time. They were teeming with lobsters.

Tim and Willis picked through each box, inspecting the lobsters for size and eggs. The smaller ones were tossed back unceremoniously and the acceptable ones were put in a box on deck where they thrashed once or twice, scooting backward like squid or gnashing their claws before settling into a stupor. The ones Tim didn't have time to weigh went into a bucket. Occasionally it would tip over, sending a few of the animals scurrying for cover. The red accents on their armor shimmered in the sun as they skittered across the white deck.

Willis picked one up and turned it over. He touched its tail a few times and pressed about its belly. "Eggs," he mumbled. Then he pulled out what looked like a set of pliers and snipped a *V* out of its tail. "It's a legal-size female," he said, showing it to Chris, who perched behind him in the pilothouse. A *V* had been cut into her already, but it was small—only a close look revealed it.

"She can breed again," he said, touching the now-undeniable notch of missing chitin. "This *V* means no one can take her."

Any lobster schooner found with her in its hold would be cited, or maybe even worse. Willis tossed her off the boat and she hit the water with a splash.

"It helps perpetuate the species," Willis said.

There is a contradiction at the heart of the hunter's profession. Willis and lobstermen like him depend on taking great sums of life out of the ocean. Fortunes are made on the size and weight of that haul. The best take in the most. But each boat's future depends on doing so responsibly. Lobstermen relied on building a resilience into their culture that kept that life ongoing. Quotas and state inspections do only so much. Willis hadn't been boarded in years. So people like him relied on nothing more than the power of their culture—the power of their example, and the pride and shame of generations before and since hanging over each boat—to keep pregnant female lobsters in the depths.

Jordan stood near Tim, watching him prep the freshly pulled traps with new bait and tying them on the back of the boat, to be laid down below once again.

"How was this for a haul?" Jordan asked, pointing at the tub of lobster. "Is this considered good?"

"Decent," Tim muttered as we motored away. He tapped out a cigarette. Twelve or so lobster were splayed atop one another in the holding tank.

We spent the morning hauling. Up came the cages and Willis and Tim would sort through their contents, throwing crabs, under-size lobsters, and claylike mud back overboard. Tim replenished each cage with fetid fish as they went through their routine. After the last cage was pulled and Tim sweetened the trap again, Willis gave the signal and Tim pushed over the first cage. They dropped like cargo out of a plane, the line between each cage writhing like a living creature as the boxes descended.

As the line whipped overboard, Tim and Willis kept their distance. As if animated by some man-made hand of the deep, when these lines spring to life they become one of the deadliest elements of a lobsterman's life. Many lobstermen have reported losing an item of clothing, getting bludgeoned against the stern by a kink in the line, or losing a crew member overboard to a biting rope. The two of us treated them like deadly snares, warily plastering ourselves against the gunwales and pilothouse as they thrashed.

As the day wore on, Willis pawed through the lobsters in the holding tank, inspecting them as they crawled over one another. "Lobsters are like rattlesnakes," Willis said. "They're hardwired. They don't feel. They're not nice to you or each other. They like eating their neighbors' brain and claws. They're primitive."

Chris didn't know whether to believe him, but as he stared down into the water at the growing mass of arthropods, they looked unthinking. Or maybe they looked defeated, unsure of the walls and limits of their captivity.

The day turned out to be a slow haul. Some cages came up empty. Others had a handful of lobsters. "I'm just grateful for what we're getting," Willis confessed.

As we motored farther away from land, Willis stretched a finger out over the blue expanse of water. "It's like the Appalachians out there— peaks and valleys. You never know where the lobsters will be, or why they move." Willis reached for a waterproof notebook. He crossed out a crate number and put his pencil on a long string of digits— coordinates. And soon we were off toward another string.

As the sun reached its meridian, Tim and Jordan were talking on deck. Chris, however, was somewhat worse for wear. The scent of the fish had turned his stomach.

"How many more?" Chris asked.

"We have 800 out there," Tim said, "but I don't know how many he's going to pull. He's only supposed to pull 100 with his heart."

"Scary."

"Especially out there." Tim pointed to the open ocean. "People will come to help you out, but for an emergency like that?"

"Four more strings," Willis yelled back. "Bait them a little heavy."

"Yes, Captain," Tim said.

We spun around and Willis frowned as we rocked in our own wake and the winch dragged up the first cage. "Tide's really ripping here."

Willis developed a slight overbite of a smile as he reeled in the traps. He and Tim worked the line masterfully, pulling traps, discarding the insides, rebaiting them, and pushing them back into place for release. Chris had decamped to the pilothouse to avoid the smell of the baitfish. From that vantage, he considered Willis's figure. With one hand on the helm and his jaw clenched at a slight angle, his other hand shot out and hooked the line. Then, with the slap of a lever, Willis set the winch sputtering to life. It was a striking image of a man at work. Each of his movements was timed, measured, and calibrated to the demands of the task, performed in one way or another for close to five centuries. This was as much an art as an act of commerce. Tim slapped open another cage, cigarette hanging from his lip, baited the box, and guided it down the gunwale with remarkable dexterity.

"It's like reading a month-old newspaper," Willis said, scanning his notebook. "Too much time has happened since we laid them. It's hard to know whether there's more to come."

"I think we did okay," Willis said as he inspected the tank, which roiled with pumped water. Through the ripples, the dark carapaces of the lobsters blended into one mass of brown freckled shells and bent arachnid-like legs. All told we pulled 22 lines that day holding about 180 traps, then laid those same traps back in the water heavy with fresh bait. Willis and Tim would pick them up again in four days or so, inspecting the slopes and valleys of the underwater mountain ranges for their next bounty.

As we approached land, a wave of relief washed over us. We couldn't imagine how exhausted Tim and Willis must have felt. But they seemed unfazed—even a little disappointed.

"We kept it short today," Willis said. "I need to ease back into it after the heart attack."

Back at the dock, Willis and Tim hunched over the tub of lobsters and packed them up individually, slipping bands on their claws to keep them from wriggling away or nabbing a finger. They expertly plucked them from the tub by their tails, keeping their fingers out of reach of the pincers. Each lobster flailed at an obscene angle before being plunged back into a crate and out of the sun once more. Their instinct to wriggle, to push backward like squid, was long gone.

Willis and Tim worked in silence, counting and tagging their haul. Above them on the wharf, fishmongers stood ready to drag each crate up and into the frozen air of the refrigerator behind them. The men amused themselves by throwing fish heads and watching the gulls fight over them like hyenas as they awaited Willis's bounty.

Four crates of lobster—the reason for our entire day—were wheeled into a darkened chamber behind the men. We waited for the final count in the sun. Willis stood on the deck, chest heaving, hat pulled low over his brow. His forearms glistened with sweat. He bobbed up and down with the gentle swells of the harbor as Tim sprayed the deck behind him.

The scene recalled a passage out of Acheson's *Lobster Gangs*. These men and women were self-made sailors without masters, but they relied upon one another. Like any commons, there was a community at stake each time one of them motored out to the fishing grounds or laid a net or a trap. "There is some truth in these stereotypes," Acheson wrote of the cowboy mythology around these men and women. "A man who cannot operate a boat and handle his fishing gear alone at sea does not last long in the business.

"Yet on the whole, such stereotypes are misleading," Acheson continued. "They obscure the fact that the lobster fisherman is caught up in a thick and complex web of social relationships. Survival in the industry depends as much on the ability to manipulate social relationships as on technical skills."

We had found it went further than this. It's not just *social manipulation*—a term only a law professor could love—but the sewing and mending of social fabric. Willis tended to his community. He wasn't a cowboy. He was an elder. A keeper of oral history and tradition. A watchman over the fisheries and an essential part of this wild system of fishing on the North Atlantic. He did not manipulate social relationships; he helped define them, nurture them, and sustain them.

"Hey," one of the fishmongers with tennis shoes and a backward hat said to us. "You've found the hardest-working man on the docks."

———

We spent the next two nights in Rockport, Massachusetts, a few miles north of Gloucester. Gloucester, like Portland, is famed for its fishing industry and was immortalized in Sebastian Junger's *The Perfect Storm*. But Rockport, just a five-minute drive up the coast, felt more like a getaway for the Kennedys and Winthrops and other American brahmins—more refined than any stretch of coast we saw in Maine.

We were nearly done with a five-week road trip, and the warm relief of being shore-bound and free from the stench of the baitfish loosened us up. We had started to come back to life at a fish shack called Susan's in Deering Junction, past the back cove of Portland. We had shambled into the airy restaurant stinking of fish and sweat. Two live lobsters in a plastic bag hung from Chris's arm, and we asked if they would cook them up. The waitress was happy to oblige, and we sprawled out over a plastic table to wait stoically for our food. Chris's stomach was sour, but he'd be damned before he'd give up his loot.

The lobsters arrived orange and set in fatty liquid. We cracked away—scalding our fingers pink on their steaming husks—and ate until our shirts and hands oozed with water and guts. The two of us slurped the claw meat and licked at what spilled. It was buttery and flavorful on its own—the fruit of the sea delivered within hours of being pulled from her depths. Chris had sworn off fish at one point while riding the swells of Casco Bay. That lobster changed his mind.

As we drove through Gloucester that night, we looped down toward the shore. Along a boardwalk, toddlers stumbled around the grass with American flags in hand. Linen-clad adults ordered barbecue from tents, threw Frisbees, and milled about the water in the pink light of sunset. The promise of weekend fireworks had brought out scores of people.

We hung a left and began to pull away from the shoreline.

"Look," Jordan said, his eyes on the rearview mirror. Chris turned around and saw it. Down the boardwalk, toward the point of the cove where the water was the gentlest, was a statue of a man cast in bronze and facing the sea.

It stood in the southwest of Gloucester, visible from all over the city. The man was green from a concoction of age and the spit of the sea sent ashore. He was bent over a ship's wheel and clad in oilskins and a brimmed sou'wester. His eyes were fixed on the horizon. He was braced as if for an oncoming wake, rough seas, or perhaps something more menacing than the tides.

The town had erected the cenotaph in the 1920s to honor three centuries of sailors and fishermen lost at sea. The dead were remembered on its base, where the sculptor had carved hundreds of names—lost on the Georges and LaHave Banks, off Cape Sable, and in the waters of the Bay of Fundy. THEY THAT GO DOWN TO THE SEA IN SHIPS, read the inscription on its pedestal. "They mount up to the heaven, they go down again to the depths, their soul is melted because of trouble," the psalm it is borrowed from continues.

This statue memorializes those who braved much to build what exists today, hailing from cities such as Gloucester and Portland and Yarmouth and countless seaside towns up and down the Eastern Seaboard. In the history of the New England coast was the courage it takes to face a capricious sea, year in and year out.

As the silhouette of the "Man at the Wheel" passed across the Boat's rearview mirror, there was the flash of something more sinister, too. In that unerring, ocean-fixed gaze was the blinding desire for wealth that led to ruin. It was the same look that drove fishermen to ignore the lines of cod eggs splayed out on unwashed decks, or developers to keep lengthening the shadow of scaffolding and high-rises encroaching on the waterfront in Portland.

History is replete with such human failure, but failure alone is no reason for shame. Willis toiled daily to shed the ugly greed and short-sightedness of his birthright, and to cherish all that made him and his fishing kin large and historic. History can be more than just a series of scars and lessons. It helps us bear hardship, find wisdom, and imagine a brighter future for the generation that follows.

Jordan had known of this statue and had kept an eye out for it as we drove. And there he was, the timeless form of the fisherman, poised for combat with a furious sea, lost in another kind of sea altogether. The new Gloucester leaned up against him, playing at his feet in boat shoes and Ray-Bans.

We were with him, and with our thoughts, for a fleeting moment. Then we turned away from the esplanade, and the "Man at the Wheel" faded from sight and passed into memory.

PART III

Augusta

First there was a shudder, and a yellow warning light flickered on the
dash. Nothing out of the ordinary for the rattling Boat. Chris was
alone and behind the wheel, driving past Augusta, Georgia, in an April
heat. It was spring of 2019, and Chris had taken the car south from
New York to meet Jordan in Atlanta, where we would begin our last
road trip. From there, the two of us planned to wheel through Mississippi and Alabama, westward across the gulf to New Orleans, on to
Tulsa and then west toward Idaho, and eventually back to San
Francisco.

As Chris set off, tornadoes, blizzards, and thunderstorms swept east
and south. A heavy rain fell in gray New York the day before Chris
left the tristate area. Despite the weather, we were brimming with
excitement to get back on the road. This trip would be uplifting—
maybe even a little triumphant. We were setting off to retrace our
steps and to tell the stories of people like Gabriel and Pete and Satori
and Frannie and others who had inspired us.

Still, Chris was conflicted. He had one goal remaining: to reconcile
his skepticism with what we had seen on the road. One America
was well catalogued in newspapers and magazines. The opioid crisis

was worsening. Violence was on the rise. Middle-class incomes were stagnant. Yet over and over again we had met optimistic people. Often they were clear-eyed about what was going on around them. Some of them expressed this optimism from the most dreary and disheartening places—prisons, empty roads, dead-end jobs. Yet there they were, giving reasons to keep plugging on.

For Jordan's part, his own initial optimism had been borne out, but Chris's wait-and-see approach had influenced him, too. He had developed a deeper understanding for the ways in which America's promise fell short. Some things went beyond political discontent. We had seen those problems manifested in Detroit, Portland, Naco, and even Page. Jordan was hoping to find some way to channel the optimism we saw among the people we met into ways we might fix the structural challenges that riddled the country.

Despite our distinct goals, traveling together had certainly given us a shared understanding of our differences and how those differences reflected the most fundamental values we held as individuals. And we could recognize those values in one another. We had internalized the lesson we learned back at Mono Lake—that finding common ground wasn't always about getting to agreement. It was about getting to the point where disagreement didn't matter as much.

By now we were old hands at these trips. We knew each other's temperaments, diets, and sleep habits. Few obstacles seemed insur-mountable, which is why Chris did not make much of that shudder as he passed over a slope on the highway in central Georgia. Especially since we had recently gotten the Boat a tune-up.

A mechanic in Long Island just off Queens Boulevard had spruced up the beloved Volvo just a week before—new spark plugs, brake pads, tire rotation, the works. Chris picked it up and found the place littered with sedans and oil slicks and a collection of mechanics insisting we were getting the best possible deal for just a few thousand dollars. Soon after, we had noticed a *clank* emanating from the back-left wheel well. Each pump of the brakes elicited a series of rhythmic *clunks*. So we had brought the car to another mechanic near the banks of the Mianus River in Connecticut, where a man with wide eyes shone a flashlight between the tires.

"Mind?" he said, making a steering-wheel gesture, and by the time he pulled the Boat back into the lot we had an answer.

"The rotor," he said. "It's the rotor."

The three of us stared at the back tire for a moment.

"Will we need to replace it?" Jordan asked.

"No—but eventually."

"We're driving to California."

"Oh," the man said. "Oh, yeah."

Jordan went inside to set up the repair.

"California, how long?" the man said to Chris.

"Ten days or so, man," Chris replied. "Long."

"Yeah, too long," the mechanic said.

He poked something inside the wheel rim.

"I drove from North Carolina—south and up. Seventeen hours. Too, too much," he continued.

"Oy, yeah."

Chris put his hands on his back and grimaced.

"Yes, yes," the man said and made the same gesture.

"It's our seventh time," Chris said, and the man shook his head.

We had driven out of his garage that day, and Chris started his drive south soon after without issue. He passed through balmy Washington, D.C., on his way toward Charleston. He drove through back woods in South Carolina past blue HURRICANE EVACUATION ROUTE signs depicting geometric cyclones. He drove until he reached the top of that hill on a Georgia highway and the shudder gave way to a sudden lurch and a grating sound echoed and the Boat plunged forward and backward and the entire car fell into an uncontrollable shake.

———

Before Chris left, we had spent three days in lower Manhattan in and around Jordan's apartment. By that time, both of us had entered the workforce. Jordan was working in New York for a venture company that invested in science, technology, and efforts to help the middle class, and Chris was based in Berkeley, writing and traveling. So while Jordan went off to work each morning, Chris wandered the mid-20s around Sixth Avenue, where the Freedom Tower loomed out of a sickly fog that clung around the city.

The weekend came and we drove north to Connecticut for a Passover Seder. On the way up, we talked about the effects of corporate money in politics, what was ailing the media, and even climate.

"We all agree there's a problem, but I think the green movement is taking the wrong approach," Jordan said. "We know some amount of climate change is happening. And even if we don't know what the effect will be in the long run, the worst-case scenario is so bad that we have to do something about it. But that can't come at the expense of economic growth. We need that to fight poverty and raise living standards around the world, too. I think our focus should be on better science and creating new technologies."

The old debate still made Chris tense. Yet by this point we knew how to go about it.

"Exactly," Chris said. "The humble approach is to say we don't know how bad the consequences can get, so let's take prudent action now. The problem is there are still people who deny it's happening."

"I actually don't think there are many people who deny it outright anymore. Most Republicans I know just reject the alarmism that's often used in these debates—like, 'We have a decade before climate change is irreversible,' or whatever—especially when the solutions offered create winners and losers that benefit Democrats politically, and hurt the U.S. competitively."

"Well, we may only have 10 years. But in either case, we need a sense of urgency to create action. Otherwise the oil-and-gas industry—these big, entrenched interests—will block any meaningful change."

"I get the urgency part, but every time claims are exaggerated and then turn out not to be right, it reduces the overall credibility of the movement. It gives opponents reason to say that we shouldn't listen to the alarmism."

"That's why we need more funding for basic research," Chris said, "so we can make reliable climate models as accurate as possible. We've got to get to a point where we agree enough about the problem that we can focus on solutions. Continuing to build trust in the science is a first step toward everything else, and that should be a bipartisan thing."

"I also think there are simple things we can do in the short term that everyone could get behind. We can invest in things that promote both economic growth and climate health—like nuclear power," Jordan said.

"Honestly," Chris said, "the biggest problem might be the politics around climate. We're either too strident and lose essential members of a would-be coalition as a result, or we have a vested interest in responding a certain way that alienates potential allies."

Jordan nodded.

The next day the two of us went to a library reference room to work for a bit. Chris's computer died, so he scanned the shelves and picked up the *Standard Dictionary of Folklore Mythology and Legend*.

"World fire," Chris murmured to himself.

"Destruction of the world in the past by fire," the entry read, "either accidentally or due to the deeds of the culture hero or trickster.... A world fire is also forecast for the end of the world as it exists today; this belief is especially prevalent in eastern North America."

He flipped on and found "The Wheel."

"The Wheel may be identified strictly as the vehicular one," he read. "But the vehicle is likely to be of cosmic or magical proportions."

All along our journeys we had found ways to reconcile the ways Americans seemed frustrated with politics but hopeful about the rest. The stories we had been told were powerful enough to reveal the wisdom in just such a perspective. Yet as Chris read to occupy himself, he was aware that even if those reasons for hope and optimism existed when we visited these places for the first time, there was no guarantee they would reveal a similar lesson this time around.

"The spinnings," Chris read, "signify the cycle of the universe or the turn of fortune."

Chris took stock as the Boat quickly lost speed and the engine roared. He pressed down on the pedal. No response. *That must have caused the lurch,* Chris thought. The car wheezed sluggishly up that Georgia hill. He pressed down harder and the RPMs flared. The CHECK ENGINE light flashed in a panicked on and off. Chris coaxed the distressed vehicle over the rise, then coasted down the slope and off the highway into an empty lot.

"We've got a problem," Chris texted Jordan. "I think the engine is shot."

"What's wrong with it?!" Jordan wrote.

"Well, the accelerator stopped working," Chris wrote back, followed by "and it's rattling a ton...and I can hear the engine knocking real bad...I'm pulled over in an abandoned parking lot."

"Jesus," Jordan wrote.

The air was getting stagnant in the car, so Chris opened the door and let the breeze in. Heat enveloped him—but not the cloying variety that lingers in battened-down cars. He could breathe, even if it left him dripping with sweat. A thought occurred to him: *Could the car's fit be cured by a few moments of downtime in the Georgia heat?* Chris took a sharp breath, put the key back in the ignition, and turned hard. The entire dash immediately lit up with warning lights and the engine shook violently.

He killed it and sat back.

"Shit."

"Well, tell me the bad news," Jordan said on the phone. He was sitting in the Atlanta airport 150 miles away, waiting for Chris, who had found shade under what looked like an olive tree in the divider between a Waffle House and a derelict gas station.

"I'm so sorry, man," Chris said.

Jordan erupted in laughter. "Throws a wrench into our optimistic start, huh?"

Chris called a tow truck, then walked to the Waffle House to wait. By the time Chris looked up from his sandwich, a driver had already started winching the Boat onto the back of his truck. Chris ran out to meet him. His name was Terry, he said, hollering over the truck's idling engine. His hair was buzzed short and held down under a tight ball cap.

"California?" he yelled.

"Yeah—how'd you know?"

He gestured at the Boat's new California license plate, which Jordan had swapped out since Idaho.

"Of course."

"Never been."

"Never?"

"Don't think they'd like me much."

"Oh?"

"Don't like guns out there."

"Some do."

"I'm a collector," he said, tightening fabric straps on the rig and examining his work. "I ain't crazy, though. Just hit the woods and stuff."

"Naturally."

Terry took Chris to a repair shop a few miles up the road, where he set about unloading the car.

"So?" Jordan said on the phone.

"The mechanics are with her now," Chris reported from the waiting area. "Not looking good, though."

"Look, dude, it's not a big deal."

215

"I just can't believe it—the Boat."

"There's still a chance."

A few moments later, Marty, a tall mechanic with oil stains on his hands like smudged henna, walked in with a photo and a gadget resembling the end of a speaker cord.

"I got bad news," he said.

Marty explained that a valve had blown, which broke and came apart and "just beat up this spark plug."

He showed Chris the photo—black-and-white, like an ultrasound.

"You need a whole new engine."

"How much will that be?"

"Thousands."

That was money we didn't have.

"Give me a second."

Chris left and conferred with Jordan via text. When he came back in, the whole room watched him.

"Think we're going to leave her behind, then."

"Good decision," Marty said, and paperwork was drawn up.

"Can I have the spark plug?" Chris asked, noticing it among the keys and forms.

A woman behind the desk gave him a puzzled look.

"Sure," she said. "Guess they won't need it to drive outta here."

"No, I figure not," Chris said. "And, well, can I go through it?"

"Sure," the woman behind the counter said. "I'll walk you over."

"We've been to around 42 states in that car," Chris said as the two of them approached the mechanic's bay where the Volvo steamed with its hood up.

"Oh, yeah? That's what you do? Drive around?"

"Yeah, I guess we do."

"How do you survive?"

"Barely—we barely do."

Chris sighed, opened his bag, and began rummaging. In the trunk was Jordan's dog-eared copy of *Travels with Charley*. Under the back seat was a wooden bag from Bags to Butterflies. And from a slit on the dash tumbled Nishan's GUNFIGHTER CANYON card—red and black.

A trip of hope begins in disaster, Chris thought. *Go figure.*

Chris stopped and looked back. Tubes snaked in and out of the car's insides. The sky was settling into the orange light of a feverish April day on the outskirts of Augusta. Something flapped in the stale wind at the entrance to the garage and an acetylene torch flared somewhere off to the side.

"I wish you were here to see her off," Chris had said over the phone to Jordan.

"Me too," Jordan responded.

Chris settled in at a tall table in the shop's waiting area. His bags were half open and the flotsam and jetsam from the bowels of the Boat tumbled out. As he waited for the rental-car company to pick him up, all of the Boat's close calls came rushing back. The midnight run through South Dakota with an overheated engine. The smoking wheel well and flayed tire near Ann Arbor, Michigan. And the various missing pieces, hull scratches, and valuables lost among the crevices. There was the grating in the wells when the Boat turned left and the tight, arthritic brakes that took a few pumps to activate fully.

On the drive away, the whistle of wind in the strange new car reminded Chris of naps in the old front seat, with Jordan across the console passing in and out of lanes. He remembered the staggering heat and the radio when it worked and the podcasts shared ear to ear with the same pair of headphones. And then the silences—the long, drawn-out drives when we had fallen quiet to listen to the wind.

———————

Chris reached the Red Lion Hotel near the Atlanta airport in the shiny blue Hyundai Elantra well past dusk. Jordan greeted him with a hug.

"Helluva day," Jordan said with a half-grin.

Chris smiled weakly. He was deflated. The day had worn him

down. We were used to the puzzles of the road, but Chris's resilience was faltering.

Jordan felt a sliver of guilt. It's not easy to be the bearer of bad news, and Chris had done all the work that day to get the Boat's affairs in order. Jordan decided to save his grief over the lost car for another day.

Yet even at this low point we could see how far we had come. By now, neither of us felt all that far apart. Our competing allegiances simply meant less to us than they had before. The essence of our relationship was history, ritual, and deepening knowledge—knowledge of who the other was and what motivated us—rather than the curio of an unusual friendship. The Boat may have been gone, and its sanctuary for debate and seeking was gone too, but we didn't need it any longer.

"I'll get them to send us the license plate," Jordan said at a pub down the road. "And we can do something to memorialize it."

Sometimes little events can change the course of your life. Just after leaving the Marines, Jordan had sold his car so he could save money while going to law school. Two months later, Jordan's grandfather had asked him to take the old Volvo, since at 87 he could no longer drive safely. At the time it had felt like a slight imposition—more expenses to pay. But that car had changed Jordan's life. Without it, we never would have set off on these trips of ours. The Boat wouldn't be finishing the journey with us, but for an inanimate object, its impact on our lives was immense.

As night set in, we discussed the plan for the next day.

"I want to see Birmingham," Chris said.

"And I'd love to go see the U.S. Space & Rocket Center in Huntsville. They're really close."

"Okay, let's head to Lee County first, then Birmingham and stay a night there. See the Pettus Bridge—"

"—and the museum?"

"Yeah, and the museum."

"And then we can head to New Orleans the next night?"

"Absolutely."

Chris rifled through his backpack and settled on something. He fished out the spark plug and held it up to the light.

"Look."

He tossed it over to Jordan, who inspected it, shook his head, and handed it back.

New Orleans

We left Atlanta the next day and headed for New Orleans by way of Alabama and the arcing shoreline of the Mississippi coast. It would be our third trip to the city together. Rain clouds stalked our drive, and torrents of water on I-65 reduced the world to the reflective lights on the road ahead of us. After a while, the rains broke and a strange, warm fog hung over the forests and under the bridges and causeways of the Gulf Coast.

"Did we drive through here with Pete?" Chris asked.

"No, that was Louisiana."

"It looks so familiar."

The last time we were in New Orleans was December 2017, just after our arduous sprint across the Southwest in Pete Mylen's truck. On our first evening in town, we had stopped into a bar on Frenchman Street to unwind.

"I was at the post office today," a band leader in sunglasses and a pink blazer had said from the stage that night. "And this woman got mad at me."

His five-man band listed against an exposed brick wall.

"Mad at you?" the horn player said.

"Yeah, man," the lead singer responded. "All I did was tell her I didn't get my kids Christmas presents from Santa, and she called me a Scrooge."

"What?"

"Yeah, a Scrooge—and that I was raising Scrooges. My kids ain't Scrooges—come on."

The room echoed.

"Well, this song isn't about Christmas at all," he said. "It's called 'Hit That Jive, Jack.'"

Pete was many miles away by then, yet the rumbling of his diesel engine still echoed in our ears like the sway of a ship many days after disembarking. The Pall Mall smoke hung in Chris's hair, the fabric of our bags, and under our fingernails. But we were back in New Orleans, and that always gave us new energy. Something about the city—simmering with heat and humidity even in December— had settled over our subconscious and drawn us back to the French Quarter's narrow cobblestone streets lit with flickering oil lamps.

Later that day in 2017, Chris was lying on a twin bed flipping through *South and West*—Joan Didion's latest book about a drive she and her husband, John Gregory Dunne, took from New Orleans to Oxford, Mississippi in 1970.

"'I had only some dim and unformed sense,'" Chris read aloud, "'that for some years the South and particularly the Gulf Coast had been for America what people were still saying California was, and what California seemed to me not to be: the future, the secret source of malevolent and benevolent energy, the psychic center.'"

Jordan lounged on the other bed in our hotel room just off Bourbon Street and looked up from his phone with weary eyes.

"She wrote that?" Jordan asked.

"Yeah."

"Read some more."

Chris flipped forward.

"'In New Orleans in June the air is heavy with sex and death, not violent death but death by decay, overripeness, rotting, death by drowning, suffocation, fever of unknown etiology.'"

Chris looked up. Seeing Jordan rapt, he continued reading.

"'The crypts above ground dominate certain vistas. In the hypnotic liquidity of the atmosphere all motion slows into choreography, all people on the street move as if suspended in a precarious emulsion, and there seems only a technical distinction between the quick and the dead.'"

"Wow," Jordan said.

Chris closed the book and listened to the sound of a trombone on the streets below.

———————

A year and a half later, we made it from Atlanta back to New Orleans. After checking into a hotel, Chris took a shower and let the music from his phone play loud. The hard guitar of "Start Me Up" by the Rolling Stones rose above the sound of the water, and Chris sang along. Jordan left to find a po'boy sandwich and headed toward the French Quarter, crossing Canal Street and weaving in and out of revelrous townies and stumbling tourists there for Jazz Fest. The beat of music emanated out of the alleys and street corners of the Quarter and hastened Jordan's pace.

We had returned to the Crescent City to run down a feeling we'd had for some time. In Mexico, Ivan, the customs agent, lightened up only at the mention of Nirvana and when Creedence played over the speakers in the *desayunador*. Poetry was Gabriel's way of making sense of his life inside and outside Parnall Prison, and Charlene just wanted to sing when she returned to Detroit after decades behind bars. And, of course, whatever was playing on the backcountry radio after our political brawls kept the two of us sane. It all seemed to crystallize for us in Denver. There, at the Leon Bridges concert in the ethereal confines of Red Rocks Amphitheatre, people of all types twisted and sang beneath red-lit trees and the glowing spits of ruby sandstone.

And like Joan Didion almost 50 years earlier, we hoped New Orleans might help us better understand all this. Here was a city that once sat at the heart of the Confederacy, where innumerable slaves were sold at auction, but that also became home to a large free black population, birthed jazz, and came through Hurricane Katrina. For us, it was a city where anything seemed possible and assuredly whatever came next would be expressed in song.

And as luck would have it, Leon Bridges was set to play at Jazz Fest. Since Denver, Leon had played in the background of our long drives across America. So we drove back to hear him play and spend time with the musicians who played the clubs and dance halls and street corners and funerals and everything in between. To us, they held the keys to Didion's dim and unformed sense of the choreography that kept the city's rhythm.

Jordan returned to the room and could hear Chris warbling from the bathroom.

"'And the women never really faint, and the villains always blink their eyes,'" Chris sang. "'But anyone who has a heart wouldn't want to turn around and break it.'"

Chris kept humming the Lou Reed melody as he came out into the room.

"You ready?" Jordan asked.

"Let's do it," Chris said.

"This weekend will be a time," Jordan responded, and we set off into the balmy evening.

———

We traipsed across the streetcar tracks on Canal Street and into the French Quarter. On Royal, a man with dreads and wearing a tie sang loudly as three little girls ate Lunchables on a blanket at his feet. A brass band led by a woman spinning an umbrella marched just off Bourbon. We had been in New Orleans only a few hours, and already our senses were overwhelmed by its color and melody.

That morning we had stopped by the Pensacola Museum of Art, where we found an exhibit on Aubrey Beardsley on the walls of the converted prison.

"He illustrated *Through the Looking Glass* at one point," Chris said, reading about the exhibit. "And he died at 25."

"And he did all of this?" Jordan said. We stood among hundreds of black-and-white prints ranging from ghoulish to erotic. We took in scenes of strange, pear-shaped figures adorned with jewels, depictions of operagoers—dour and mute—women with hair made of fruited grapevines and gnarled, sharpened fingers—all in black ink.

"'Of course I have one aim—the grotesque,'" Chris read. "'If I am not grotesque, I am nothing.'"

He stared at it for a moment.

"Why, of course."

A more living kind of art marked the French Quarter that night. It was an art that sprang from the pavement in full color. Shotgun houses on quiet streets echoed with scratchy recordings. On Bourbon Street itself the notes of brass instruments caromed off the iron balconies and competed with the rock pumping from the beer-washed dance halls just down the way.

We stepped into 801 Royal, a French Quarter bar, where pop music played over the speakers and raucous drinkers filtered in and out on their way to and from Jazz Fest. We were looking for Storie Gonsoulin, a bartender and musician, who John-Michael had said would be working that night. On a flight many years before, Chris had struck up a conversation with John-Michael Early, a New Orleans rock musician, and the two of them had stayed in touch. Chris reached out ahead of our trip, and John-Michael delivered musician after musician—friends and collaborators—all willing to talk.

Behind the bar, a man of about 40 with long hair in a bun made eye contact.

"Chris?"

"Storie?"

"Take a seat," he said.

In an instant, Storie Gonsoulin was off to greet another group that had just come in from the street. So we climbed up on two stools next to three brothers from Philadelphia.

"You here for Jazz Fest?" one of them asked Jordan.

"We came here for Storie, actually."

"What do you guys want with Storie?"

"He's a musician," Chris said.

"Retired," Storie interrupted, reappearing.

"What?"

"I retired two years ago from playing full-time," he said.

"How come?" Jordan asked.

"I make four times more here at the bar than in a year of performing."

Storie had been raised in southwestern Louisiana—"a Cajun Creole from the swamp," as he affectionately put it. His childhood memories were stitched together by the notes of zydeco (a unique sound featuring fiddles and washboards), which had emerged from the bayous and swamps—much like Storie himself. Early on, Storie learned the guitar from Paul "Lil Buck" Sinegal, who became like a father to Storie, and soon a passion became a profession. Storie took to the road for gigs with bands and other acts. He played guitar and drums and later a washboard, traveling and performing full-time. At one point he played upward of 200 shows a year.

Until it all became too much.

"January 15," Storie said, looking at the ceiling to jog his memory while he washed glasses. "That was two years of retirement."

The artist's life is difficult. By one count, the average musician in

New Orleans makes around half of what the average American house-hold does. Club-level bands have to play more than 40 shows to make just around $16,000. Storie wore himself thin touring and cutting albums—and politicking.

"I'm pretty much done with playing in a band," was how he put it. "I can't deal with four other egos."

Instead, Storie kept bar and cut experimental hip-hop albums made up of the melodies of Louisiana-raised artists.

"All American music has come from jazz and blues, which was played down here," Storie said. "The only music that can trace its roots back anywhere but Louisiana is hip-hop, which was invented in the Bronx. But what people fail to realize is that they were sampling the Meters, who are from New Orleans, to make those hip-hop beats."

Storie expressed great pride in the city. He wasn't a full-time musician any longer, but the Creole culture that had created zydeco kept him in the city he called home.

"I got a couple sitting down here from New York last week and they said, 'Do you like New York?'" Storie told us. "And I said, 'Yeah, New York is cool, but it's not New Orleans.'"

The first syllable of *Orleans* came from somewhere deep in his gullet.

"She said, 'What makes it cool down here?' And I said, 'Well, in New York, you got diversity. Here we've got diversity too. But in New York, you got Irish neighborhoods, Venezuelan, Puerto Rican, and you've got Jewish neighborhoods and stuff. But it doesn't ever blend and mix and become a culture. Coming here, there's a mix of African, French, Spanish, Caribbean, all this shit. It's melted, and it invented a whole culture of food, language, music, everything—unlike anywhere else in the United States.'"

This was certainly part of our infatuation with the city. It was a community knitted together by too many cultures and heritages and ethnicities to count. New Orleans was welcoming in its spirit, and in its music. Its magnetism for men and women like Storie was in its openness. All could be loud there, especially if one kept a beat.

We watched as Storie ministered to all who stopped by with wide gestures and loud welcomes. He was boisterous and charming. Eventually he stopped by our end of the bar and leaned in so only we could hear him.

"Hey, y'all," he said. "I gotta run out for a bit."

And in a moment Storie disappeared out onto Royal and into the night.

———————

Around midnight that same evening, three musicians trotted up to the stage at Buffa's Bar & Restaurant on Esplanade, just a quarter-mile off Frenchman Street. The two of us sat at a table two rows from the front. A family band was still packing up their violins from the last set.

"Hurry up," a large man in a black T-shirt barked from behind the bar. "You're running late."

A plump woman stared back at him from the stage.

"Don't you have some silverware to roll?" she sneered.

"Naw, I'm doing paperwork," he said. "Don't we have some drinking to do?"

Soon after, Keith Burnstein, 39, plopped himself down at the piano and started playing scales. He wore a baseball cap and a gold varsity jacket over his wiry frame. Chris, a tall man with rolled short sleeves and a pomade-slicked side-part, arranged a drum set. Charles, a young man with a halo of hair and a twisty beard, ferried over plastic cups of water with limes for Keith and Chris and a beer for himself before tuning his bass. By the time Charles started plucking the first notes of a song Keith wrote, only a handful of people remained. A majority of the tables were empty, yet the three musicians warmed up as if Carnegie Hall lay just beyond the curtain behind the stage.

An hour earlier we had met Keith on a bench beneath a streetlamp outside the bar, where a handful of drunks and slouches loitered, asking for cigarettes, a buck or two, or a light. Storie had nodded along when we quizzed him about music, but his utterings ended up sounding as cryptic as he was. If we hoped to learn more, perhaps Keith could explain it to us.

Born in Philadelphia and raised in New Jersey, Keith had discovered New Orleans while on tour with his old band, the Mumbles, and moved down soon afterward. It was a good city for a piano player: Keith had recently bought a home with what he made from gigs, albums, and touring.

"If you can play, people don't care what you think personally," Keith told us. "If you can do the job, then most people are cool to you."

Music was a great equalizer, Keith said, and you could feel its reach across the city.

"I work with this cat sometimes as my side hustle," Keith said. "We deliver organs, like church organs. He's an older guy, and this dude's got like a shelf full of Glenn Beck books. We meet a lot of people, and he occasionally will say some things that are a little bit insensitive, and I'll be like, 'Dude, think about what you just said.'

"But I'll tell you, we were in a church the other day, and everybody looks super suspicious of him for some reason. It's this old rundown shotgun-like church in a rough part of town. And so we bring the organ in, and they're all stressed because they're setting up their congregation somewhere else for whatever reason. So there's just some weird vibes, and then finally he turns the organ on to show them that it works, and he starts playing 'Amazing Grace' like really beautifully, you know what I mean?

"Everybody just stopped. There was like six or seven people beside me, and they all just stopped, and they all came around the organ. And they were just like, 'That sounds great.' And when we got back in the car, I was like, 'Yo, man, that was a smooth move.' And he's like, 'You gotta do that sometimes to make sure people know you're all right. Music breaks every color barrier, every socioeconomic barrier, whatever it is. It makes people trust you, for whatever reason.' He's like, 'If you do this more, play the organ when you deliver it, it'll be all good, like 95 percent of the time.'"

Chris's mother had sung "Amazing Grace" to him as a child, and he knew its soothing melody well. Perhaps it was how raw and vulnerable a song can be that gives it such force. We're drawn to unalloyed expressions of joy or sadness—loss, bereavement, coping, and at times elation. There's no pretense or artifice to the notes of "Amazing Grace" echoing through the transepts and naves of an unoccupied church. A melody is welcoming in a way no gesture or slogan ever could be.

As Keith wrapped up his story, Charles showed up with a bass slung over his shoulder.

"Don't you guys warm up?" Chris asked.

"I'm warm," Charles said.

"Charles wakes up warm," Keith said, grinning.

We all went inside for the show. A few young people walked in and out, ordering Coors Lights and other three-dollar beers. The preparations ready, Keith introduced the band and they started playing. Keith sang and the others watched him for cues. In many ways it was a warm-up gig for Jazz Fest—Keith and Charles were playing backup for various artists on enormous stages the next day, and they wanted to stretch their fingers and feel and hear the familiar chords. They seemed undaunted by the silent room. *Live music is like a conversation,* Keith had said outside, and now the three of them were having it among themselves. They played their set until after 2 a.m. for scattered applause, often singing over the occasional peal of laughter from outside the open front door, and none of it mattered. What they were creating mattered to them, even if few saw it and even fewer would remember it.

"Charles, whatcha want?" Keith said, standing up to look over the piano. Charles looked over and wordlessly leaned back, baring his teeth and riffing away on the stand-up bass.

The walls of the St. Louis Cemetery No. 2 were made of bricks strangled with moss and failing mortar. Crypts with chipped plaster facades were failing up like blotches of crumbling dried paint on a canvas. It had become a tradition for us to walk the burial grounds of New Orleans.

We entered through the gates in the stone wall and parted ways to walk around the crypts. Jordan hugged the walls while Chris went down the middle. Jordan paused to observe the memorials carved into the high brick walls. The sun beat down, and the bouquets and carnations curdled and browned in the heat. The stone was sandpaper to the touch as Chris grazed his hand over it. GONE BUT NOT FORGOTTEN was written above the tomb of a John Franklin. His name bled a black rust over the green-white tablet. Jordan crouched down to look at a family tomb where generations going all the way back to the founding were buried.

We met again in a pool of shade by the mouth of the graveyard.

"This place goes back more than 200 years," Jordan said. "Someone born in 1804 is buried here, and a descendant dies in 2009 and goes in right next to them."

Jordan pointed at the dates in front of him.

"All that history."

"The only cemetery I ever really spent time in is this one near Hot Springs, Virginia, where my grandparents are buried," Chris said. "It's the only cemetery I ever felt connected to. But I only know a few of the tombstones. The rest are just names."

The same black-headed gulls of Mobile and Pensacola flew above our heads on forked wings.

"Are you thinking about your grandfather?" Chris asked.

Two weeks earlier, Jordan's grandfather, Dr. Arthur Aufses Jr., had passed away, and Jordan's family had laid him to rest in New Montefiore Cemetery in West Babylon, New York. Nearly a century earlier,

Jordan's great-great-grandfather, Samuel Whitman, had purchased a plot there.

"I was thinking about the burial plot my great-great-grandfather started," Jordan said, "and how amazing it was to see three generations represented there. I felt rooted somehow."

"Is that where you want to be buried?"

"I don't know," Jordan said, looking down as he considered it. "Part of me is drawn to the idea of creating a new plot."

Arthur had been a guiding influence in Jordan's life. He represented the kind of person Jordan hoped to become: a respected professional, a compassionate but firm man, and a loving husband and father for seven decades. Yet Jordan had made a conscious choice not to follow in his footsteps. Jordan often joked that he broke his mother's heart the day he chose to join the Marines and forgo medical school. He often found himself conflicted in this way. Tradition kept him afloat. It gave him his faith and his moral compass. It offered him an idea of the good life, even while he remained his own man who desired to make his own way.

But Arthur never saw tradition and self-realization as incompatible. He never showed a hint of disappointment in Jordan's choices, no matter what path he chose. After all, it was Arthur who had bequeathed Jordan the Boat four years earlier, and who often waxed poetic about his own youthful road trips across Germany, where he'd been stationed as a surgeon during the Korean War.

Chris watched his friend's pained expression. It had been three years since Jordan's Oregon-highway tale about his sister's vendetta against his middle-school tormentors. The two of us had shared so much since then. The road had become our own ritual, our own rambling sacred space. So too was New Orleans. Over the past three years, we had developed a rhythm, coming back to the city every six months or so, even when 3,000 miles separated the two of us for most of the year. It was here that our most tender moments seemed to take place. The city's hidden recesses exposed our most vulnerable selves.

"Do you want to talk about him?"

Jordan shook his head with eyes downcast, emotion strangling the words in his throat, and Chris knew Jordan's troubles were his own again.

"I remember when we were here last, we went to that cemetery in the Garden District," Chris said, "and we stopped in front of one of these mausoleums for a man who was born in the 1800s and lived through both world wars. I remember thinking how he had seen the rise of fascism, Nazism, the Great Depression. He had seen all this—seen America at these times of great upheaval and triumph too—and I just wondered how his perspective on this country changed."

Jordan looked over.

"And I wonder if future generations will look back on us and think, *They had 9/11, they had the Iraq War, they had the War on Terror, they had the global financial crisis, they had Donald Trump. How did they deal with it all?*" Chris said. "Will the last 20 years be seen as this dramatic upheaval that shocked every sense of who we were in a way similar to back then?"

As we spoke, a man in a white T-shirt and jeans entered the cemetery grounds.

"Lockin' up," he yelled, looking down the pathways. "We're lockin' up."

"Or are their troubles in the future going to make these look like placid times?" Chris said.

"I think it depends on how we choose to interpret that history," Jordan said.

"How so?"

"History is written in hindsight, and how it's written affects the way we see the present."

Chris half-nodded.

"Take the American founding. If you think America's history is fundamentally rooted in slavery, genocide, and racism, then your conception of who we are today is shaped by that perspective. But if you believe instead that American history is defined by an uneven but continuous fight to expand civil rights, then you have a very different sense of American identity. History becomes the vocabulary by which we describe ourselves, and the story we tell. The same will be true for our generation."

How does one ever reconcile those two histories? Placing good beside evil had always confounded Chris. He struggled to capture how that alloy seemed so human, yet so ominous all the same.

But in that plot of above-ground crypts, with death surrounding us—in a city where the "distinction between the quick and the dead" merged, as Didion put it—a harmony seemed to exist. Statues of the virgin mother draped in robes, carved words pregnant with poetry, and stark crosses all captured what death could be. This city was heavy with the afterlife, Didion wrote, though it offered a remembrance of life, too. Contradictory ideas lived as one here. And perhaps that was a lesson to both of us as we reckoned with who we were and would soon be. Perhaps this unknowable, inarticulable knowledge was the nameless menace that seemed to haunt our time on the road, and maybe we could be at peace with it only when we confronted things unsaid; things that were instead carved, strummed, painted, or hummed.

We both had come to believe that art, culture, and music were the best way to convey the complexity of who we are, where we've come from, and where we may be headed. Perhaps that was why we were turning away from politics. In 2019, it was bereft of what really mattered—honesty, dialogue, nuance.

"So we're either born of original sin," Jordan concluded, "or something else. Maybe we're something new."

"Or both," Chris said.

And with that, we slipped out behind the groundskeeper.

The neighborhoods around the city's fairgrounds throbbed with music. Another Saturday of Jazz Fest was upon the city, and practically everyone in the Sixth Ward seemed to have a Solo cup in hand and a party to attend. John-Michael Early sat beside us on the green-cushioned couches on the porch of his family home. Festivalgoers streamed by, and a piano played somewhere not far off.

Over the course of our time in New Orleans, we had been told a lot about John-Michael. He had set us up with Storie and Keith and others, and everyone had a story or two about the man. He was a musician of some local acclaim, playing with his band, Flow Tribe, and traveling the country for shows. Some thought he was destined for politics, and he did seem to know everyone who walked by as we settled into the shade.

"Where you at, cuz?" he shouted.

A man down the street waved back.

"That's my cousin," he said, turning back to us.

The entire block seemed more intimate and familiar.

"I think music activates a different part of people," John-Michael said. "Kind of brings you back to childhood wonder.

"And there's nothing really dualistic about music or art. There's a million ways to arrive at the same place with a song or a piece of art. What's happening in the country now is that people are being forced to pick a side. It kind of comes down to a binary kind of thinking: *It's right or it's wrong.* But really there's so much gray area."

Music is expansive, John-Michael seemed to suggest. It is an infinite medium in which all comers can lend something—a tradition, a riff, a new worldview. In music, such offerings are rarely uninspiring. Novel, encompassing sounds give new life. And that philosophy—that lifestyle—gave John-Michael great sums of hope.

"You ever read *Freakonomics*?" John-Michael tried. "Remember the bagel story in New York?"

Both of us shook our heads.

"This dude ran a bagel company, would go to different offices in

New York City and would just put fresh-made bagels down, and a sign like, BAGELS $1.00, CREAM CHEESE $0.50 or whatever. And every day he would leave out a can—total honor system. Did it for like 10 or 12 years and kept scrupulous records. And across the board it was like, 89 percent of people would pay.

"Those are good numbers," he said. "We've got a damn solid majority of people who will pay for a bagel when no one's watching. That's our country."

John-Michael made a living performing for strangers in bars and concert halls across the South and the Eastern Seaboard and as far away as Wisconsin. He had played for thousands of different people who cared only if he could give them a good time.

"When you really just talk person-to-person," he told us, "and you strip away whatever flag or label that you're flying for whatever reason, you can sit down with somebody."

The two of us had always said we were at our worst when we were speaking for a flag or group. Instead, we were at our most understanding when we spoke from our other passions, from the most fundamental parts of our identities.

Jordan's service had spawned his optimism about the country. He had watched Americans from all different backgrounds act selflessly under terrible circumstances. Some of his friends had given their lives for it. Anything that could inspire that kind of sacrifice had to be good. Underneath the tarnish of it all, we had to be good. *Good* meant they hadn't died in vain.

Chris was a journalist—an unconventional one, but a journalist all the same. That was the origin of his skepticism and his devotion to seeing things for himself. His temperament was ultimately that of the unaffiliated, the seeker, the teller of what was said and done in distant places.

These were the kinds of authentic selves both of us could not only relate to and understand, but communicate with. And that meant there was room to be wrong, to be challenged, and sometimes even to be changed.

The notes of a piano and the vocals of an older man wafted across the porch.

"Is that a recording?" Chris asked.

"That's next door," John-Michael said, gesturing up at a screen window on the second floor of his neighbor's home. He explained it was the lead singer of the Radiators. He was losing his hearing, but he played up there all the time with the window thrown open. As we listened, he played "Jumpin' Jack Flash" and sang in a deep, resonant voice.

"The Radiators always used to close Jazz Fest," John-Michael said. And since the Rolling Stones had canceled their set closing the festival, perhaps he was practicing to close once more.

"Know which way the wind blows," the man sang from his perch behind the screen window as he embarked on his latest tune.

Later that afternoon, we arrived at Jazz Fest just as Leon Bridges and his band took the stage. We edged around the crowd until we found an open space. A hundred yards away was Leon, doing his wild, locking, stumbling, stepping dance—elbows up and knees out—in a bucket hat, a white shirt, and linen pants.

"I feel like playing some blues tonight," Leon called out. "Can I play some blues?"

And the songs of our trip echoed out from the Gentilly Stage in front of us.

We looked out over the crowd and found young and old, hair past waists, all shades of skin, and tufts of chest hair emerging out of untucked button-downs. It was warm, and people wore little. Every few minutes a baby stroller went by. Teens roamed about with backpacks. Others had straw hats and pens trailing vapor. Cell phones came out for "Coming Home" and passersby mouthed the lyrics.

We took a stroll and passed stages featuring Steve Earle, Logic, and Katy Perry. We walked by art vendors, food trucks, and small folk bands. We walked and walked, as we had in Yuma and Phoenix outside the convention center among the maddening numbers of protesters and politicos, and Lorain where a Confederate flag hung on the siding of a booth, and downtown Detroit where lofty monuments and high-rises whistled with wind off the river, and cemeteries just down the road elsewhere in Louisiana, and countless other boulevards and trails and fairgrounds where people gathered and celebrated and spirited themselves away to another place. Eventually we made our way back to Leon's stage. He had a guitar around his neck and the crowd was quiet. Voices went up in harmony for the stripped-down guitar chords and Bridges's reverb voice.

"I wanna go," Leon sang. "Lord, please let me know."

The music faded.

"I wanna know," he sang, and applause followed the final line and filled his silent wake.

Two years earlier, still recovering from our voyage with Pete Mylen, Jordan had asked Chris if he could borrow *South and West* as we returned to our hotel off Bourbon Street after dinner one night. He sat down near the balcony, where a full brass band could be heard beyond.

"Listen to this," Jordan said, flipping through it. "'Joan Didion went to the South to understand something about California and she ended up understanding something about America.'"

He was reading from the book's foreword, by Nathaniel Rich.

"'The future always looks good in the golden land,' Didion wrote in 'Some Dreamers of the Golden Dream,' 'because no one remembers the past.'"

Jordan paused before reading Rich's last line.

"'In the South no one can forget it.'"

Didion had sensed a "peculiar childlike cruelty and innocence" in New Orleans, but that seemed off the mark to the two of us: *innocence* was the wrong word. What we witnessed was an awareness of the city's faults and sorrows, its beauty and richness, and how time and expression brought it all together. Storie had waxed rhapsodic about a line of Frenchmen, and soon-to-be Cajuns, who had left Nova Scotia for Louisiana and the pride he took in being descended from one of their leaders, a man named Joseph Bruskee.

When Jordan heard that, he thought of Captain Willis Spear back in Portland, Maine. People cared about tracing their lineage and commemorating their ancestors who put down roots. No matter where people came from, or what corners they were flung from, their descendants often revered those women and men for having settled and made a home. But what we saw in New Orleans was a culture that could allow pride to live alongside complexity—where traditions interplayed with other traditions and even formed new ones to express this unique fusion.

Years before, we had deduced that politics was not the solution to any of our problems, personal or national. Any hope of harmony, of belonging and community, would have to spring from something else. What bound the two of us together had always been shared passions and a curiosity about what kept the other one animated—literature, philosophy, ideas. And as we packed up to leave New Orleans in 2019, years after Didion had piqued our curiosity, that insight seemed to have greater relevance to us than ever before. The kind of American future the two of us dreamed of would emerge from a tradition like that of New Orleans, which was made up of a medley—a chorus—of different people, voices, customs, art, and ways of being and learning and knowing. In that diversity, a new way could take shape. New Orleans beguiled us, and always would.

We left again, headed for Tulsa, Oklahoma. As we took I-10 out of town, two massive cemeteries flanked the highway on either side.

"That's the Metairie Cemetery," Jordan said. "One of the biggest in the city."

We stared out over rows and rows of crosses and memorials, mausoleums and crypts, carnations and grassy pathways, stone pyramids and bare crosses that rose above the fence line like vines seeking sunlight. It was another above-ground burial plot on the Louisiana floodlands, where groundwater tended to raise even the most weighted-down coffin out of its soil after a rain.

And there, on grounds that were once a racetrack, were Spanish-style tombs. Tombs etched with the names of Cajuns and Creoles sat next to the stand-alone graves of pirates, governors, and musicians. Nameless vaults were stacked six high in the same tomb. All were encircled by the same iron fence. All were built on land both primordial and ever-changing. All belonged there, together.

Tulsa

We left Louisiana and took off down straight highways into Oklahoma, where abstruse road signs urged us not to "drive into smoke." As we pulled into Tulsa a few hours later, storms battered the area just north of town and spilled flurries of rain over the city.

Our first stop was a familiar one—the Greenwood Cultural Center and the Black Wall Street Memorial. We had first visited eight months earlier, in August 2018. Back then we had arrived during a deluge and rushed to take cover inside.

This time, with gray skies overhead, we were able to look around outside. Across the way, on the wall of a parking lot below a quiet highway overpass, was a mural. BLACK WALL STREET it read in big black letters, with a flaming K emitting a plume of smoke.

We were in Greenwood to see Jamaal, a newly ordained pastor who was in his last week as a project manager on the Tulsa Race Riot Centennial Commission. Greenwood Cultural Center, where we had first met Jamaal, was a shrine to the hundreds of African Americans murdered and more than 10,000 left homeless in 1921 during the sacking of the Greenwood neighborhood, then known as Black Wall Street. Those 36 blocks had once been a thriving economic center for a growing African American middle class. Then a violent white mob descended on the community with little warning, reducing more than 1,000 places of worship, grocery stores, homes, and hospitals to rubble. After that fateful day in 1921, a culture of silence gripped Tulsa and Greenwood. Jamaal told us he had interviewed one of the last living survivors of the massacre. Her parents had told her to never discuss it, she explained.

The year before, Jamaal and his colleague, Brandon, had walked us through the relics in the museum, telling disturbing stories.

"It's one thing for us as descendants and black Greenwood residents to talk about it," Jamaal had said as we walked past the exhibits, rain falling in sluices outside as we spoke. "It's another when we have allies to talk about it as well."

"This isn't just black history," he added. "It's American history."

Nine months later, we returned and found the memorial empty. A silence pervaded the green-carpeted room.

"Oh, hello," a woman said, poking her head out of a bathroom down the hall.

"Hi, there."

"Can I help you?"

"Just here to look around and see if Jamaal is here."

"Oh no, he doesn't have an office here anymore."

"Mind if we still look around?"

"Not at all," she said, coming out to shake our hands. "We're all kinda hiding in the bathroom."

"I'm sorry?" Chris said.

"For the tornado warning."

"The what?" Jordan said.

"One touched down in Luther—should be on your phones."

"We're not from around here," Jordan said.

"Oh dear," she said. "Well, it's dangerous with all the glass, so feel free to join us. The bathroom is the safest."

The woman watched us make for the exhibits—perhaps too cavalier about what was brewing in the skies above. We walked past framed newspaper clippings with black-and-white photos of burning buildings, streets reduced to rubble, and another of a black man in suspenders, hat in hand, arms raised above his head in a gesture of surrender.

We were headed for a particular room at the end of the hall, a room we had seen before. The first time we had found it lit with halogen lights and filled with the staccato of rain above. The room was lined with portraits of survivors. Their faces were their own testament—bespectacled at times, stern, dignified, unbowed. Many had been young at the time of the massacre, and their stories were the experiences of children. We read their stories out loud to each other, and tears fell down Jordan's cheeks.

Back again in the room, Chris found the portrait that had touched him most last time around. It was of an older woman, with parted hair, deep-set eyes, and thin-rimmed glasses, taken many years after the massacre. Her name was Beulah.

"That riot cheated us out of our childhood innocence," she was quoted as saying. "My life dreams were destroyed too by that riot."

"I can't believe this," Chris whispered. "I can't believe this happened here."

Jordan shook his head.

We had come to know Tulsa as a city riven by race and class. Once the oil capital of the world, the great wealth coming out of its soils never reached certain communities. The pillaging of the Greenwood neighborhood in the 1920s was only the most prominent instance of the deep and oftentimes violent divisions that ran through the city. Housing policies, poll taxes, voter disenfranchisement, and discriminatory hiring practices had marginalized the black population. As recently as 2019, the median white household in Oklahoma possessed 18 to 20 times more wealth than the median black household.

Tulsa might have seemed like a peculiar town to visit on a trip devoted to hope. Yet despite the tragedy there was a spirit of civic pride and engagement. A small, devoted core of residents saw promise in the city—residents like Jamaal and Brandon. And among them was the woman we had come back to see—a woman who had devoted her life to an organization called Women in Recovery (WIR), a prison-diversion program for addicted and abused women and mothers. We were returning to Oklahoma because of a woman named Mimi Tarrasch.

Later that day, clouds kept swirling over Tulsa as tornadoes stalked the state. On our way to meet Mimi, we watched a video of a huge cyclone touching down near Ada, 120 miles south of Tulsa, as the wind thrashed the camellias and street signs outside the windows of our rental car. Rain came and went all afternoon.

"Listen to this," Chris said, reading a speech off his phone. Mimi was set to give remarks later that week at a gala put on by the Tulsa Chapter of the Association for Women in Communications to honor women for their good works. She had sent a draft to us earlier that day for Chris's thoughts.

"'In a perfect world, I wouldn't be standing here today,'" Chris read. "'And if it were a perfect world, women would not be the fastest-growing segment of the prison population nationally, with a 700 percent increase over the last 40 years.'"

"I hope that's a relative number," Jordan said. "If there's one woman in prison and three get convicted, that's a vast statistical leap in name only."

"'In this world,'" Chris read on, "'there would not be 215 women in the Tulsa county jail today or another 2,943 women in Oklahoma's prisons across the state.'"

Jordan hung his head. "Guess not."

The first time we visited Mimi in Oklahoma was just after our drive through northern Mexico in 2018. We had left Denver in the middle of the night and descended into the red lights of wind turbines blinking on and off in the distance, as they had in the Texas Panhandle. Burlington, Colorado, just shy of the Kansas border, was our stop for the night when the fatigue became too much. The woman who checked us in at three o'clock in the morning had the word *addicted* tattooed into the almond flesh of her neck.

The next morning, Kansas was flat and long, all corn and the stench of cattle. Homemade signs, stark and strident, marked I-70.

HELL IS REAL

ABORTION STOPS BEATING HEARTS

JESUS IS REAL

We had stopped for lunch in Hays, Kansas—an old frontier town thick with history. The kind of town that had a graveyard for those who had died in gun battles.

Tulsa was supposed to be another quick stopover. One of Jordan's friends had introduced us to Mimi, though, so we decided to stay an extra day. We first met her the next day at Women in Recovery, located above a trauma center behind a few rows of glass doors southwest of downtown. Mimi was tall and her curly hair fell around her ears.

"Come on," she said. "I'll take you around."

Mimi was elegant and possessed a fiery, almost rebellious spirit. There appeared to be a deep need for women like her in Oklahoma, a state with the highest female-incarceration rate in the country—nearly twice the national average. Women in Recovery was designed as a last-resort diversion program to keep women, especially those with children, out of prison. The women who Mimi helped keep out of prison received comprehensive services: everything from professional training to parenting skills and outpatient-clinic treatment for trauma, addiction, and mental illness. Around 70 percent of women who entered the program finished. Only 7 percent ended up reoffending. Mimi explained this to us as we walked through the halls of the complex. Behind glass doors we saw women in front of computers, mopping floors, and chopping vegetables.

A woman came up as we lingered at the corner of the complex.

"Mimi," she said. "Mimi, I saw my kids—all four."

"That's wonderful."

"The first time in over a year."

"And how did it go?"

"My son didn't connect," she said.

There was much to do when it came to recovery. The women had counseling and job training to attend. They were also responsible for performing a task considered essential to their healing and, simultaneously, to perpetuating the program: They were encouraged to tell their stories.

Mimi led us into a room and two women stood up to greet us. There was Anna, with tattoos running along her arms, and Jackie, who was shy and demure.* We shook hands and sat down around the table with Mimi off at an angle.

"Where would you be if not for here?" Mimi asked.

"Prison-bound," Anna said.

"How long were you in your addiction?" Mimi asked.

"I've been an addict off and on most of my life. But when I got the DUI three years ago is when I really got into my addiction. I lost my children, and I turned to meth. And it's like I procrastinated ever since that day. I don't even know how three years went by."

"And how many times were you in jail?"

"I went to jail once before the DUI, and I went to jail three times total because of the DUI. The time before that was for shoplifting."

On average, the women at the facility had been to jail between 13 and 15 times, Mimi explained. Oftentimes judges would show them leniency, but no services met them where they were. As a result, some women landed back in court again and again, making returning to prison next to inevitable.

"It's a vicious cycle that ends with a life destroyed," Mimi said.

---

* The names of Women in Recovery participants have been changed to protect their identity.

Anna told us how she would hop from abandoned house to abandoned house, "because you don't really sleep when you're on meth." At one point she hadn't slept in a bed for more than a year. Instead she would haunt 24-hour casinos, where she found free coffee and soda and bathrooms, and people had plenty of money to hand out for spare drinks. She would go from casinos to strange couches and back again.

"That sounds exhausting," Jordan said.

"It was," Anna said. "It really was."

Then she was accepted at Women in Recovery.

"At first I was angry," Anna explained. "Nobody wants to give up their addiction. But after three weeks of being sober, I felt so good. I smiled for the first time in I can't tell you how long."

"This program is hard by design," Mimi explained. "But addiction's really hard too. Where you gonna get your next high? Where are you gonna get your clothes? Where are your kids? This is structured, this is hard, this is a lack of chaos."

Up until that point, Jackie had sat quietly. Anna had been in the program for more than a year and was confident, even gregarious. Jackie, who had been in WIR for just two months, was hesitant at first, but it began to seem like a relief to let her words out.

"I've always had a supportive family," she said. "I ran away when I was 12 because I didn't want to abide by my mother's rules."

Soon Jackie was drinking and shoplifting. She was sent to a juvenile detention center at 17, then an adult facility for the better part of eight years. In between those stints, she was introduced to meth by an ex-girlfriend. When she finally got out of prison, she was an addict. Like the women at Bags to Butterflies, her problems only intensified out of prison. She was fired from her first job when they found out she was a felon, and her uncle's death sent her into a tailspin.

"This addiction is not a joke; it's not a joke at all," she said. "I was that person that said, 'I'll never do this—and I'll never shoot up,' and at the end of my addiction before I came into this program, I started to do that. This addiction will take everything from you. It'll leave you with nothing."

After her latest arrest, Jackie was sent to Women in Recovery.

"They don't really teach you anything in prison to become a perfect citizen in the world," Jackie explained. "Here, they work through the pain and all the bad that I've done. They give me a different outlook on life and coping tools instead of sending me back out on the streets with nothing."

Her words kept getting caught in her throat.

"We could walk out of the door if we wanted to, but we have the option to change our lives, and I know that I want that in my life. I just want to be better. I want my mother to see somebody better than what I was. It's all I have out there.

"It's a blessing to me," she concluded, tears on her cheeks. "I'm sorry—I didn't mean to cry."

"Don't be sorry," Jordan said.

Listening to Anna and Jackie was sobering. The hardships they had faced were unimaginable, and they had suffered deeply. But like Charlene, Brenda, and Tonya in Detroit—and in ways the men in Parnall dreamed—they were turning things around. Jackie, for one, had found her blessings and named them. With the right help, these women were doing better. "I want to do something meaningful with my life," Anna had said.

We got a different perspective the next day, when we met with three lawyers and legal assistants at a group called Still She Rises, a largely female indigent-defense group that provides legal representation exclusively to mothers in Oklahoma.

"That's a nice narrative," one of them had said as we recounted our sense of redemption at work in Tulsa. The three of them then proceeded to tell us how women ensnared in Oklahoma's criminal-justice system were rarely ever released again for good. Warrants began a cycle of fees and fines that would pile up and keep the poor in various forms of obligation to the state for decades. Some in Tulsa, inspired by a malignant form of faith, took destitution as a mark of God's ill will and handed down punitive sentences from the jury box.

"We're up against four generations of belief," one of the lawyers told us.

Having come to Tulsa from elsewhere, these lawyers were shocked by the depth of the problem and the degree of opposition they faced. The idea of personal responsibility had been weaponized and turned against the women they represented. A palpable anger permeated the room on behalf of the women—the mothers—whom the state had shackled in perpetuity.

As we left town that afternoon, Chris felt the toxicity of these ugly things leaching through his understanding of the entire country. There in that small corner of Oklahoma was a broken system. Some women would recover; many would not. Almost a century before, thousands of black families had been burned out of their homes and lost their loved ones. And now, in 2019, women with children were being imprisoned rather than helped. Chris thought of Gabriel and what lay ahead for him, and of Charlene's dream of a career in entertainment. The optimism he felt speaking to Mimi and Anna and Jackie seemed impotent in the face of these stronger, more devastating forces.

Chris had been aware of some of this in the abstract. But to see it—to fully face what was once merely an uncomfortable kernel of knowledge—rendered it unignorable. The skeptic in him was reignited, and that familiar fear and sadness came to him in a rush.

Jordan felt differently. As the Still She Rises team told story after story about the unjust nature of Oklahoma's legal system, a well of resistance built up in his chest. It was a feeling Jordan had come to know well—a gut rejection to the progressive worldview. The advocates were so certain that they were right, and that the system was utterly and thoroughly wrong. That bothered him. But another, less-familiar sensation gripped Jordan, too: Anna and Jackie had shaken something loose, and the lawyers who followed left Jordan disturbed by the severity and callousness of it all. If they were right, if it really was as these lawyers said, then he felt that something was deeply wrong. Despite his usual predisposition toward law enforcement, Jordan wondered if there might be a glaring lack of mercy in Oklahoma, and that possibility sent a tremor through the foundation of his belief system.

Back in the car, we settled into a stupor. Outside Women in Recovery, two paramedics had led a shirtless man—his emaciated, tattooed form bent and shivering—by the elbow into the hospital below. Rain dripped down his back. His knees buckled. He seemed to be suffering immensely. And as we took to the road again, the monastic silences of Vermont and the gasping anxiety of Detroit gripped us. We had faced the nameless menace once again, and neither of us could fully reckon with it quite yet.

Upon our return to Tulsa in 2019, we met Mimi on the darkened plains, where thunder lingered and rainwater swelled the gullies along the country roads. Mimi ushered us into a warmly appointed room—dark wooden panels, beige carpets, walls lined with bookshelves and paintings of Western scenes.

We sat down around a table and our tales came and went. Sometimes our stories from these trips felt wearisome, and we'd look back and forth hoping the other had the energy to explain. But we relished recounting them to Mimi, who listened and asked questions and challenged us when things didn't add up. We told her about Gabriel and his poetry, and the time when we realized that trucker Pete was a complete stranger a day into our journey with him, and our search to find Willis on the timbered docks of Portland. We had our own history by then, and we tripped over one another to tell it.

"And just as we were leaving Leon's set at the fairgrounds—" Chris said, talking about New Orleans.

"Which was amazing in its own right," Jordan added.

"—we came across these two men. One had an electric violin and the other was playing an upturned bucket like a drum. And they were outstanding."

"I've never seen anything like it," Jordan said. "The emotion—they were lost in it."

"At one point, Jordan tapped me on the shoulder and I turned around—we had been the only ones watching on this street corner at first—and this massive crowd had formed on all sides."

"Music is really just so powerful," Mimi said, shaking her head.

"Do you know which article is one of *The Washington Post*'s most read?" Chris asked.

"Yes!" Mimi said. "The one about the violinist—oh, what's his name? Joshua Bell!"

"How'd you know?"

"I have his CD. Though I think they did the experiment wrong."

Jordan looked at Chris.

"They sent this world-class violinist into a busy Metro stop in Washington, D.C., to play," Chris said, "and recorded who stopped to listen."

"Which was the problem," Mimi said. "People have places to go."

"And who did stop?"

"Children wanted to stop," Mimi said. "The children understood."

On the morning described in the Gene Weingarten article, at Washington's L'Enfant Plaza Metro stop, more than 1,000 people walked by violinist Bell without stopping. But Evan, three years old, lingered before his mother whisked him away, and a cashier at a store across the way leaned out a door to hear the music more clearly. Then there was a government employee named John, who stopped and listened intently for three minutes, while nearly 100 people passed by without a second look. "Whatever it was," John later said, "it made me feel at peace."

Jordan wandered off to call his girlfriend, and Mimi and Chris stayed at the table.

"Do you ever feel it?" Chris asked her at length. "Or do you not have time?"

"I don't really have time," she said, understanding what he meant.

"I guess I ask," Chris continued, "because when Jordan and I were in Detroit, we heard these stories, the stories of the men at Parnall and the women who served all that time, nearly a century, and we had just come from seeing you. And, well, we got to Vermont, and we didn't talk for hours. I'd wake up and feel refreshed and then fall apart again. Jordan would tell you the same thing. And it wasn't for a few weeks that we could articulate it. We felt this responsibility. This trauma— well, that's not right—but some kind of *vicarious* trauma."

Chris paused.

"And maybe it was because we weren't doing much about it," he said. "But it stuck with us. That pain lingered. I think it probably still does deep down somewhere."

"That's what I want," Mimi said, as a peal of thunder rattled the walls. "I want legislators to feel that. I want them to bear it, and take it with them. That's why we tell stories. No amount of numbers can accomplish that. I can talk to them all day about *recidivism this* and *average that,* but the stories and that nagging feeling are what makes someone do something."

"But it hurts," Chris said.

"And maybe it should."

Later, Chris joined Mimi to practice her speech. She stood up and spoke.

"After almost 10 years, hundreds of women come through our doors," Mimi read. "I've seen how trauma is the most common pathway that entangles women in the criminal-justice system. From early childhood neglect, sexual and physical abuse, rape, trafficking at the hands of 'loved ones,' getting arrested, witnessing violence and experiencing it, and being told to maintain a code of silence. It takes an enormous effort to break these patterns. But they can be broken. I've seen it time and time again."

Mimi kept at it, stumbled from time to time, and picked things back up. Chris tried to be expressionless, to neither encourage her or demoralize her.

"How do I sound?" she said, finishing.

"I think you sound terrific."

"Do you think?"

"Absolutely. And you'll only be better in the moment."

Chris and Mimi went over it twice more. As Mimi was wrapping up her last lines, Jordan returned and leaned against a doorjamb. She stopped, looked over at Chris—who gave her a thumbs-up—and set her papers down.

"I want to show you both something," she said.

Mimi left and came back with a series of posters for Women in Recovery. She turned them around and revealed a half a dozen portraits of women's faces.

"I think this one is so powerful," she said, pointing at a portrait on the far end.

It was of a blond woman—not young, not old. She looked like someone who had seen much. She neither smiled nor frowned, just looked on. Her face was knowing in a way the others were not. They were stern or hopeful, but this woman's image spoke to a vastness.

"Yes, it is," Jordan said. "It really is."

And the rain pattered and a clap of distant thunder roared off over the Oklahoma wildland—out over Tulsa and into the firmament.

———————

We wanted to see one other person while we were in Tulsa. His name was Rodrigo Rojas. On our first trip to town in 2018, we had met him at the Gathering Place—a 100-acre, $465 million public park on the banks of the Arkansas River. That year it had still been a construction site, and Rodrigo—the park's director of community relations—had handed out hard hats and taken us around. We walked through a series of rock totems and cliff walls cut from Oklahoma sandstone and past a boathouse, a five-acre playground, and trails snaking around ponds. We passed a skate park and indoor lounges with carved-wood ceilings. The park was designed in the Olmsted tradition—a democratic space for gathering and community. It reminded Chris of the public spaces of Washington, D.C. Chris's mother, Holly, had worked for nearly 30 years at the Trust for Public Land, a nonprofit devoted to creating places for people to spend time outside. There was something essential about such spaces to free and open communities. These were the locations where we expressed outrage or support, honored and retold our history and our futures, and simply saw one another.

"There's a lot of misperceptions about Oklahoma," Rodrigo had said that day. "It's not all cowboys and Indians. There's so much more to it."

When we returned to the Gathering Place in 2019, Rodrigo was beaming.

"The public is taking care of the park," he said, leading us down familiar paths. "They're picking up trash because they have a sense of pride in the place."

In a room that had once been wrapped in cellophane and occupied by heavy equipment, we found a sewing club of older women sitting and chatting, a few teenagers eating bananas and sandwiches, and a woman with blond-tipped hair tinkering with a piece of jewelry.

"This is what we wanted," he said, looking around. "The last time you were here, this was the goal."

We stopped on a balcony overlooking a three-acre pond. "It's nice to hear the children," Rodrigo said, gazing at the now-completed playground in the distance. And it felt like the right moment to pose our most burning question.

"I want to ask you point-blank," Chris began. "What you see

going on in the city—does that overwhelm the pessimism around this country right now?"

"I think there's a lot of optimism here in Tulsa," Rodrigo said, "especially with something like this."

What about Tulsa's history, though? Chris asked. Rodrigo considered it. It was Rodrigo who had told us that the city was littered with "invisible barriers" that segregated people from one another.

"There's been a lot of history," Rodrigo started. "And now the city's talking about it. Instead of being afraid of history, we're actually talking about history—not putting it behind us, but moving forward with that in mind."

Perhaps this was a new piece of the puzzle. We had come to view history as a powerful source of identity. Satori and Willis and John-Michael and others had suggested as much. But what do we do when that history is pocked with darkness and terrible things? We had seen how those historical legacies can leave people traumatized, embittered, and broken. Rodrigo, though, spoke of a way to overcome that tension. There was still a lot of work to be done in Tulsa, he admitted. Not everything was going well. Tulsa's immigrant population, for instance, had been targeted by legislation that separated families. The Tulsa County Sheriff was making immigration arrests on behalf of U.S. Immigration and Customs Enforcement (ICE), which was dividing residents of the city. Tulsa had to find a way to welcome everyone, he told us.

"But the first step is talking about it," Rodrigo said. "The first step is getting it out in the open."

For Rodrigo, the anti-immigrant legislation was personal. His parents had come to the United States from Argentina and Bolivia. Rodrigo's father, Guillermo, had worked as an investigative journalist in Argentina at a time when the dictatorship there was "disappearing" people. When life became too dangerous, they left for Tulsa, where others in his family had already settled. Guillermo's relatives ran a restaurant, so he went into the family business. Then in 1995 he gave journalism another go, starting a bilingual newspaper, *La Semana del Sur*.

"He's been really fortunate to have that opportunity to continue his career in journalism," Rodrigo said. "It has been important to give the community an outlet to share their voice."

And it all began to click for Chris. Tulsa, like any city, may be lashed to its history, but that didn't consign it to repeat the tragedies of its past. Chris felt a spirit of renewal in the town, and it started with an open conversation—a reckoning.

Back in August, when we met Jamaal and Brandon at Greenwood, their story was not just one of tragedy; it was one of rebirth. In 1921, with Black Wall Street in ruins, the African American community had a choice, the two of them told us. They could leave or rebuild. Some wanted to go. Why stay in a community that was capable of such a thing? Others advocated to stay and rebuild. Rebuilding was perhaps quixotic, and definitely dangerous. On the heels of the violence came more slights and acts of oppression. The attack was designated a "riot," and most insurance companies refused to pay out to rebuild Greenwood's storefronts. The massacre never made school textbooks. Government officials took decades to acknowledge it. The campaign to forget what happened began hastily.

"They could have left," Jamaal had said. "But they stayed."

People rebuilt, and their descendants continued that work. The Tulsa Race Riot Centennial Commission was determined to tell Tulsa and the world what had transpired—not simply to heal transgenerational wounds but to bind Tulsa closer as one city, for progress could not begin without first acknowledging what had taken place.

"Reconciliation," Jamaal had said matter-of-factly, "starts when you're uncomfortable."

Chris thought back to an email exchange he'd had with Jamaal earlier that spring. Jamaal's signature included a quote by Dr. Olivia J. Hooker, a survivor of the massacre.

"And so when this terrible thing happened, it really destroyed my faith in humanity," she said. "And it took a good long while for me to get over it."

On first read, Chris made nothing of it other than here was a woman who had experienced the worst, survived it, and had her faith destroyed. On that balcony with Rodrigo, though, it took on new meaning: Hooker's faith in humanity had indeed been destroyed, but then—after "a good long while"—it came back. The grace of her statement was overwhelming.

Then there was the memorial itself. Just outside the Greenwood Cultural Center, ringed in by a horseshoe of benches, was a slab of black marble that, from afar, resembled the texture of Joe Louis's fist in Detroit. "The Black Wall Street Memorial," Chris read off the marble to Jordan, "reaches for the unity of all God's people."

We walked farther through the park with Rodrigo, past a pond and through the new playground, where we were swarmed by dodging children—their voices all around us.

"There are a lot of great cities all over this nation that are putting people first and thinking about how they can actually make this a better place for the future," Rodrigo said. "I think that's what America is, right? It's about what's happening here in your town and your city, because that's where you can make the biggest impact. Tulsans are taking that to heart and trying to make an impact for the long term."

There was hope in Tulsa not because it was pure, but because despite the dark past and issue-riddled present, there were those who would work to shape it in their image.

As Jordan thought it over, it wasn't optimism that they exhibited. It was something more powerful than that. There was *work* behind what Mimi, Jamaal, Brandon, and Rodrigo were all doing. They weren't taking progress for granted. They knew the scope and scale and magnitude of the challenges they faced. They understood them better than anyone, and they were sober about how long and how hard they would have to work to truly change things. Yet they remained undaunted.

There, in their words and their toil, was the compassion and mercy Jordan craved, and the grace that would keep Chris going despite the dark clouds gathering all around us.

At the end of a road that snaked up and down a grassy slope, flanked on all sides by the sand traps, greens, and roughs of a golf course, stretched Southern Hills Country Club. We pulled our mud-streaked rental car up to a clubhouse colored pink and tan, where valets in green-and-white uniforms fussed over our keys.

"I should have packed a jacket," Chris said, pulling at his short-sleeved button-up while Jordan slipped a sports coat over his tucked-in collared shirt.

"You look fine."

"Road-trip chic, I hope."

We milled around a reception space where suited waiters served sweating crystal glasses of water and ice tea before the Association for Women in Communications honored Mimi. The room was filled with elegant women in bright dresses and sparkling accessories. When her time came, Mimi got up from her table at the front of the room and took the stage.

"In a perfect world," Mimi began, speaking the words she had practiced over and over with Chris, "I wouldn't be standing here today."

In the crowd that morning was Elizabeth, a former addict and felon who, during her time at Women in Recovery, had become an advocate for women like herself, meeting with legislators and engaging politically. She was reaching back, as Brenda in Detroit had, and advocating for those whose fortunes hadn't yet turned. Another honoree was 96-year-old Marina Metevelis, the longest-serving employee at Tulsa Community College. Dubbed "Tulsa's Rosie the Riveter," she had built warplanes during World War II. Around the room were other women who looked like the denizens of high society. Yet one of them told us she was entering her second year of sobriety. As it turned out, scores of women were there to support Mimi—women who volunteered, who weathered their own struggles but gave back all the same.

"The stories that we tell today," Mimi said on stage, "they're powerful. Stories speak to the heart and stories certainly help me drive my work every day. Now don't be thinking that the work is over—it's not. We still need to improve criminal-justice practices for women in our community, in our state, and in our nation."

Jordan thought back to something Anna had said to us the year before.

"I remember a stranger once gave me some money on the bus. And he was like, 'People aren't as bad as you think they are.' It was raining. I'm wet and sitting there crying. I just remember him giving me this money and telling me that, and I remember thinking, *You don't know nothing—people are horrible.* But there he was doing that.

"I'm starting to see things differently now since I've been in here," Anna said to us. "I know the women in this program genuinely care about each and every one of us. But when you're in your addiction, you don't see that at all. You think everything's bad and horrible."

And that was the problem, Jordan realized, not just here in Tulsa but across the country. It's easy to forget that people are just people, and that not all of them are bad. But systems have a way of replacing humanity with cruel, harsh, and unfair ways, and the same is true in reverse. Those fighting the system can too easily forget that systems and institutions are made up of people, just people, and they're not all bad either.

Mimi saw the flaws in the system but also knew the people within it. She knew the judges personally. She had the district attorneys on speed dial. She had built a hard, structured program at Women in Recovery, but one designed with care and personal attention. She had brought people to the fore in her work, and in doing so elevated the one thing that Jordan had felt was missing. Through her strength, she was able to show compassion and mercy. In the end, whether the Still She Rises women were right or wrong about Oklahoma was besides the point. They had reminded Jordan that justice untempered by compassion can become cruel. Mimi had shown him how to weave them together and bring humanity back into a system. She had demonstrated how leadership could change lives and turn around even the most hopeless situation.

Mimi exuded an uncommon good that drew in people around her. To us, she represented everything we had hoped to find on the road—kindness, hospitality, hope, and the promise of redemption.

Idaho

In Nebraska, the wildflowers were purple. Farther south, they were red and orange. Up north, where the season was still cold, the blooms sprawled out beyond the fallow rows of gray pasture in a shock of color.

"Look," Chris said, pointing. Jordan peeked his head over the wheel to peer upward. Large birds with black wing stripes rode thermals over the chilly grasslands.

"Sandhill cranes."

"What are they like?"

"Beautiful."

Snow dimpled the hills in Wyoming, where everything appeared to be on a diagonal slant toward the hazy mountains ahead. Lattice snow guards lined the range where antelope and cattle grazed. And as we drove from Jackson for Idaho Falls through a snowcapped pass, the two of us hashed out a plan for the last stop on our journeys.

The man we knew only as "the Idaho state trooper" had pulled us over almost three years before, and now we wanted to find him. We had driven nearly 1,000 miles out of our way to track down a person we had met only once before, and who would very likely not recognize us. But something compelled us north, toward him. In many ways, his frustrated statement—*None of this makes any goddamn sense*—echoed throughout our journeys. If two Californians were a puzzlement to that Idahoan, as we assumed him to be, then we felt compelled to find more confounding places, stories, and people, in order to listen. Those seven words had spun us out on the road. Now they were leading us right back to him.

"What should we say?" Chris asked. "If we find him, that is."

"Not entirely sure."

There were fires in the hills of the Targhee forests outside Victor, Idaho. The smoke was blue and yellow, and the fire-touched evergreens turned gray.

"What if we don't find him?" Chris said at length.

"We will."

Jordan felt this was one of those times when confidence would pay off. With persistence, we could track him down.

"I don't know, man," Chris said.

He had a sinking suspicion that this man was lost to time. Too much could have transpired in the years since. He could have moved away, retired, taken on a new profession, or worse. More likely he might not *want* to be found, let alone talk to us. The pursuit itself still seemed worth our while—one last improbable adventure.

The search for the unknown officer was frustrated, in part, by our broken memories. Chris had been far too wrapped up in his own fear to recall much detail, and neither of us thought we'd ever attempt to find him later on.

"Remember which region we were in? District Three is the westernmost section of I-84," Chris said to Jordan before we left. "It seems to fit with our itinerary from that trip."

"I've been racking my brain," Jordan said. "I remember we came into Idaho near Missoula and we definitely went to Craters of the Moon. The ticket happened somewhere in between."

"No ticket," Chris said.

"That's right."

Chris tried to picture the man. Chris had looked up over the trooper's barrel chest at round features—or were they sharp?—into dark, reflective glasses. He was tall—very tall, in fact—and stern, with a short haircut. He spoke with a deep voice, but not quite a bass. And he drove a white Ford Bronco–like truck.

"Did he have a hat?" Chris asked Jordan once.

"Was his car even white?"

"I'm sure of it."

"I'm not."

A month before arriving, Chris had reached out to the Idaho State Police in Meridian. Chris typed out a long note to a man named Tim, who ran the department's external relations. "My name is Chris Haugh, and I'm writing a book with Jordan Blashek about how people on opposite sides of the political aisle can find common ground."

Good clean start, Chris thought. He kept writing.

"As part of this story, we were hoping to talk with one of your officers who pulled us over in Idaho in May 2016. He was very pleasant and treated us very fairly. And that first trip across the country, when we met him, was very formative for this project. Now, in May, we are returning to Idaho after three years of driving, and we hoped we could see him again to discuss his impressions of the two of us and maybe what has changed since then."

Chris's heart sank as he typed the next paragraph.

"Sadly," he began, "we didn't catch his name, rank, badge number, or anything else, so this is all the information I can provide right now:

We met him in mid–May 2016. He was driving a white truck. We were driving a Volvo S60."

The response was as expected: Because a ticket had not been issued, Tim wrote back, our names did not come up in their database.

"There's no trace of the incident," Tim typed. "Sorry…"

"What if he sent out an all-call?" Jordan said to Chris on the phone later that day.

"A what?"

"Like an email to the whole department."

"I don't think he'll do that."

"Worth a try."

"I hate to be a pest," Chris started his latest to Tim, "but would you be willing to forward an email from the two of us on to the force?"

"What I'm understanding from you is," came Tim's response, and Chris already knew it was a bridge too far, "you'd like me to blast out an email to all 600 of our employees (to include over 300 troopers) on a hunt for the trooper who didn't issue you a citation and therefore has no trace in our system of meeting you. Is that right?"

Chris gulped.

"As you may be able to tell," Tim continued. "I'm doubtful this will be fruitful and I'm very reticent to send such an email blast which will contribute to the many emails we expect our employees to read and which sometimes fall through the cracks. In the absence of you being able to provide some mitigating factor to help me overcome my reticence, I shall not bog down our email system with your request."

Chris sat back in his chair and texted Jordan: no dice.

The possibility of finding the trooper was dimming by the moment—until Tim responded again.

"Sir," he wrote, and this felt like a change of tone. "After all that, in reading your original email once again I picked out a detail that I had missed, regarding the white truck driven by the officer. Since our troopers drive black vehicles with white stripes, it could not have been an ISP trooper."

A breakthrough, Chris thought. If we could find the law-enforcement branch with white trucks, we could find him. The problem, some research revealed, was that in Idaho there were 117 state law-enforcement agencies with well over 3,000 sworn officers.

Idly, Chris clicked over to the Idaho Sheriffs Association website and scrolled. *Aha,* Chris thought. There on the home page was an image of a white truck in the lower-left corner. It had a blue streak across the body and a badge on the front door. Behind it were snowy mountains, and the whole scene felt familiar. He was a sheriff, Chris knew. So he found a link to a list of the state's districts, and his heart sank once again. Staring back at him were 44 men and women in dark suits on blue backgrounds. There were at least 20 possible sheriff's offices along the highways we traveled that May.

A month later, as we drove across that snowy pass and came into the first river valley of Idaho, Chris had a list of 18 addresses to visit. The valley gave way to wide golden fields where tractors spit up soil and dust like the smoldering fire in the hills behind us. Jordan, though, had narrowed in on a part of the highway that he thought was the best bet and wanted to test that hypothesis.

"Let's start with the Bonneville Sheriff," Jordan said. "Then the others going up I-15 North. And toward Boise in the morning."

"I can do the first one," Chris said.

"You mean, tell the first story?"

"Yeah, I can do it."

Jordan smiled. Not long ago, Chris had quaked in the presence of law enforcement. Now, he was taking the lead on questioning potentially dozens of officers. Still, neither of us knew how we would be received, and our email exchange with the staties had not exactly been encouraging. It was a strange conversation to have, to be sure, and one a sheriff might not relish.

Chris snorted and pointed out the window.

The hills had turned green and there, out on distant slopes, were large wind turbines turning slowly in the sun.

"What?"

"Tilting at windmills."

———————

In Idaho Falls, just down the Snake River from a low waterfall with an apron of rocks, was the Bonneville Sheriff's office. The downtown area was full of two-story brick buildings above quiet streets. We walked in from the parking lot—Chris ahead and Jordan a few steps behind.

"How about that?" Chris said.

Jordan looked over and saw white police trucks parked in diagonal rows.

"Look right?"

"Kinda."

Inside, Chris sidled up to a city information officer in a black uniform and tried to act nonchalant—as if what he was about to ask was an everyday question suited for a sworn officer of the state of Idaho.

"Hello, sir," Chris went with, a smile plastered on his face. "I have what may sound like a very strange request."

The man lowered his mustached face and looked at him from over his glasses.

"My friend and I here had a run-in—a conversation, really—with an officer who we believe was a sheriff of some sort on a highway coming through this area just about three years ago."

Chris paused to let that sink in.

"And now we're hoping you can help us find him."

The officer looked at him.

"Did he give you a ticket?"

"No, he very kindly let us off."

"Which highway?"

"We're not really that sure."

"Get a name?"

"Sadly not."

The man leaned back. "I have no idea who that could be."

"Well, he had a white truck," Chris tried. "Does that help? It was definitely white."

Chris looked back at Jordan, who grimaced.

"We *think* it was white," Jordan said.

"That's Idaho Falls."

"Excuse me?"

"That's an Idaho Falls officer—white truck? Yeah, Idaho Falls. City cop."

"Oh, I see. Well, would a city officer be on the highway?"

"Can't imagine why."

"Oh, well—that's no good."

The man looked at us, and his mien broke.

"Gosh, I wonder who it could be!" he said in a burst. With a smile, he continued: "Best bet is to try the sheriffs down the way."

"Not a bad start," Chris said to Jordan as we walked away.

"Could have been worse."

A few feet beyond, behind a plexiglass window, a young woman in glasses sat in front of shelves of records and files.

"Can I help you?" she said, and Chris pasted on the same smile and started his now-familiar yarn. "I have what may sound like a very strange request..."

"County sheriffs have blue cars," she said after Chris finished his spiel. "IFPD have white cars?"

"Yeah, white cars," said another woman behind her. "IFPD's got white ones."

"We actually don't think we were in Idaho Falls," Jordan interjected. "We were definitely pulled over by a sheriff somewhere north of here along I-15."

"You said three years?" the woman said.

"Almost exactly," Jordan said.

"May 24," Chris added.

"And which highway?"

"We're not entirely sure."

"Likely headed down I-15," Jordan said.

"Likely?"

"Probably."

She looked at us and back at her desk.

"Do you have the license-plate number?"

"I can get it," Jordan said and walked out.

"And you," she said. "I need you to write down your names and driver's-license info on this."

She flipped a business card over and put it on the counter. And with that she sat down and started dialing.

"Hi, Dispatch—Erin in Idaho Falls. I have something I'm hoping you can look up for me."

The caper was on.

Chris scribbled away and slid the card across the counter.

"Yes, a record. It's *Christopher*—traditional spelling—*Haugh*," she said. "Are you sure the 24th?"

"I think so? Could have been the 22nd or 23rd."

It seemed like this man was out there and tangible again. If we could just identify who had been working that day and where we'd been, we could track him down. But the words of a researcher Chris had met once echoed in his head. "If they want to be found, I can find them," the man had said. "But sometimes people don't want to be found."

"I remember he was tall and blond," Chris said as Erin waited for Dispatch to run our information.

Erin shot her colleague, Karly, a glance.

"That's the guy!" Karly yelled, looking at a picture on her phone.

"The guy?" Chris asked excitedly.

"The guy!" Karly shouted back.

"*Which* guy?" Chris said, and Erin and Karly laughed between themselves.

The quick burst of energy, and the realization that this was nothing more than two clerks passing the time late on a Friday, returned Chris to his skepticism. This was a wild-goose chase, to be sure, but we were deep in it now—an organ of the state was engaged.

"They were going southbound from Montana," Erin said over the line. "Yeah, and writing a book now. Yeah, a book. ISP said no—wasn't them. Hmm, that's what I thought."

Jordan returned and the two of us sat down on a bench carved with initials and errant cuts made by those waiting to hear back on far-less-frivolous pursuits.

"Could be Clark County," Jordan said, looking down at a map on his phone. He zoomed in and out on its details.

"Think we're spending all day in police offices," Chris said.

"Madison is your best bet," Karly said over the window, still running down leads. "They have white cars and they patrol the highway all the time—I live down there."

"If it helps," Chris said, "I got invited into the front seat and he had an intimidating number of weapons just sitting there between us. Shotguns—lots of them."

"Do you remember exactly how tall he was?"

"Not really—just how terrified I was," Chris said. "He could have been five feet tall, but I swear he looked to be six-six."

"He was tall," Jordan said.

"Did he have a K-9?" Erin asked from behind the glass.

"Oh, no. Yeah, definitely not—I was in the car, after all. Only a ton of shotguns."

Karly leaned in, and Chris leaned in to meet her.

"Did you guys go to jail?" she whispered as Erin talked on the phone behind her.

"Lord, no."

"Too bad," she said, leaning back again. "Would make things a lot easier."

Karly, Jordan, and Chris started looking through Facebook photos while Erin continued talking on the phone. We showed photos back and forth from various departments—Ada County and Boise, Canyon County and Twin Falls. Photos of tall men and stout ones, bearded and fit, clean-shaven and pot-bellied.

"Is this him?" Jordan said.

"Could be," Chris responded.

"Or him?"

"That guy looks really familiar."

"It's not him," Jordan said.

"How are you so sure?"

"I just know."

"You weren't even sure the damn truck was white but you're sure this isn't him?" Chris said.

"How are you *not* sure?"

Details one or the other of us thought were immutable—never to be forgotten—were suddenly amorphous and blurry. Each photo seemed to reveal something. Often a trait would click, and one of us would feel a rush of familiarity while the other shrugged. This seemed hopeless. If we were going to find him, it would take more than a Facebook post or two.

"Guys, if you leave now," Erin said, "you can get to Clark before they close up. Ask for Shane."

"Clark could be right," Jordan said.

"And Madison is your next best bet," Erin said. "Their cars are right."

"Okay, J, should we go?"

Jordan nodded.

"And we'll call you if we hear back," Erin said.

"Thank you—really can't say that enough."

"Promise you'll let us know if you find him?"

"Of course."

The drive north coursed with memories—or false memories, as the case may have been.

"It's Clark County," Jordan said.

"How do you know?"

"I remember that overpass. Don't you?"

Chris shook his head.

"I remember it being more rural," Chris added as trucks headed south and sedans kept up alongside us. "I remember a curve in the road out ahead and scrub for miles."

"Kinda like this?"

"Yeah, kinda like this."

We had 40 minutes to consider what was to come. Forty minutes until we arrived at Clark County, trying to find a sheriff, or a deputy, who had pulled us over 36 months before.

"Cop," Chris said, pointing one out across the divider as a car sped past. "White car with a blue stripe."

"Looks right," Jordan said.

———————

"They're expecting you," Erin said over the speakerphone as we pulled off the highway for Clark County.

"Terrific," Chris said. "I think?"

"He's a deputy."

"What?"

"And his name," Erin said, "is John Clements."

John Clements. Chris kept saying the name to himself, as if it might awaken old slivers of memory.

"How do you think they know?" Chris asked Jordan.

"I have no idea," Jordan said.

The sheriff's office was in what looked like a one-road town called Dubois. The sun was low. It being a Friday, we expected little from the one-story building of red brick. As we pulled up, Chris noticed a sheriff's truck parked in the back. It was gray and outfitted with technology, lights, and rigging.

"Look right?" Jordan asked.

"No, not really."

Inside we found Shane, the dispatcher Erin told us to speak with, along with the sheriff and an administrator.

"You the two looking for John?" Shane said, and we nodded.

"Is he here?" Jordan asked.

"No," the sheriff said. "John left a while ago."

"He had a week from hell," said the administrator.

"But it's him," Shane added.

The three of them had gone back through their logs and found who was working that day—John Clements, a deputy, had been the only one on patrol.

As Chris explained to the dubious administrator who we were— liberally using *No, ma'am* and *Thank you, ma'am*—Jordan pulled up a photo on his phone. There was Deputy Clements—roughly 40 years old, tall, maybe six-three, with blond hair and a kindly face. In the photo he was receiving an award and smiling at the crowd.

"Look," Jordan said, showing Chris the photo. "That's him—tall, skinny, those glasses."

"Well, John won't be back from the north until Monday," the sheriff said.

"Too bad."

"If you want, I can pull you over and you can talk to me," the sheriff offered. "Just give me 15 minutes to get out ahead of you."

Still laughing, we headed back to the car, then looked once more at the photo on Jordan's phone.

"Is that him?"

"The smile looks right."

"And he looks kinda quiet—gruff, even."

Deputy John Clements, Chris mouthed to himself. A few weeks before, he had recounted our mission to a couple of professional searchers. "Well, I hope you have his name," one of them said, and Chris had to admit we didn't have even that. But now we did—or at least we hoped we did.

"How did they know it was us? And him?"

"They didn't," Jordan said, having had the same thought. "Did you hear Shane? They just pulled who was working that day—May 24, 2016."

"So it wasn't necessarily us."

"No, not at all."

"John didn't confirm it?"

"Nope."

"And we could have been halfway across the state."

As we headed for Idaho Falls for the night, Jordan marveled at the number of people who had tried to find the trooper. People with no reason to help. Perhaps it was just the dose of excitement they needed on a calm Friday afternoon. But Jordan felt it meant something to them, too. Whatever happened with Deputy Clements—whether it was him or not—did not really matter. People had helped, and that meant something to us.

Chris was unconvinced our man was Deputy Clements. There were still thousands of Idaho police officers out there. To say it was Clements was too much of a stretch—qualifying words such as *suspected* and *alleged* came to mind. It was something to hang on to, though. We had tried, and we had come close. There are times for searches like this, and times for asking *What if?* The in-between times, especially when life spits you out on the road for the better part of three years, are for dreaming. We had taken a chance at a good tale and fodder for conversations for years to come.

Maybe the three of us would have gotten along, and maybe taking that chance would have given us something we would cherish. A little risk had led us to Pete and that smoke-choked voyage across the Southwest. It had led us to Willis and the waters off Maine, and even into Frannie's prison classroom and across the table from Mimi and on a balcony with Rodrigo. Quite frankly, it led us to one another. Perhaps Idaho was frivolous, even unnecessary, but it was an adventure that kept us moving forward.

Disappointed as we were, there was one last game of chance to play. So as we drove south toward Idaho Falls, Jordan handed Chris the piece of paper on which the Clark County sheriff had scribbled Deputy Clements's email address.

With Jordan behind the wheel, Chris wrote.

"Deputy Clements," he typed. "You may remember us from May 2016. We were driving down I-15 in Idaho and met a very kind officer who let us off from a speeding ticket after a long chat. It was that interaction that inspired us to write this book. Your dispatcher, Shane, just told us that you were working that day and that you may have been that officer. Your sheriff confirmed that you might be the one. If this was in fact you, and you had any interest in seeing us again, we'd love to buy you a coffee."

Chris paused and watched Idaho go by the window. When marooned in Augusta, he had wondered about the central conceit of this final trip—that there was something optimistic to be said about the country. With sweat trickling down his chest and the Boat in a mechanic's bay a few feet away, Chris had not felt hopeful. And in the misery and tragedy of others elsewhere on the trips, he hadn't always found reason for it either. Much spoke of calamity and misfortune, but on that Idaho road he found clarity.

"This book is all about hope," Chris wrote to Deputy Clements after a beat, "and it's our hope simply to chat and talk about these journeys of ours."

"Sent," Chris said.

The giant wind turbines down near the Raft River weren't turning as we passed by the next morning. Mountains woolly with snow flanked the white blades in the midmorning sun. Below them were open red-brown fields kept moist with gigantic metal sprinklers, which seemed to rise and fall as we drove by. Down there, rows were dug into the soil for planting. Swallows flew over and under the bridges.

Idaho

We were on the last leg of our journey, homeward bound for California. We kept at it all day and drove down into Nevada and up over the Sierras past Reno on one side and Truckee and Donner Pass on the other. Around 4 p.m. we emerged from the bronzed foothills and into our home state. Our goal was to catch a blood-orange sunset over the San Francisco Bay before we arrived at Chris's childhood home around nightfall. We had only three hours left on the road together.

"Well, brother, it's coming to an end," Jordan said. He put a hand on Chris's shoulder.

"How do you feel?"

"Nostalgic."

"I wonder when we'll be back on the road together again?"

"Soon, I think."

When we had first set off three years earlier, we had been running away from things in our lives that we didn't want to define us. We were getting away from suffocating ideological debates, politics, and the drawing of lines. Yes, we were searching for something too, but that something was undefined. We were looking for a space for our friendship and an antidote to the division we saw all around us. Three years ago we knew how to leave things behind, but not how to arrive at something new.

That had changed. The two of us had stopped fleeing from things and started heading toward something. It began as a vague notion that the two of us were building a friendship that brought out the better versions of ourselves, not because we radically changed each other's views, or because we each moved to the center, but because we helped each other understand our own values at a deeper level. And as we did, we found that it made our friendship more compassionate and more unshakable. Through that bond, we built our shared understanding of the kind of home, the kind of nation, that we wanted to see someday—and that we believed other Americans wanted as well.

"It would have been fun to meet Clements," Chris said as we

approached Vallejo and the mouth of the Napa River. We were near home, and Jordan would be leaving the next day.

"We could always go back."

"Maybe."

Yet as we made our way down I-80, speeding west toward the sunset, we both knew that it had never really been about finding him. It was just an excuse to spend another long stretch on the road together.

Perhaps the same was true about all of these trips. Perhaps all of it had been nothing more than an excuse to set off on this journey together. First to get away from it all, and then to move toward something together. But somehow that didn't feel quite right. Every stop, every mile we drove, we had met people and learned things that were meaningful. There was something deeper in those interactions than just kindling for a friendship. Our trips had been about the two of us, but they were made possible by the kindness, generosity, and grace of strangers along the way. People had supported us, brought us into their homes, taken us into their lives, and expressed the American spirit that we hoped to find.

"My God," Chris said, looking down at his phone.

"What is it?"

Chris looked at Jordan.

"It's him."

"No, it's not."

"'This is Deputy Clements,'" Chris read. "'I would be willing to meet with you again possibly.'"

"That doesn't mean it's him," Jordan said.

"He wrote *again*."

Chris looked down and kept reading.

"'I was the officer you met,'" Chris read at full pitch. "'When and where were you wanting to meet? John Clements.'"

The two of us looked at each other.

"We found him," Jordan said.

"We did."

CONCLUSION

The sun was setting over Kansas as we passed by Independence, a small town named after the declaration, and signs for the Little House on the Prairie. We drove across highway spans that straddled swollen rivers with muddy overflows, submerged trees in dark water, and tilted over power-lines.

"We haven't been to Missouri," Chris said as we went.

"How's that possible?"

Three years on the road had taken us to 42 states and across nearly 17,000 miles. At that moment, we were on our way north to see two new ones, Nebraska and Iowa, then on to Idaho—our last 1,000-mile leg.

"You know," Chris said. "Forty-five states sounds a whole lot better than 44."

So we veered east toward the Missouri River to touch the soil of the Show-Me State, if only for a moment. It would be a quick detour, we surmised. No more than an hour, which would put us in Omaha before midnight.

"I don't understand," Chris said, scrolling through Google Maps for a route. "Why can't we get across the Missouri River?"

There was no direct route to the other side, even though we were around 25 miles away. The map kept sending us hours north in a giant 250-mile loop.

"There are a dozen bridges all along the route."

"Let's just try one," Jordan said.

"Which one?"

"Is one closer?"

"Rulo," Chris offered. "Looks like there's at least a footbridge—we could walk it?"

"Sure—why not?"

So we turned off Highway 75 and onto a two-lane road that passed through soggy fields. We took a right down a dirt road that cut through homesteads and barbed-wire fencing and the odd copse of trees. The car shuddered as it passed over rocks and potholes.

"This isn't good," Jordan said, holding the wheel tightly.

We came up to our turn and skidded against the rocks to a stop 20 feet past the intersection. Jordan reversed course and took us down the single-lane dirt road past a farmhouse and a slope upward that disappeared out of view 100 yards ahead. As Jordan took the curve, Chris noticed a sign on the right: MINIMUM MAINTENANCE TRAVEL AT YOUR OWN RISK. It took him a second too long to process. Jordan had already hit the accelerator.

"Wait, don't!"

The car crested the rise and began sliding down a gradual hill, hydroplaning diagonally as the wheels lost traction. Jordan furiously pumped the brakes, then tried the accelerator, which threw brown liquid out into the air in a steep arc.

"Stop, stop, stop!"

We kept sliding until we came to the bottom of the hill. Jordan stepped out. The mud was thick and sticky. Chris followed, his shoes sinking an inch or two deep into the mire with each step. Jordan slumped against the side of the car with a dry smile.

"We're not getting out of this."

We climbed back into the car as the sun gave way to darkness.

Conclusion

Mud was everywhere. Jordan peeled it off his shoes; Chris picked it out of the grooves in his phone case. The floor of the car was slick with it, and the windows were spotted with large gobs. We wiped dirty fingers against our jeans as owls and coyotes called in the distance and mosquitoes swarmed around our ears. The car started making odd noises, so Jordan turned off the engine and we watched a light rain falling in the headlight beams.

Chris shook his head. Night was setting in and blackness enveloped the car, which echoed with the clicking of the hazard lights. Chris felt deflated. His resilience was flagging, and his friend's silence seemed to confirm a sneaking suspicion.

"It's time to go home," Chris said, and Jordan clenched his jaw.

We got out of the mud that night thanks to a taciturn man named Lonnie with a hearty ATV and tow strap, but in that moment we knew our trips were coming to a close. As we spent the night crouched at a 24-hour car wash power-spraying the undercarriage of the sedan—and praying the shudder in the engine would let up once the mud and soil was flushed from it—there didn't seem to be much else out there for us. We had been on the road for parts of the last three years, and it was time to return home. It was time to rest. We were fatigued, and the road seemed more frightening than ever before.

Kansas had been another near miss. We had started our final road trip filled with optimism, yet our car sputtered to a stop on the first day. Then our windshield cracked not long afterward—the result of a missile-like rock that had escaped the mud flaps of a truck ahead of us. At one point, a pickup towing a boat drove us off the road and into a median in Mississippi. Pools of water in the gullies of rain-drenched highways sent us skittering. The rush of passing trucks rattled the car and reminded us of the perils of one-lane roads taken in the middle of the night.

Conclusion

The near misses were familiar but growing in frequency. Within four hours of setting off on our first voyage three years earlier, that trailer on a long-haul truck had fishtailed into our lane and nearly sent us into a wooded shoulder. Then there were brushes with wildlife, tighter turns than expected in Montana, and belongings sloughed off the back of cars and pickups to dodge. Such moments were nothing new. They were simply becoming more unnerving.

So we headed home.

This felt timely, since something seemed amiss across the nation. It wasn't obvious unless you strung it together state by state—south to north, north to south. Plagues of weather followed us across the continent. That mire in Kansas was one small consequence of it. Rains pounded the Midwest and the Gulf Coast for weeks, sending roiled water gurgling up and out of manholes and storm drains as far south as New Orleans and as far north as Council Bluffs, Iowa. Flooding rendered the Missouri River impassable and the Mississippi untamed. To our north, spring blizzards spread snow from the Sierras to Maine and coated the Dakotas, parts of Minnesota, and the flatlands beyond. Hail the size of golf balls pelted Amarillo, while tornadoes touched down on the outskirts of Sulphur, Oklahoma.

As we drove through Selma, Alabama, the weather service advised church pastors to watch the sky. Storms might threaten Sunday services.

We stood on the gangway of the Edmund Pettus Bridge, along a bend in the muddy Alabama River where civil-rights protesters were met with police truncheons in 1965, and looked past the leaning, vine-strewn houses toward a dark blue sky verging on black.

We felt this power most as we drove through Lee County, Alabama. Two months earlier, on March 3, a tornado had ripped through in the middle of the night. What was a sleepy hamlet of a dozen or so churches, Angus cattle, and lumberyards became first a cacophony of sirens and then a series of open wounds, mourning families, cleanup scams, and speculators.

Conclusion

That day, we came over a rise near County Road 38 and were met by an expanse of damage. Cordwood and mattresses and siding and black tree branches were stacked on the side of the road. Trash bags distended with the contents of gutted homes littered the ground. Messy, gory heaps—the impulse toward small order in the face of destruction.

We crouched on the side of the road.

"Think that's a grave?" Chris said.

Up on a muddy rise was a small wooden cross, held together with what looked like a single nail. Carnations and colorful trinkets lined the patted-down earth around it. Broken foundations and jagged beams flanked its bare form.

"A memorial."

"Yeah."

"There's a bunch."

Across the hillside, going down into the valley, were dozens of makeshift crosses.

"Jesus."

Twenty-three people were dead, including a six-year-old.

"It must have blown right through that house there."

Chris followed Jordan's gaze. Two stone lions sat atop the pillars of a gate at the entrance of a barren plot. Behind them was emptiness, except for the remains of a car cantilevered into the trunk of a tree.

As we drove away down County Road 38, we felt it in our gut. Jordan looked out the window and saw kids' toys scattered on the ground and smeared with mud. There, hanging from a tree limb, was a paper star with the word *hope* written on it.

A few days later, in a Tulsa hotel room, we watched a Weather Channel segment on Lee County. Shots of a Bible and sunflowers and a celebration of life flickered across the screen in tribute.

One woman, Evony, had brought her mother back to the road for the first time.

"I stand here on these grounds of people that I would wave to every day," Evony said. "You can't help but be part of the rebuilding of this area. This is right. This is home. It will forever be home."

Then there were the regular reminders of what we humans have done to one another. Billboards advertising naloxone, an opioid-overdose treatment, lined Nevada highways. Shrines and crosses yellowed with rain dotted the shoulders of Mexican freeways. Signs forbidding hitchhiking in Texas tolled the presence of a sprawling detention facility. A man with oily hair sprawled on a New York sidewalk, scratching with stained fingers at a tattoo etched across his alabaster forearm.

And in Montgomery, Alabama, we bore witness to a larger kind of destruction. There, on a quiet knoll just outside downtown, was the National Memorial for Peace and Justice, where hanging Corten steel pillars were engraved with the names of the 4,400 victims of lynching between Reconstruction and 1950. They looked as if the tablets of the above-ground cemeteries in New Orleans had been colored shades of red-brown, each one's pigment having then bled in the rain and streaked each face with long, stained lines.

"It seems like it's going to rust and peel off," a college-age docent named Tiana told us. "But there's another layer there, like a scab. There's skin underneath, and it changes colors."

Placards told of lynchings over a missing overcoat in a hotel room or marrying a person of a different race.

"I wasn't sure I could do it after the first few weeks," Tiana continued. "I went home, and I was dreaming about this."

We walked on through monument park, where each county had its own iron block laid prone like a casket.

"I wonder if there's one from where my family is from—Bath County."

"Virginia?"

Chris nodded. We walked to the curve in the memorial. Chris lingered, and Jordan kept on.

"Look," Chris murmured to himself. "Virginia."

And he traced each county down the line—Campbell, Brunswick, Bland—until he pulled up short.

"There."

Bath County read the dark, unmistakable letters. Chris couldn't see the name on the top—the name of the man or woman who had been lynched. He stood on his toes and still couldn't. He wanted to carry it with him, so he wouldn't forget whoever they were and what happened on that soil where his ancestors were buried.

A mockingbird called from a tree down the hill as Jordan walked alone. Jordan thought about this place in the context of Holocaust museums. Each one is meant to evoke some feeling. The one in Washington, D.C., universalizes the message of *Never again*. The one in Jerusalem, which looks out over the Judean hills, speaks to the triumph of hope out of despair. Here, the Memorial for Peace and Justice seemed to us an injunction to remember our own somber history.

Across the continent, we had set out to find stories that might uplift our fellow citizens, and we had also witnessed stories of great tragedy as we went. The two seemed to follow on one another's heels. No story of uplift went unchallenged by a coda of struggle. Struggle, in turn, seemed accompanied by words and poetry of hope and renewal. There was a mosaic to this country, one that took us the better part of three years to reconcile and, in many ways, remains our ongoing project of hope and faith. It was this puzzle—the promise and the tragedy—that took us so long to understand. It's what kept us driving.

———————

"I finally picked up one of those Bibles," Chris said. "You know, the ones in the motel-room drawers."

"Really?"

We were in southern Idaho, where the soil was dark—our last day on the road.

"I started reading Genesis while you were out."

Conclusion

"What did you think?" Jordan asked.

"I'm no man of God. But even I can see the beauty and moral urgency of the language and the story."

"Agreed," Jordan said.

"But I found it curious."

"How so?"

"Well, look at the earliest days of creation: God made man and then saw it was 'good.' And then in those first years we do so many bad things, as far as God is concerned. Adam and Eve ate from the Tree of Knowledge, and we're expelled from Eden. Cain kills Abel. And their descendants enrage God to such a violent extent that he destroys the whole earth, save for Noah and his menagerie."

The car hummed with the melodies of Leon Bridges playing low.

"God often seems mystified by us," Chris continued. "But doesn't it seem like eating from the Tree of Knowledge was our first act? Isn't knowledge of our world, or our desire for it, what really makes us human? Separates us from the beasts and all that? And if we're made in God's image, that only seems right—that we'd be curious and explor-atory. That we might not take instructions well, that we'd misbehave, that we'd want to look around and declare things good and bad."

"That's the paradox of Genesis," Jordan said. "God created man in his image, so we have free will and the ability to create good, beautiful things. But that also means we have the ability to disobey—and to do evil things, too. It's the heart of the drama—will we use our freedom to create order or will we use it to create chaos?"

"But knowledge, we're told, is bad," Chris said. "It's original sin."

"Jews don't really believe in original sin. We believe that humans are born with the capacity for both good and evil, and that we can choose between them."

"It just seems wrong to me that curiosity would be punished," Chris said.

"Depends on your interpretation of the story, I guess."

"How do you explain it?"

Jordan considered it for a moment.

"Maybe it's about the failure to heed rules we don't understand. It's odd, isn't it, that God created us in his image—meaning with the capacity for good or evil—but then tells us not to eat from the tree? Perhaps there was wisdom or purpose in that rule we didn't understand. The problem was not that we acquired knowledge of a sort, but that we didn't listen."

"But wouldn't that mean he just expects us to obey him? To have blind obedience?"

"No, I don't think so. One thing I've always loved about the Torah is that the greatest prophets all argue with God at various points. The word *Israel* means *to struggle with God*. The most revered among us are not those who have blind obedience, but those who argue and protest."

"I can get behind that."

"That's faith, I guess. God tells the Israelites to go on journeys filled with hardships. He makes all these promises to the Jewish people, but those promises take decades, even millennia to fulfill. In fact, those promises might never be fully realized, but each generation is tasked with remembering and struggling to realize them and wrestling with our faith in spite of it all."

"I like that—the promise and protest across generations," Chris said.

"Exactly."

A familiar melody played over the stereo, and Idaho fell away as we talked.

———————

Our last day on the road together was a long one. We left Idaho Falls for California. The plan was to stop for the night, but we never did. We drove across farmlands and in and out of great spired mountains and their attendant hillocks. We stopped along the Snake River, just over Hansen Bridge, where terrace rocks with grasses and hanging plants arced down hundreds of feet toward the white water below.

"Can you imagine how ancient that river has to be to cut walls like that?" Chris said, and Jordan stared down at the gorge as he had at Horseshoe Bend before.

We kept on through the Nevada wastes on highways vaguely resembling those we had fought on three years before, where twisters rose and fell in white-gray plumes way out on the horizon. We drove on over the sloughs outside Sacramento, and the sun dipped behind the green hills and the rust-colored narrows between their flanks.

That night, as we killed the engine for the last time, we found that spring had crept across the coast and into Berkeley. The tree branches of the mock orange of Chris's home hung low with white blossoms, and petals fell along the stone pathways. We were home, at last. Home for the last time, and we were changed.

When we left New York for the first time, Jordan had been sure that we would find positive signs about America everywhere we went, and Chris was worried we might witness America's coming apart. Three years on, our politics were more nuanced but our positions hadn't changed all that much.

But both of us had moved.

Jordan's favorite rabbi may have said it best. "Optimism is the belief that things are changing for the better," Jordan once recounted. "Hope is the belief that, together, we can change things for the better." This made sense to us. Optimism is based on faith about what the future will hold. Hope recognizes things as they are, but also how they could be if we act together to make it so. Hope is neither naive nor blind. It requires courage, resilience, and patience. To have hope is to see what has gone wrong, and to believe in what can go right.

That's where the two of us had ended up—sober and hopeful for the United States. Much still worries us about the state of our country. Much reminds us of tragedy and failure and the ways in which we've sown our own discord, division, and maybe even downfall. This nation wears the brutality of the world and our history like scars. We are witnesses to this legacy, and any hope must be tempered by it.

Despite these historical scars, we've seen much that inspires us, too. Hope lives on. No matter the depth and breadth of tragedy, the two of us more often than not found a spirit of rebirth and renewal. That is where our two perspectives became one. We shared a conviction that the balance of our union is good—that amid the ugliness is that which could be our salvation. We heard voices cajoling us to do what love required, to see the humanity in addiction and mistakes, to carve out new forms of community and rituals to bring one another close, to hold fast to what works and what propels us forward. People shared their life stories, and they shared their failures, great achievements, and ethics. And what they imparted inspired us to keep imagining and dreaming up new possibilities next to old wisdoms.

Progress is never inevitable, and promises aren't always fulfilled in a lifetime. Though neither is failure or dissolution. Redemption, progress, wisdom—these things abide in our culture. So as long as there are those who will dream, those who will act, and those who will listen, the two of us will have hope. That's the story of our journey, and it's the story of America we will tell going forward.

Hope is how we found union.

ACKNOWLEDGMENTS

We owe a debt of gratitude to a number of people who deserve more recognition than a few characters of print could ever express.

Elias Altman, our agent, once took us to a display of hardcovers near Union Square and told us to imagine our book on those shelves someday. We were still graduate students at the time, and the idea seemed far-fetched—until he made it happen. Without Elias, there would be no *Union*.

Vanessa Mobley, our editor at Little, Brown, was our guiding light. She, too, saw something in these stories that we had yet to fully realize ourselves. Her kindness, beautifully savage red pen, wisdom, and passion mark every sentence of this book.

The entire team at Little, Brown was instrumental in creating *Union,* including Reagan Arthur, Ira Boudah, Sabrina Callahan, Judy Clain, Allan Fallow, Elizabeth Garriga, Elizabeth Gassman, Shannon Hennessey, Sareena Kamath, Gregg Kulick, Miya Kumangai, Carolyn Levin, Michael Noon, Abby Reilly, Stacy Schuck, Mary Tondorf-Dick, Betsy Uhrig, Tyneka Woods, and Craig Young.

We also owe a deep debt to three individuals: Evelyn Duffy read *Union* more times than anyone else and helped us find our voice. We'd like to thank our fact-checkers Rob Garver and Jake Leffew, who sacrificed a portion of his holidays to ensure we met our deadline.

Acknowledgments

Many people read drafts, outlines, and notes of *Union* and deserve enormous credit. They include Jason Berkenfeld, Cassie Crockett, Alex Galimberti, Adam Hammer, Jaclyn Harris, Dr. Andrew Imbrie, Andrew Kappel, Jodie Rosenberg, and Caroline Betsy Holland—our best listener—and her brother Brady.

One of the most common questions we get is: "How hard is it to co-write a book?" The answer would be "very" if Google Docs didn't exist. We'd like to thank the engineers responsible as well as Jordan's boss, Eric Schmidt, for this technology.

We're also thankful for all the people who opened their homes and pantries to us, and the many people who let us tell their stories. There were Ben Stolurow, John Adams, and Matt Blumenthal in Chicago, Illinois; Miranda Carson in Bozeman, Montana; Sebastian Heil in Napa, California; John Powell in San Diego, California; Carla Medina and Chuck Dominique in Sparks, Nevada; Nishan, Joey, Bob, Caleb, Mike, and the rest of the gunfighters in Page, Arizona; Peter Mylen across the Southwest; Jeff Leachman in Slidell, Louisiana; Pam Saunders in Santa Fe, New Mexico; Zabiullah "Zee" Mazari in Nashville, Tennessee; Ben Stewart, Rodrigo Rojas, Jamaal and Brandon, and Mimi Tarrasch and the entire Women in Recovery community in Tulsa, Oklahoma; Franny Shepherd-Bates and the men we met at Parnall in Jackson, Michigan; Chrissie Johnson Zoufal and Natalie in Grosse Pointe, Michigan; Eli Savit, Michelle Smart and the women of Bags to Butterflies, Satori Shakoor, and Ari Simon in Detroit, Michigan; Willis, Christine, and the rest of the Spear family, Tim, and Captain Kevin Battle and his deputy Charlie in Portland, Maine; Maggie Madden in Saint Paul, Minnesota; Lonnie in Kansas; Dr. Paula Traktman and Dr. Stephen A. Duncan in Charleston, South Carolina; Erin Rix and Karly Jarnagin in Twin Falls, Idaho; Sheriff Bart May, Chief Deputy John Clements, and the Clark County Sheriff's Office in Dubois, Idaho; Colin McCarthy, Adam Rice, and Alex Baron in Denver, Colorado; Professor Tanina Rostain, Dr. Richard Schottenfeld, and Joe Schottenfeld near Peru, Vermont; Matt and Carla McGirr as well as Joe and

Acknowledgments

Sandra Jurczynski outside Schenectady, New York; David Hartstein, Lisa Saunders-Hartstein, Don Saunders, Liv Ullmann, Tal Hartstein, Nate Enos, and Ariel Hartstein in Gloucester, Massachusetts; Terry, Marty, C & C Automotive, and the Enterprise team in Augusta and Martinez, Georgia; Walter Isaacson and his family, John-Michael Early, Keith Burnstein, Storie Gonsoulin, the Radiators, the other musicians we spoke with, and Ben Marcovitz and his family in New Orleans, Louisiana; Chris, Catherine, and Jack Leavell in Louisville, Colorado; Ava and Luke Plasse in New York City; the staff of the National Memorial for Peace and Justice in Montgomery, Alabama; Nelson, Josh, Marisol, Noel, Ivan, and the volunteers of Desayunador Salesiano Padre Chava in Tijuana, Mexico; Mark, Lindsay, and 1/8 Pizza Pub in El Paso, Texas; the Pensacola Museum of Art in Pensacola, Florida; as well as Finn Murphy, Joan Didion, Zeke Hutchins, Leon Bridges, Khruangbin, William Zinsser, Red Roof Inns across the country, and HotelTonight—our constant companion.

Countless men and women supported us, put up with us, inspired us, and challenged us. We'd like to thank all of them, even if we've forgotten or never knew their names.

We're also grateful to the scores of friends, mentors, and colleagues who supported us in ways small and large. Richard Frohlichstein may not always agree with either of us, but he was the only other person who lived these stories with us; his friendship means the world to us. Paul Gewirtz was our earliest believer. Dr. Mark Oppenheimer opened our first doors. We must mention Alex Schiller and Alex Bigler, with whom we had dinner on the very first night of our journey, Ben Levander, who nearly joined us on the first trip, Lauren Baer, Andrew Moore, Lauren Volo, Amy Chua, and Stef Feldman.

Jordan would like to thank, in no particular order, Eric Braverman, Eric and Wendy Schmidt, Alison Laporte and Barbara Bodine, Jamie Macfarlane, Frank Luntz, Ronnie Weissbrod, Geoff Abraham, Nimit Mehta, Paul Harraka, Rebecca Weidler, Michael Monagle, Joe Kristol, Carter Cleveland, Josh Lavine, Beverly Fitzsimmons, Marty Martin,

Acknowledgments

Josh Mandel, Joe Weilgus, Hassan Jameel, Gary and Nancy Levy, Gal Treger, and many more terrific friends and supporters.

Chris would like to thank a number of people—also in no particular order—including Bob Woodward and Elsa Walsh, Heather Gerken, Ori Brafman and Hilary Roberts, David Schleicher, Eugene Rusyn, Jason Corbett, Garrett West, Steve Lance, Michael O'Leary, Alison Hornstein, Claire Priest, Michael Lewis, Leo Goi, Nick Gulino, David Lewis, Steve Krupin, Stephanie Epner, Patrick Granfield, Bill Woodward, Jon Finer, Jonathan Powell, Ariana Berengaut, Terry Szuplat, Sarah Hurwitz, Tyler Lechtenberg, Cody Keenan, Aneesh Raman, David Litt, Kyle O'Connor, Laura Dean, Josh Rubin, Matan Chorev, Dan Benaim, John McConnell, Dave Bloom, Kate Moore, Jorge Rodríguez, Malik Ali, Dennis Shannon, Steve Henrikson, Nina Rennert, Jo Bradley, and so many others who taught him how to write and encouraged him on.

Besides both of our mothers—Holly and Carolyn—our families were critical to this endeavor. They gave us the confidence to embark on these journeys and the wisdom to finish them. Jordan's love and appreciation go to his family, including Jenna, Eric, and Justin Guja, Robert Blashek, Harriet Aufses and Arthur Aufses, Bob and Barbara Blashek, and Annie Blashek. Chris's love and gratitude go out to Daniel Johnson, who is family to him, Kyle Edwards, who Chris appreciates for so many reasons, Michael Haugh, Sarah Haugh, Kim Haugh, Mary Law, Maggie Law and Ritu Bhargava, the Hutchinsons, Anthony Woods, Steve, Sarah, and Jim-Bob Hoskins, the whole Johnson clan, Alfie, Jordy Yager, and, to some extent or another, that Kentucky warbler.

ABOUT THE AUTHORS

Jordan Blashek is a businessman, an attorney, and a military veteran from Los Angeles. After college, he spent five years in the U.S. Marine Corps as an infantry officer, serving two combat tours overseas. He holds degrees from Yale Law School, Stanford Graduate School of Business, and Princeton University. Blashek is based in New York City, where he invests in entrepreneurial efforts to grow the American middle class as part of Schmidt Futures.

Christopher Haugh is a writer from Kensington, California. After graduating with highest honors from the University of California, Berkeley, he attended Oxford University and started speechwriting as an intern in the Obama White House. He went on to join the U.S. Department of State's Policy Planning Staff, where he served as a speechwriter to the Secretary. In 2018, Haugh graduated from Yale Law School, where he was a Yale Journalism Scholar. He is based in the San Francisco Bay Area and New York.